750
eu

MIRACLE IN THE EARLY CHRISTIAN WORLD

Miracle in the
Early Christian World

A Study in Sociohistorical Method

HOWARD CLARK KEE

Yale University Press
New Haven and London

Designed by Nancy Ovedovitz and set in Baskerville type. Printed
in the United States of America by Edwards Brothers, Inc., Ann
Arbor, Michigan.

Library of Congress Cataloging in Publication Data

Kee, Howard Clark.
    Miracle in the Early Christian world.
    Includes bibliographical references and index.
    1. Miracles—History. 2. Religion—Methodology—History. 3. Isis—
Cult—Rome. 4. Aesculapius (Greek deity)—Cult—Rome. I. Title.
BL487.K43 1983   291.2'11'0722   83–40004
ISBN 0–300–03008–8
        0–300–03632–9 (pbk.)

10   9   8   7   6   5   4   3   2

CONTENTS

PREFACE

The study of history, and particularly the history of religion, has been stimulated by mounting evidence of the ancient world: archaeological and inscriptional discoveries, and especially the recovery of major collections of writings, as from Qumran, Nag Hammadi, and most recently, from Ebla in Syria. These finds have in turn given rise to reappraisal of chronological, philological, and conceptual perceptions of human life in the past. What has failed to keep pace with the emergence of new data, however, is the refining of historical method for the interpretation of the evidence, old and new. What has often passed for historical analysis is little more than a classification system of phenomena along formal or simplistic conceptual lines. Historians have read modern categories and values back into ancient cultural epochs, rather than making the effort to enter empathetically into the world of a past time, place, and outlook.

This book is an effort to achieve that goal, and to do so by self-conscious development of historical methods which make the historian aware of differences between his own culture and the one he is studying. Rather than proceeding on a broad, generalized front, the subject matter of this work concentrates on a phenomenon that was widespread in the ancient world and figures importantly in the literature of the Graeco-Roman period which is the focus of our interest here: miracle. The aim is to enter into the ways in which miracle was understood in this period rather than to impose on the data modern judgments about the claims made by or on behalf of miracle-workers. It is hoped that the results will not only shed some light on this particular subject but will also have implications for historical investigation of other subjects, especially in the study of religions in the ancient world.

More than three decades ago at Yale, two brilliant professors sought to instruct me and other students in how to read texts from the Hellenistic and Roman periods. One stressed the historical and archaeological dimensions; the other aroused sensitivity for the symbolic and affective aspects of the works. It is to the memory of these esteemed mentors, Carl Hermann Kraeling and Erwin Ramsdell Goodenough, that this work is dedicated.

Boston University   H. C. K.
October 1, 1982

ACKNOWLEDGMENTS

My gratitude is hereby expressed to the following:

To the President and Trustees of Boston University for the grant of a sabbatical leave for the academic year 1980–81

To the staff of the Boston Athenaeum for access to that fine collection and for study space in that handsome structure

To the McMaster University project on "Jewish and Christian Self-Definition," which stimulated my research on Asklepios

To the Boston University Institute for Philosophy and Theology for the invitation to lecture on Isis, Wisdom, and the Logos, and on the importance of Max Weber for historical study

To the Theological Faculty at the University of Tübingen, for the invitation to lecture on Roman and early Christian historiography

To my doctoral students in seminars on miracle in the Early Christian world

To Professor Stephen D. Crites of Wesleyan University and to Professors Emily Hanawalt and Charles Beye of Boston University for helpful, critical reading of portions of the manuscript

LIST OF ABBREVIATIONS

BZNW	*Beiheft zur Zeitschrift für die neutestamentliche Wissenschaft*
FRLANT	*Forschungen zur Religion und Literatur des Alten Testament und Neuen Testament,* 1903 ff.
IG	*Inscriptiones Graecae,* ed. Preussische Akademie d. Wissenschaften zu Berlin, 1873 ff.
JBL	*Journal of Biblical Literature*
NTS	*New Testament Studies*
P. Oxy.	*The Oxyrynchus Papyri,* ed. B. Grenfell and A. Hunt, 1898 ff.
SBLDS	Society of Biblical Literature Dissertation Series
SEG	*Supplementum epigraphicum Graecum*
SIG	*Sylloge inscriptionum Graecorum,* ed. G. Dittenberger, I–III. Leipzig, 1915–24
ZPE	*Zeitschrift für Papyrologie und Epigraphik*

CHAPTER ONE

When the Golden Bough Breaks
The Decline and Fall of the History-of-Religions Methods

This study in the history of religion has two major aims: to offer a critique of what have been, for the past century and more, the prevailing historical methods in the study of religion; and to propose a historical method which more faithfully portrays and interprets religious phenomena in their original setting and which seeks to develop safeguards against imposing modern categories on ancient data. To lend concreteness to the enterprise, a central focus of the work is a particular set of phenomena that even the casual observer will note as highly significant in the religious developments during the centuries just prior to, and subsequent to, the rise of Christianity—namely, miracle.

The first section of the book (chaps. 1 and 2) traces the rise and points out the serious flaws in the traditional history-of-religions methods and then describes the possibilities for a responsible strategy for historical reconstruction and interpretation. There follows a series of brief sketches of some changing perceptions of human nature and destiny among pagans, Jews, and Christians around the turn of our era. Chapters 3 and 4 point up the various evolutionary stages of the Asklepios and Isis cults. The basic orientation of primitive Christianity in an apocalyptic world-view is presented in chapter 5, while chapter 6 shows the increasing impact of Roman literary and religious traditions on the reworking of the gospel traditions. The profound importance of symbolic thought and interpretation of older religious tradition is traced in chapter 7, in relation to both Christian (Gospel of John) and Roman sources (Plutarch). The further influence of the pagan literary and conceptual traditions on early Christian writings—the romances—is depicted in chapter 8. A brief concluding chapter suggests some of the implications of this study for a substantially revised method in the historical study of religion.

BEYOND THE ISSUE OF FACTICITY

In the course of his vivid description of the cures effected by the Corybantes to the accompaniment of orgiastic music and dance, as reported by Plato and others,[1] E. R. Dodds paused to comment concerning these reports of miracle: "The whole proceeding, and the presuppositions on which it rested, are highly primitive. But we cannot dismiss it . . . either as a piece of back-street atavism or as the morbid vagary of a few neurotics."[2] Dodd's observation is revealing with respect to both ancient and modern assessment of miracles and miracle-workers. Disbelief in miracle and dismissal of it as chicanery or fraud are not modern conceits. Skepticism about miracle goes back to classical Greece, as Plato's relegation of the Corybantic cures to the realm of psychological alleviation of phobias and anxieties attests.[3] Credulity about miracles, especially healing, is as modern as television evangelists, while doubt-dispensing response to miracle stories is artfully attested in George Gershwin's folk opera, *Porgy and Bess*, where the embodiment of evil, Sportin' Life, rounds off his retelling of the biblical miracles with the refrain, "It ain't necessarily so."

What Dodd's observation calls for is that the historian give primary attention to the world-view assumed by both the performer of the miracle and the reporter of the event. It is by no means adequate for the historian to ask merely whether miracles can or cannot occur. What is reported to have taken place can never be separated from the larger framework of meaning, the assumptions about reality, the values, the attitudes toward evil, the hopes of deliverance that comprise the network of assumptions in which the experience took place and in which the event is recounted. Even among ancient skeptics—to say nothing of ancient believers in miracle—there was no single operative system of thought. The disbelievers were not at one on the

1. Plato *Symposium* 215E; Aristophanes *Wasps* 119; Plutarch *Dialogue on Love* 758F.
2. E. R. Dodds, *The Greeks and the Irrational* (Berkeley: University of California Press, 1951, 1964), p. 79.
3. Plato *Laws* 790E.

ground of their disbelief. Some vivid examples of both credulity and skepticism, from a range of points of view, are sketched in chapter 8.

But is it sufficient to ask concerning miracle—or any other phenomenon from the ancient world—"Did it really happen"? The hermeneutically prior and far more important question is "What did the ancient writer who reported the event understand to have occurred?" Too often historians of religion have not asked the latter question. Instead, they have occupied themselves with discerning abstract patterns—mythic, cultic, literary—in ancient accounts of religious experience. Or their attention has been centered on a timeless truth to which the reported event supposedly refers.

How did such interpretive methods arise? Tracing the development of the long-dominant methods of historians of religion will occupy me for the remainder of this chapter. Only then can we turn to consider an alternative method which has been in the process of formulation for the past century but which has only in recent years begun to take defined shape. This method insists that the essential requirement for interpretation of a text is to read it in context: not merely in literary context, but in the wider, deeper social and cultural context in which both author and audience lived, and in which the language they employed took on the connotations to which the interpreter must seek to be sensitive.

THE LOGICAL AND EMPIRICIST ANTECEDENTS OF CRITICAL-HISTORICAL INQUIRY

The very different modern—or more specifically, post-Enlightenment—modes of interpretation are those which have dominated historical studies and analyses of Graeco-Roman and early Christian literature down to the present. To assess the array of factors involved in the analysis of modern religious phenomena in general and of miracle in particular requires us to go back well before the Enlightenment itself, when both the attack on and the defense of miracle began in an explicit and systematic way. Two major thinkers whose work had formative influence on the intellectual climate in which the question of miracle was raised in the early nineteenth century were John Locke and René Descartes.

In 1619 Descartes, at age twenty-three, conceived the basic theory which shaped his subsequent mathematical and philosophical work: that all nature could be perceived in terms of geometry, and that all sciences could thereby be unified in terms of universal reason. It is ironical that this precocious mathematical genius, whose lifelong goal was to analyze the universe in terms of rational order, should have received in a dream the fundamental theoretical insight on which his later work was built. The point of departure for Descartes's philosophical system was his principle that all things must be doubted (*de omnibus dubitandum*). That procedure, however, led him to arrive at the indubitable conviction that the self exists, and from that he deduced the existence of God (the sum of perfection) and of bodies (the world of matter). This, the greatest of French philosophers, sought nothing less than the unification of all the sciences, a goal to be achieved by what he regarded as the clear, rational, empirical methods that he derived from mathematics. The starting point of this rational enterprise, nevertheless, was doubt.

The stance of radical doubt from which Descartes set out to answer his fundamental ontological and epistemological questions not only had an enduring effect in and of itself but also was akin to the profound uncertainty resulting from the sixteenth-century challenges to intellectual authority represented in the ecclesiastical and theological areas by Luther and Calvin. Descartes's response to the challenge of that uncertainty is epitomized in his famous dictum, *Cogito ergo sum*, or even better in Spinoza's variant of it, *Ego sum cogitans*. The self's existence is disclosed directly without any intermediary factor. Anything else that he may perceive with equal clarity is equally true. Since self-knowledge has been achieved as a self-contained thinking being with no knowledge of the outside world, it follows that the self is wholly independent of that world, and that "mind is distinct from and superior to matter."[4] That I as an imperfect being have

---

4. F. E. Sutcliffe, in Introduction to Descartes's *Discoveries on Method* (New York: Penguin, 1968, 1975), p. 19.

the capacity to conceive of perfection is a sign that a Being exists who could have produced the idea and who possesses that quality. That Being is God, who in his perfection is unable to deceive us, so that we may be confident in the truth of the clear and distinct ideas that arise in our minds. The world of sensory experience, however, is an obstacle to the acquisition of knowledge, which comes by intuition alone. The goal of the human mind, therefore, is to master the world of nature. Descartes's agenda of dominating the physical world sounds like an intellectualistic equivalent of the divine injunction to Adam to subdue the earth and exercise dominion over it (Gn 1:28). And both undertakings were forthwith perverted by human hubris.

Descartes's impact on later critical studies, especially those focused on the question of miracle in the early Christian documents, was twofold: his locating truth in the noumenal world denigrated the phenomenal world in which miracles were reported to occur; his drive to master the world of nature—in spite of its lowly ontological status—contributed to the prideful notion of many natural scientists that they quite literally had everything under control. As violations of natural law, miracles simply cannot occur.

Ironically, the epistemological theories of Descartes's contemporary, John Locke (1632–1704), though they set out on a very different path from that chosen by Descartes, came to reinforce the attitudes toward miracle that were shaped by the Enlightenment. Locke's *Essay concerning Human Understanding* declared that knowledge of the world begins in sense-perception, while knowledge of ourselves is based on introspection and reflection. There are no such things as innate ideas, however; but experience and reflection, though not knowledge in themselves, furnish the mind with the materials of knowledge. There is no other source of ideas than sense-experience and reflection. Among these experiences is the experience of God through his Spirit, which compensates for the inadequacies of human reason. Furthermore, revelation and reason are compatible and mutually reinforcing. Although knowledge of empirical reality may approach certainty, it remains in the realm of the probable. Accordingly, human assent to truth rests on probability, which is based on either observation or human testimony, but it may also be

grounded on things beyond the discovery of our senses. The
wider the basis of assent, the higher the degree of probability,
with universal assent offering the highest degree.[5] Knowledge,
therefore, builds on empirical evidence; its mode of construction is rational, critical evaluation (and weighing) of evidence.
Although Locke's starting point in probabilistic empiricism differs fundamentally from Descartes's point of departure in subjective certitude, the epistemological results are similar, in that
both approaches aim at mastery of the phenomenal world by
rational means. What does this imply concerning miracle?

Fortunately for our purposes, Locke discussed explicitly the
question of miracle, and in so doing anticipated recent developments in analytical thinking that were not picked up by his
immediate contemporaries or by the generations of empiricists
who followed him. The preoccupation of the Deists with the order of nature and the supremacy of reason led them to ignore,
or perhaps to repress, one significant strand in Locke's system:
the supernatural event. In contrast with testimony concerning
events which are consonant with ordinary expectations are reports that run counter to normal experience:

> Though the common Experience, and the Course of Things have
> justly a mighty Influence on the minds of men, to make them give
> or refuse Credit to anything proposed to their Belief; yet is there
> one Case wherein the strangeness of the Fact lessens not the As-
> sent to a fair Testimony given of it. For where such supernatural
> Events are suitable to ends aim'd at by him, who has the Power to
> change the course of Nature, there, under such circumstances, they
> may be fitter to procure Belief, by how much more they are be-
> yond, or contrary to ordinary Observations. This is the proper
> Case of Miracles, which well attested, do not only find Credit
> themselves; but give it to other Truths which need such Confir-
> mation.[6]

Locke expanded on these remarks in shorter works. In *The
Reasonableness of Christianity, as Delivered in the Scriptures*, building
in large part on passages from the Gospel of John (3:36; 4:25,

5. John Locke, Book 4, 16.661.
6. Ibid., p. 667.

26, 39, 40–42; 10:24–26), he declares that the miracles are performed as evidence of Jesus' messiahship. Commenting on Peter's confession of Jesus as the Christ in Matthew 16:16–18, Locke observes: "To convince men of this, he did his miracles: and their assent to, or not assenting to this, made them to be, or not to be, of his church."[7] His performance of miracles is the first factor in the declaration of his messiahship, based on the expectations from the Jewish scriptures.[8] The outlook toward miracle is in keeping with Locke's conciliatory, broad church stance which, though opposed to fanaticism and "enthusiasm," was based in tradition.

In a brief tract, *A Discourse of Miracles*, however, Locke offers a definition of miracle involving analytical dimensions that were not to be developed fully and explicitly until the rise of the phenomenological school under Edmund Husserl and its child, the sociology-of-knowledge, as represented in the present century by the work of Alfred Schutz, Thomas Luckmann, and Peter Berger. The significance of this movement for historical study will be discussed below in detail, but here it may suffice to note the central importance for interpreting miracle that Locke assigns *to the world-view of the observer or analyst*. He defines miracle as "a sensible operation, which, being above the comprehension of the spectator, and in his opinion contrary to the established course of nature, is taken by him to be divine."[9] He goes on to note that, since everyone judges which are nature's laws on the basis of his own acquaintance with nature, what may be a miracle to one will not be so to another. Rather than settle for subjective preference, Locke makes the claim for a unique function of miracle in the biblical world-view. Repeating his affirmation of the sign value of miracle as a confirmation of revelation, he writes, "To know that any revelation is from God, it is necessary to know that the messenger that delivers it is sent from God, and that cannot be known but by credentials given by God himself."[10]

7. Locke, *Works* (London: Tegg, Sharpe & Son, 1823), 7:7–18.
8. Ibid., pp. 32–33.
9. Ibid., 9: 256.
10. Ibid., p. 257.

Locke then proceeds to the extraordinary claim that no other miracles done in this world are concerned with divine revelation: "I do not remember any miracles recorded in the Greek or Roman writers, as done to confirm anyone's mission or doctrine." That claim is made only in behalf of Moses and Christ.[11] Quite apart from the question of the validity of Locke's conclusion about the unique evidential power of biblical miracles, what is important for our purpose is to observe that he recognizes that phenomena which are overtly similar may function in importantly different ways in different thought systems or—to use the sociology-of-knowledge term—"life-worlds." We shall return to this claim of Locke's about the uniqueness of biblical miracle, inquiring especially about the propriety of such a distinction and the demonstrability of his specific assertion about the evidential function. Surprisingly, this aspect of Locke's discussion of knowledge in general and of knowledge of miracle in particular seems not to have been taken up by those otherwise powerfully influenced by his empiricism.

THE SUBJECTION OF THE DIVINE TO NATURAL LAW

The stance of the Deists toward miracle was markedly different from that of Locke. The title, and especially the subtitle, of Matthew Tindal's work provides a clear indication of his position: *Christianity as Old as Creation: or, The Gospel, a Republication of the Religion of Nature.* Published only a few decades after the appearance of Locke's Essay (that is, in 1732), Tindal's treatise is far closer to Descartes. The essence of natural religion is belief in the existence of God and the practice of those duties which result from the knowledge that we, through our reason, have of him and his perfection. Since he is infinitely good and wise, he can design nothing by his laws but our good, and by his power he can bring to pass all he designs for our good. Although Tindal skirts, or at least avoids, mention of the New Testament miracles, he scoffs at miracles claimed by Saint Simeon Stylites and

11. Ibid., p. 258.

others as "impudent forgeries" (p. 77) and calls the story of the
sun standing still (Joshua 10) "elegant fiction" (p. 249). Prayers
at tombs of the saints, extreme unction, penance, and confession
and absolution are dismissed as nonsense: "Natural religion puts
the whole stress on internal penitence and true virtue of soul"
(pp. 111–13). Implicitly, miracle is ruled out because it is in conflict with the divine consistency: "If God acts arbitrarily in any
one instance, he must, or at least he may, do so in all" (p. 108).
Explicitly, Tindal declares that no doctrine should be believed
on the basis of miracle or angelic message. Quoting one Doctor
Claget, whom he characterizes as "judicious," Tindal reports,
"When men pretend to work miracles and talk of immediate
revelations, of knowing the truth by inspiration, we ought not
. . . to be afraid of calling these things into question which are
set off with high-flown pretenses. . . . The tricks and cheats of
superstitious persons, their enthusiastic motions, ridiculous actions, exorcisms and lustrations, and such like; give them occasion to believe it better that there should be no god than such a
god as the author of such a superstitious religion must necessarily be" (pp. 193–95). We should admit nothing to our religion
"except what our reason tells us is worthy of having God as its
author," Tindal declares (p. 197). Obviously, that leaves no room
for miracle, from his point of view.

The certainty of the law of reason was affirmed by other Deists
as well. For Thomas Chubb, the purpose of revelation was to
bring mankind back to reason.[12] To that supreme law the Deity
is subject absolutely and perfectly, thereby manifesting his own
moral perfection[13]—in a phrase reminiscent of Descartes. Although Chubb does not discuss miracle as such, there is in his
description of the value of the Eucharist a hint of the psychological interpretation of scripture that was to provide many with
an appealing option in the twentieth century. Chubb observes
that to participate in the "Bread and Wine" provides no benefit

12. Thomas Chubb, *A Discourse concerning Reason, with regard to Revelation and
Divine Reason* (London: printed for T. Cox, 1731), p. 15.
13. Ibid., p. 57.

unless one is "led to an imitation of the mind and life of Christ, and consequently to a conformity of his affections and actions *to the law of reason*"[14] (italics mine).

The dualistic assumptions of Thomas Morgan,[15] according to which he differentiates the spiritual kingdom proclaimed by Jesus from the temporal political kingdom that Jesus' "Nazarene" Jewish Apostles expected, do not prevent him from depicting Jesus as rebuking the Devil and curing the sick, the blind, the lame. Since he does not explicitly allegorize or psychologize these actions of Jesus, the contrast that Morgan wants to make is apparently between a national-political reign—which he thinks Jesus rejected—and a personal-need-oriented kingdom. We shall have occasion to note how appealing devotees of some of the Graeco-Roman deities found that second option in the Antonine period of imperial Rome, but it is enough to note here that some of the Deists had no quarrel with the miracles of Jesus, together with his death, burial, and resurrection, whereas for others the sole legitimate focus of religion was on the ethics of natural law.

In this same period, however, others engaged in the task of interpreting the scriptures were calling for just the reverse of this imposition of limits that characterized the Deists' project. Jean Alphonse Turretini (1671–1737) began by insisting that the Bible be interpreted like any other document, and that the principles of "natural reason" were the norms by which truth in scripture was to be discerned. But he went on to insist that "No judgment on the basis of the axioms and systems of our day is to be passed on the meaning of the sacred writers, but one must put oneself into the times and into the surroundings in which they wrote, and one must see what concepts could arise in the souls of those who lived at that time." To impose modern doctrines "is certainly the most perverse kind of interpretation and the one least suited to the discovery of truth." The prerequisite

14. Ibid., pp. 64–67.

15. Thomas Morgan, *The Moral Philosopher in a Dialogue between Philalethes a Christian Deist and Theophanes a Christian Jew*, 2d ed., 3 vols. (London, 1738), 1: 88, 377.

is to divest oneself of preconceived opinions: "If, however, we lay aside the ideas of all the opinions and systems of our day and put ourselves into those times and surroundings in which the prophets and apostles wrote, that would certainly be the true way of entering into and recognizing their meaning. . . . Consequently, in the reading of scripture one must keep this rule carefully in mind. An empty head, if I may so express myself, must be brought to scripture; one's head must be, as it were, a *tabula rasa* if it is to comprehend the true and original meaning of scripture." [16]

Turretini's advice went largely unheeded, however, since a major impact of Locke's empiricism was to bring the scriptural narratives to the court of judgment by eighteenth-century rationalist norms, rather than to encourage the interpreter to seek to enter empathetically into the biblical world. Chief spokesman for this skeptical extension of Locke's proposals about knowledge as probability was David Hume, whose discussion of probability and miracle appeared in an essay with a title obviously borrowed from the treatise of Locke, *Essay concerning Human Understanding*. In Hume's "An Enquiry concerning Human Understanding" appear many of Locke's lines of reasoning concerning empirical evidence and degrees of probability. But on the issue of miracle, Hume is diametrically opposed to Locke's position: "A miracle is a violation of natural law: and as a firm and unalterable experience has established these laws, the proof against a miracle, from the very nature of the fact, is as entire as any argument from experience can possibly be imagined." Hume said he could believe a miracle only if the testifier's credibility was so great that it would be a greater miracle for him to tell a falsehood. But "There is not to be found, in all history, any miracle attested by a sufficient number of men of such unquestioned good sense, education and learning, as to secure against all delusion in themselves; of such undoubted integrity, as to

16. Jean Alphonse Turretini, *De Sacrae Scripturae interpretandae methodo tractatus bipartitus*, . . . (Concerning the method of interpreting the Holy Scriptures) (Frankfurt: C. G. Straus [1728], 1776). The translation is from W. G. Kümmel's *The New Testament: The History of the Investigation of Its Problems*, trans. S. M. Gilmour and H. C. Kee (Nashville: Abingdon Press, 1972), pp. 333–34.

place them beyond all suspicion of any design to deceive others; of such credit and reputation in the eyes of mankind, as to have a great deal to lose in case of their being detected in any falsehood; and at the same time attesting facts performed in a public manner, and in so celebrated a part of the world, as to render detection unavoidable."[17] In contrast to the overwhelming improbability of there being truth to any miraculous claims, Hume notes that there is in human beings "a passion of surprise and wonder" which inclines the mind to give credence to miracles: "If the spirit of religion join itself to the love of wonder, there is an end of common sense." Not surprisingly, reports of miracle are most common among the ignorant and the barbarians. Hume has special praise for Lucian of Samasota, who exposed the tricks of the charlatan Alexander to the gullible Paphlagonians. Not only is there no testimony of any kind for a miracle which has ever amounted to a probability, much less a proof, but "No human testimony can have such force as to prove a miracle, and make it a just foundation for any system of religion."[18]

THE RISE OF HISTORICAL-CRITICAL METHOD

The problem of miracle in the nineteenth century is inseparably linked with the rise of critical-historical study of the Bible in the two preceding centuries. Concurrent with the emergence of the skeptical estimate of scripture, especially with regard to the miraculous element, represented by Hume was the rise of a self-consciously critical method for analysis of the biblical texts. This had begun in the later seventeenth century, but in the work of Richard Simon (1658–1712) and J. A. Bengel (1687–1752) criticism was largely devoted to questions of text and canon.[19] The eighteenth-century studies of J. S. Semler (1725–88) and J. D. Michaelis (1717–91) prepared the way for historical study of the individual books but made no more than a beginning at that

---

17. David Hume, *Essays and Treatises on Several Subjects*, vol. 2 (London: printed for T. Cadell, C. Elliott, T. Kay and Co., 1788), pt. 10, pp. 114–35. Quotation is from pp. 120–31.

18. Ibid., pp. 122–23, 131.

19. Kümmel, *New Testament*, pp. 40–50.

larger undertaking of differentiating among the various life-worlds of the writers. Semler, for example, rejected the notion of the "uniformity and homogeneity" of the biblical books as "without historical justification." He thought moral judgments would lead others, like himself, to regard the Apocalypse, with its vindictive judgment scenes, as "unpleasant and repulsive."[20] He did plead, however, for scholars to examine the writings in their own historical and linguistic contexts: "An interpreter ought not to interject anything of his own ideas into the writing he wishes to interpret, but to make all he gets from it part of his current thinking and make himself sufficiently certain concerning it solely on the basis of its content and meaning."[21] Even though Semler's goal of presuppositionlessness may be unattainable, it does anticipate the method of the phenomenologists, who seek to bracket out for analytical purposes their own assumptions and values.[22] His undertaking was marred, however, by his insistence on a sharp differentiation between the literal and the spiritual meaning of scripture: that is, the "sensual," political mode in which Jesus was heard by his Jewish contemporaries and the pure, "spiritual" significance intended by Jesus.[23] On this distinction Semler was in agreement with H. S. Reimarus (1694–1768), whose famous essay (never published during his lifetime) was seen by Albert Schweitzer to mark the beginning of "The Quest of the Historical Jesus."[24] Here we have an analogy with, and perhaps even a remote descendant of, the Cartesian dualism, according to which only the clear and distinct ideas of the mind are free of the error inevitably involved in what is conveyed to the self through the senses.[25] Though it is not expressly

20. Ibid., pp. 63–65.

21. Ibid., p. 66.

22. Albert Schweitzer, *Quest of the Historical Jesus*, English trans. by W. Montgomery (New York: Macmillan, 1948; London: A. and C. Black, 1910), p. 25. (Original German title *Von Reimarus zu Wrede. Eine Geschichte der Leben-Jesu-Forschung.*)

23. Ibid., p. 26.

24. Ibid., p. 23. Cf. Kümmel, *New Testament*, pp. 89–90.

25. Descartes, *Sixth Meditation*, ed. F. E. Sutcliffe (New York: Penguin [1968], 1979), p. 161.

stated, the implication of both Semler and Reimarus is that historical analysis is carried out in order to differentiate between the external, historical phenomena and the spiritual core concealed within.

In 1800 appeared the first volume of a commentary on the first three Gospels by H. E. G. Paulus (1761–1851), who announced his project as "a historical and pragmatic survey of the life of Jesus." His undertaking was dominated, however, by his conviction that every word of the gospels is an accurate representation of the historical Jesus.[26] But since he was a thoroughgoing rationalist who could not believe that the miracles occurred as reported, Paulus undertook a systematic explanation for the miracles to show that what happened in each case was merely a credulous misunderstanding by Jesus' contemporaries of what was actually a natural event. For example, what the disciples mistook for a miraculous illumination of Jesus at the Transfiguration was a natural play of light and mist on the mountaintop. At the empty tomb, the winding sheets left behind were transformed into angels by the pious, superstitious visitors. The short-run discrediting of the New Testament accounts by skeptics and rationalists did not undercut for him the importance of the biblical witness, however, since the long-run result was to encourage and enable the interpreter to separate out historical chaff from eternal grain.

THE LOCUS OF HISTORY: MIND OR FACT?

Paradoxically, it was G. W. F. Hegel (1770–1831) who, in spite of his scornful attitude toward historical criticism—what he called "replacing historical data by subjective fancies"[27]—was the one whose philosophy of history provided the decisive impetus and the dominating method for the historico-critical enterprise. The tensions between phenomena and rationality, between mind and

26. H. E. G. Paulus, *Philologisch-Kritischer und historischer Kommentar bei die drey esten Evangelien*, 4 vols. (Heidelberg: A. Oswald, 1828). Excerpts in Kümmel, *New Testament*, p. 91.

27. G. W. F. Hegel, *Reason in History*, trans. Robert S. Hartmann, in "The Three Methods of Writing History" (Indianapolis: Bobbs-Merrill, [1953]), p. 9.

spirit, between ancient religion and nineteenth-century intellectual sophistication, did not have to be circumvented or explained away but could be exulted in as part of the dialectical process of history itself. As R. A. Hartman observed in comparing Hegel and Kant (1724–1804), "Hegel rejects Kant's program of examining the faculty of understanding before examining the nature of things. For him things and thought are dialectically interrelated." The historical process moves according to the divine laws of reason; by it the Divine Mind constitutes reality. "Since the divine thought progresses according to its own laws, which are the laws of the world, all that is must be and all is as it ought to be. But what is real in existence is only that which is divine in it. Only this it is which develops. Everything else is contingent and must perish."[28]

For Hegel, mankind "constitutes the antithesis to the natural world; he is the being that lifts it up to the second world. We have in our universal consciousness two realms, the realm of nature and the realm of Spirit. The realm of Spirit consists in what is produced by man. One may have all sorts of ideas about the Kingdom of God, but it is always a realm of Spirit to be realized and brought about in man."[29] This rosy view of the free unfolding of the Spirit in history stood in direct conflict with the biblical picture of the Fall, and with other mythological portrayals of a pristine paradise. Hegel denounced those images as "monstrous errors and perversions" but acknowledged that valuable information had been turned up in the process of searching out these themes in oriental and ancient religious traditions. Nevertheless, the material produced by these investigations into the alleged origins of humanity remains in the realm of "prehistory" and therefore lies outside the historical process.[30]

Although Hegel does not deal directly with the question of miracle, he has a view of history as the working out of the ultimate purpose of God: "We know of God that He is the most perfect; He can will only Himself and what is like Him." Yet that

28. Hegel, *Reason*, in "The Idea of History and Its Realization," p. 20.
29. Hegel, *Reason*, in "The Course of World History," p. 72.
30. Ibid., pp. 3, 73–74.

will manifest itself through the human spirit and in the idea of human freedom. Spirit is at work "to make itself (actually) into what it is (potentially)," so that "world history is the exhibition of spirit striving to attain knowledge of its own nature."[31] Hegel is interested in this broad intellectualized equivalent of biblical eschatology, according to which the movement of history is the unfolding of the Divine Mind, the outcome of which will be the Kingdom of God. Of specific events in which this is foreshadowed by way of miracle, he evinces no interest.

Several factors are operative in Hegel's philosophical system, however, that were to have major influence on the methods of nineteenth-century historical criticism in general and on the analysis of miracle in particular. First, there was new methodological justification for examining all possible evidence in the field of religion, since it was believed a priori that behind the diverse and complex phenomena was the work of the Divine Mind that was striving toward the accomplishment of a unified scheme of history. Second, there was a rationale for distinguishing a core of spiritual significance from the culture-conditioned, contingent features of the account by which the eternal truth is imperfectly conveyed. These positions were adopted as axioms by D. F. Strauss (1808–74), who produced the first fully historical analysis of the gospel narratives, and who—important to our line of inquiry—devoted special attention to the miracle stories.[32]

MYTH AND HISTORY

Adopting from Hegel a triadic pattern as his mode of critical analysis, Strauss set over against each other (1) the position of orthodoxy, with its assumption of the supernatural element in the gospel accounts as both the dynamic that gave rise to the history and the guarantee of its accuracy, and (2) the rationalist

31. Ibid., pp. 21–23.
32. David Frederick Strauss, *Das Leben Jesu, kritisch bearbeitet*, vol. 1, 1835; vol. 2, 1836. English translation: *The Life of Jesus, Critically Examined*, ed. and intro. Peter C. Hodgson; trans. George Eliot (Philadelphia: Fortress Press, 1972).

position, which wanted to retain the credibility of the stories, but did so by resorting to natural explanations for the apparently miraculous occurrences. The solution that Strauss offered was (3) what he called mythical, by which he meant that the stories were to be regarded as metaphorical vehicles through which spiritual truths about Jesus were conveyed to the discerning reader. Among the natural explanations offered for the seeming miracles of Jesus by Strauss's rationalistic contemporaries are two concerning the transfer of the demons into the herd of pigs (Mark 5): (1) the swine had fallen into the sea during a storm as Jesus approached Gerasa, and he or his followers persuaded the demoniac that the demons had gone into the deep with the drowned pigs; (2) the swineherds had come down to the sea to meet Jesus on arrival, and some of their untended herds had fallen into the water about the same time Jesus was expelling the demons, with the result that onlookers made a cause-and-effect connection.[33] Strauss's own solution to the supernaturalist-rationalist controversy he found in the Johannine miracle stories—especially the turning of water into wine—and the Lukan account of the cursing of the barren fig-tree: to treat the miracles as symbolic or parabolic representations rather than as literal accounts.

Strauss's positive alternative to either supernaturalistic or rationalistic interpretation of miracle stories in the Gospels was his mythic approach. He defined myth in the Gospels as "a narrative relating, directly or indirectly to Jesus which may be considered not as the expression of a fact, but as the product of an idea of his earliest followers."[34] Pure myth has two sources: (1) the messianic ideas and expectations existing among Jews prior to the time of Jesus, and (2) the impression left on his followers by Jesus' personal character, actions, and fate. Historical myth mingles fact and conceptions culled from the idea of the Messiah. By contrast with both, legend does not serve to clothe an idea but is the addition of the author to lend clarity or climax to his representation of Jesus. Among the miracle stories affected by Old Testament prophecies and messianic expectations are those

33. Ibid., p. 430.
34. Ibid., pp. 86–87.

which describe the cure of the blind and the lepers, based on
the models of Elijah and Elisha and such prophecies as Is 35:5–
6. For stories of demonic possession he offered a rational, psychological explanation: the power of Jesus' personality helped
the victims overcome their neurotic obsessions.[35] Clearly, Strauss
is most comfortable with those miracle stories which are already
treated symbolically within the text of the New Testament: the
signs of Jesus in the Gospel of John.

Ferdinand Christian Baur, also deeply influenced by Hegel,
adopted a different approach to historical analysis of the New
Testament. Building more directly on the Hegelian scheme of
thesis-antithesis-synthesis, he undertook a reconstruction of early
Christian history on the assumption that the initial dynamic of
the early Christian movement arose from the dialectic between
Paul's law-free gospel, on the one hand, and the hybrid of Jewish legalism and messianism that constituted Paul's opposition in
the Corinthian correspondence and in Galatians, on the other.
Of more direct relevance for our investigation, however, is his
conclusion that each of the Gospels has a tendency (Matthew's is
Jewish; Luke is trying to mediate between Jewish and Gentile
Christianity). The specifics of his proposals are of mixed value,
but his insight that each writer in the New Testament represents
a view which must be examined for its own sake and in its own
historical context is of enduring validity. The question of miracle as such is not a major concern of Baur.

What is central for Baur's analysis of the Gospels is his conviction that the essence of these documents lies in their report of
Jesus' mission: "He has come only in order, by the moral demands he made on men, to introduce 'the kingship of God,' to
invite them to enter it, and thereby to open it. The 'Gospel' as
such, the proclamation of the kingship of God as a morally religious community based on the teaching of Jesus, is here all that
counts."[36] This interpretive method, by which the essence of the

35. Ibid., p. 436.
36. F. C. Baur, *Kritische Untersuchungen über die Kanonischen Evangelien, ihr
Verhältniss zu einander, ihren Charakter und Ursprung* (Tübingen: Ludw. Fr. Fues,
1847), pp. 108, 239.

text is reduced to a moral or theological formulation, was to dominate New Testament studies for more than a century after the publication of his work. Although it has been rarely acknowledged by practitioners of the history-of-religions method, for which Baur's work was an important preparatory factor, this reductionist strategy has in fact provided the unacknowledged norms by which many ostensibly objective historical judgments have been made. When the central interest is theological ideas, miracle can either be treated as a metaphorical vehicle for religious truth (as Strauss did) or it can be pushed to the periphery as disposable excess baggage, a regrettable accretion of the Christian tradition as it passed through the Graeco-Roman world.

The same charge of reductionism may also fittingly be leveled against the opponents of the Baur school, as is evident in the work of Adolf von Harnack. In summing up the results of the enormous and immensely learned volumes on the history of dogma,[37] Harnack in his popular lectures insists that the gospel of Jesus is timeless, that Hellenistic influences on Paul, if they exist, are indirect through Judaism, and that while Jesus probably believed in the Devil and other features of eschatological conflict and triumph, these were no more than primitive notions of his time and culture. But the essence of Christianity is Jesus' message of the kingdom of God and its coming—that is, its coming to the heart of the individual. Thus "the whole of Jesus' message can be reduced to these two heads: God as the Father, and the human soul so ennobled that it can and does unite with him."[38] Harnack affirms the operation of the supernatural but not in terms of miracle. Rather, "It is a purely religious blessing, the inner link with the living God." Like Hegel before him, Harnack perceives miracle and supernatural public acts as merely

37. A. von Harnack, *History of Dogma*, 2d ed. (Freiburg: J. C. B. Mohr, 1893) vol. 1.
38. A. von Harnack, *Das Wesen des Christentums?* (What is Cʰ ᵗ zig: J. C. Hinrichs, 1900), English trans. T. B. Saund Putman's Sons [New York] and Williams and Norg. with introduction by R. Bultmann (New York: Harpe 241 in Kümmel, *New Testament*.

contingent features of the gospel narratives, and as such they must perish.

THE FOCUS ON HISTORICAL CONTEXT

Among scholars engaged in the historical study of Christian origins, Otto Pfleiderer was a major forerunner of what was later to be known as the history-of-religions school. Though he was a pupil of F. C. Baur—one of the last—he disagreed with his mentor in that he rejected the neat thesis-antithesis pattern of Baur's historical reconstruction and pointed out the range of diverse cultural influences that were operative among the early Christians. While Baur's impact on historical study had been chiefly to raise theological and institutional questions about the emerging church, Pfleiderer shifted attention to wider social, cultural, and contextual questions.

His explorations of the possible influence of Hellenistic culture on Paul were matched by studies among classicists of Graeco-Roman religions and the possible links between them and nascent Christianity. Pfleiderer raised the rhetorical question of whether Paul when he wrote in Romans 6 about baptism and new birth "was not familiar with the rite of the Eleusinian mysteries."[39] He had no doubt that the Eucharist was analogous to the pagan sacrificial meals. Obviously what was emerging in the later nineteenth century was the historical method that explains the phenomena of early Christianity *by analogy with religious practices, concepts, and institutions in the Jewish but especially in the Graeco-Roman world.* From the outset, however, one can discern that more is going on in the history-of-religions enterprise than the assembling of massive data for classification and comparison purposes. One of the pioneers of the movement, Hermann Usener, announced that he was exploring the background of such New Testament ideas as virgin birth and Son of God in Greek

39. Otto Pfleiderer, *Des Urchristenthum, seine Schriften und Lehre, in geschichtlichem Zusammenhang beschrieben* (Primitive Christianity, its literature and doctrine described in historical interrelationship) (Berlin: G. Reimer, 1887). English trans. Montgomery (New York: G. P. Putman's Sons, 1906; and London: Williams Norgate, 1911), 1: 436–64.

culture, with the aim of discovering the universal religious ideas and aspirations, so that "the divine kernel of our religion, freed from the husk of poetry and dogma, will prove itself only all the more effective to coming, more advanced generations as a source of salvation and as a means of lifting the soul to God."[40]

In a survey of methods employed in the study of Greek religion during the nineteenth and early twentieth centuries, Walter Burkert has indicated the shift that occurred from an initial mixture of Christian apologetics and counterpositions defending paganism (as in Goethe and Schiller) to a responsible effort to make available the basic texts and to arrange them in chronological order. Analytical processes during this period, however, were informed by a range of historical and methodological assumptions: among the romantics, the aim was to show that the myths were expressions of a particular *Volksgeist* or ritual pattern[41]; among those at work in the important and maturing field of linguistics, a dominant emphasis was on myth as an allegorical expression of nature (growth, fertility). In England an attempt was made to identify totemism or animism and/or some related concept of soul or spirit as the primal element of religion. In this linking of myth with ritual, the goal was to uncover the oldest forms of religion, such as the ritual murder of the king and the dying-and-rising god. Although the influence of these British-based hypotheses, as exemplified in the work of Sir James Frazer and of Jane Harrison, continues to be strong, the combination of careful investigation of texts and of studies based on abundant archaeological evidence has—in Burkert's view, properly—led to basic distrust of these simplistic generalizations.

THE SEARCH FOR PRIMAL PATTERNS: MYTH VERSUS HISTORY

The romanticizing of the study of religion is dramatically evident even in the choice of title of Frazer's magnum opus, *The*

---

40. H. Usener, *Religionsgeschischtliche Untersuchungen I* (Bonn: F. Cohen, 1899), p. 187.

41. Walter Burkert, *Griechische Religion der archäischen und klassichen Epoche* (Stuttgart: Kohlhammer, 1977), pp. 22–25.

Golden Bough, taken from the painting of the same name by J. M. W. Turner, in which is pictured a romantic spot in the Alban Hills sacred to the memory of Diana. Frazer describes the artist's work as "suffused with the golden glow of imagination in which the divine mind of Turner steeped and transfigured even the fairest natural landscape," though he goes on to report that this idyllic spot was the scene of the recurrent ritual slaying of the king-priest.[42] This ritual had no historical basis, however, but "belongs to that large class of myths which are made up to explain the ritual." Their "real value" is twofold: they provide the standard for demonstrating the nature of worship, and they illustrate that the origins of worship are "lost in the myths of fabulous antiquity."[43] Frazer's discussion of this and other themes, such as the sacred trees, is set in an atmosphere of pleasurable romantic tragedy.

A striking feature of Frazer's encyclopedic work is the complete absence of historical consciousness. References to tragic figures in religious and mythical traditions appear from the first to the last pages of this monumental study, but with no hint of historical change or of the effects of social forces. B. Malinowski noted appreciatively Frazer's extraordinary gift for depicting in vivid, emotionally evocative fashion the backdrop against which the myth and ritual he described took place. It was as intuitive artist rather than as theoretician that Frazer earned praise from Malinowski. Thus, for example, although one can infer from Frazer's material the insight that "religious and magical belief has always functioned as a principle of order, of integration, and of organization at primitive and at higher levels of human de-

42. Frazer's basic thesis of the murdered and restored king was explored in his *Adonis, Attis, Osiris*, for which the subtitle "Studies in Oriental Religion" indicates what he considers to be the important influence of Eastern religions on Greek mythology (London: Macmillan, 1907; p. 2). Frazer's more famous work, *The Golden Bough*, grew from edition to edition, changing from an original two volumes in 1898 to twelve from 1911–36. An abridged one-volume edition was published in 1922 and issued in a new edition, edited by T. H. Gaster in 1959, which is here quoted (p. 1).

43. Frazer, *Golden Bough* (1922), p. 5.

velopment,"[44] Frazer did not make that theoretical base explicit. Rather, he failed to take into account methodologically the social-psychological or the sociological implications of the folklore and mythology that he was reporting in such a colorful, sympathetic way. When treating what ought justly to be recognized as social factors—such as property rights or the society's reliance on the king for both social and cosmic order—Frazer explained these phenomena as resting on the "rotten foundations" of superstition.

On our theme of miracle, Malinowski had clearly and forcefully articulated views, on the basis of which he more explicitly criticized Frazer. He reports Frazer as making this distinction between magic and religion: the former involves the direct coercion of natural forces, based on the assumptions that like produces like, and that things once together influence each other after they have been separated; the latter is based on the propitiation of the gods by the believer.[45] Malinowski thinks that Frazer is wrong in assuming that the difference rests on "an essentially different attitude towards the universe," but he then goes on to describe religion as "a system of belief defining the place of man in the universe, the provenience of man, and his goal." Since Malinowski had such a restricted definition of religion—public or private ceremonial, prayer, sacrifice, and sacrament[46]—he failed to recognize what is only inchoate in Frazer's treatment of magic and religion but has the potential of achieving more fully the very goal which Malinowski announced as his own: the perception of magic and religion as socially grounded, as the ground of human life moves from a purely biological base to one of increasing complexity socially and culturally, and as the need for organization and stability thereby intensifies.[47] What Frazer hinted at and Malinowski missed is

44. Bronislaw Malinowski, *A Scientific Theory of Culture* (Chapel Hill: University of North Carolina Press, 1944). Quotations are from reprint (New York: Oxford University Press, 1960), p. 191.

45. Ibid., pp. 196, 200.

46. Ibid., pp. 200–01.

47. Ibid., p. 175.

that magic and religion are two different modes of the social construction of reality in the attempt to bring order and meaning to personal and social existence. Shunning the issues of social and cultural change, Frazer chose instead to concentrate on what he deemed to be the perennial. For Frazer what mattered most was eternal recurrence, as expressed in the traditional cry with which his book closes: "Le roi est mort, vive le roi!"[48]

THE ESCAPE FROM HISTORY

Although Frazer himself was avowedly impatient or even uncomfortable with psychological interpretation of myth, his work was exploited fully by Freud and his school, who treated ancient mythology as an allegorical statement of timeless human anxieties and aspirations and, ironically, drew from Frazer's work the anthropological data to demonstrate this view. C. Kerenyi's study of Asklepios, though carried out with the explicit denial that it was employing the methods of Jungian psychology, shows by its title ("Archetypal Image of the Physician's Existence") and by its announced interest in "primordial mythology" ("In mythology man's own being and the reality of a being that enfolds him are expressed simultaneously in the modality peculiar to mythology")[49] that the work's overarching goal is analogous to that of Jung: to discern psychological master-images through the historical, inscriptional, and textual data. Kerenyi's interest in Asklepios's miracles of healing is minor and is subsumed under his primary concern with archetypal images.

The contemporary equivalent of Frazer in the field of history-of-religion is Mircea Eliade. Like Frazer, Eliade's vast researches and encyclopedic collections of data revolve around a major motif: not the dying-and-rising king (so Frazer), but the triumph over and transformation of historical time into "primordial mythical time made present." This occurs through "every reli-

48. Frazer, *Golden Bough* (1922), p. 714.
49. C. Kerenyi, *Asklepios* (New York: Pantheon/Bollingen Foundation, 1959), p. xxvi.

gious festival, any liturgical time" which represents "the reactualization of a sacred event that took place in a mythical past, 'in a beginning.'"[50] What is unique about Christianity is that time itself is ontologized, "is made to *be*, which means it ceases to become, it transforms itself into eternity." The Judaeo-Christian tradition thus presents us with the supreme hierophany: "the transfiguration of the historical event into the hierophany."[51] Without his directly saying so, Eliade apparently assumes that "this abolition of history, this viewpoint according to which for every Christian individually . . . the paradise regained . . . may be attained from this moment," carries with it the dissolution of the need to analyze religious data by means of historical methods. Or as he expresses it elsewhere, "Ritual abolishes profane, chronological time and recovers the sacred Time of myth. Man becomes contemporary with the exploits that the gods performed *in illo tempore*. On the one hand, this revolt against the irreversibility of time helps man to 'construct reality'; on the other, it frees him from the weight of dead Time, assures him that he is able to abolish the past, to begin his life anew, and to re-create his world."[52] There is no place in Eliade's enterprise for a consideration of social or cultural transformation or of historical development. On the specific subject of miracle, Eliade is explicit: "Indeed, the Christian admits that, after the incarnation, miracles are no longer easy to recognize; the greatest of all miracles having been, in fact, the Incarnation itself, all that *which was clearly manifested as miraculous* before Jesus Christ is of no further use or meaning after his coming." For Eliade it is sufficient that, if one is "close to Christ," one should seek to "recognize the marvelous" and approach "every historical event . . . with 'fear and trembling.'"[53]

Like Frazer and Kerenyi, Eliade declares that he is opposed to reductionism in the study of religion, such as the attempts to

50. All quotations from M. Eliade are from the Eliade Reader, *Myths, Rites and Symbols*, ed. W. Beane and W. Doty, 3 vols. (New York: Harper, 1975), p. 33.

51. Ibid., p. 75.

52. Ibid., pp. 38–39.

53. Ibid., p. 77.

portray religious behavior or ideology as projections of the unconscious or as covers for political or social factors. Yet the result
of all three of these men's scholarly enterprises is to play down
or even to eliminate the factor of historical change, whereby social and cultural transformations occur in human existence down
through the ages and affect substantively the way in which the
cosmos and man's place within it are perceived. To retreat into
"the spiritual unity" which is allegedly "subjacent to the history
of humanity"[54] is to evade the responsibility of the intellectual
historian, not to discharge it.

A recently emergent variant of these antihistorical approaches to the study of religion is carried on in the name of
Claude Lévi-Strauss, whose structuralist method has had wide
influence in the field of anthropology. Although Lévi-Strauss's
own work evinces little interest in miracle as such, interpreters
who have adopted his method as a hermeneutical base have found
it useful for handling miracle tradition. It is essential to our inquiry, therefore, to survey the structuralist enterprise, since it
has directly affected interpretive and historical methods in recent scholarship. In the opening chapters of his *Introduction to
Structuralism*,[55] Michael Lane has conveniently set out both the
agenda and the procedures of the structuralists, specifically that
of Lévi-Strauss. Lane perceives that five basic questions are addressed: (1) How can the social behavior of any human group
be most exactly, meaningfully, and intelligently described? (2)
How can these social phenomena be accounted for and explained? (3) How do the different sets of social phenomena within
a group—its myths, kinship-system, and so on—relate to one
another and to the totality? (4) What are the interrelationships,
if any, that exist between social groups as wholes (whether they
be primitive tribes, feudal states, or advanced industrial soci-
eties)? (5) What have they in common that might provide a basis
for meaningful comparison? Structuralism regards itself as a
method for organizing raw material to provide answers to these

54. Ibid., p. 121.
55. M. Lane, *Introduction to Structuralism* (New York: Basic Books, 1970). Published in Great Britain under the title *Structuralism: A Reader*.

questions, which are the traditional ones raised by sociology and social anthropology.[56]

The relevance of these questions for our study is evident. The question is, how effectively does the structuralist method contribute to solutions? Lane helps define what he regards as the distinctive method of structuralism. It is a method whose scope includes all human social phenomena, no matter what their form—not only the social sciences but also the humanities and fine arts. The basic assumption, building on the linguistic theories of Ferdinand de Saussure,[57] is that all social phenomena— whether clothing, kinship systems, literature, marriage systems—constitute language in a formal sense. Accordingly, the theory runs, their regularities may be reduced to the same set of abstract rules that define and govern what we normally think of as a language in the sense of a "socially employed system of communication" with its own code and vocabulary. All the members of a society constitute the lexicon or repertory of permissible terms.[58] For example, kinship rules constitute the syntax or grammar which determines the relationships of the components. Instead of making inductive judgments about the whole on the basis of analysis of the parts, structuralism insists that the whole and its parts can be understood only in terms of the relationships between the parts and of the parts to the whole. It studies, therefore, "not the elements of the whole, but the complex network of relationships that link and unite these elements."

More radical, however, is the assertion that analysis must not at all focus on the components or on the phenomena at the observational level, but on the structures "below and behind empirical reality." The ordinary observer sees only the external, superficial evidence, which is the product of the true structure. What is basic is the deep structure. Here the enterprise of structuralism receives strong support from the linguistic theory of

56. Ibid., pp. 12–13.
57. Ferdinand de Saussure, *Cours de linguistique générale*, pt. 1 (Paris: Payot, 1916). English trans. W. Baskin (New York: Philosophical Library, 1960).
58. Lane, *Structuralism*, p. 14.

Noam Chomsky: "There is in man an innate, genetically transmitted and determined mechanism that acts as a structuring force."[59] Just as in natural language, the possible ways of structuring speech represent only a narrow spectrum of what might theoretically be conceivable, so in human social communication systems "we can imagine a hierarchy in which the innate structure generates a specialized structure for a particular type of activity," which in turn produces the limited repertory of observable social phenomena at the surface level.

What bearing does this set of assumptions have on the historical task? We get our first clues when the structuralists tell us that if we compare two different patterns of social relationships or of authority, separated by time and space, we should not argue that some factor caused the one to differ from the other. Rather, we can only say that a certain structure has been transformed into another structure. Repeated observations of comparable changes enable us to determine the laws of transformation.[60] What this means for Lévi-Strauss is astonishingly simple: that all structures characterized by relationships are "ultimately reducible to binary opposition," including society, myth, and the entire inventory of social relationships, concepts, and institutions. Since the structure of language—the paradigm for the entire enterprise of the structuralists—is synchronic (concerned with mutual and simultaneous relationships) rather than diachronic (tracing developments in temporal succession), the structuralist's goal is "the realization of the whole inventory of social relations that the unconscious reason both makes possible and restricts." Ideally this can be reduced to algebraic formulation, according to Lévi-Strauss[61]—which is not a style readily adaptable to historical analysis.[62]

---

59. Noam Chomsky, *Reflections on Language* (New York: Pantheon, 1975); quoted from Lane, *Structuralism*, p. 15. Developed in *Reflections on Language*, pp. 29–35.

60. Lane, *Structuralism*, pp. 16–17.

61. Ibid., p. 34.

62. An attempt at schematic reduction of social relationships to diagrammatic representation is offered by Peter Abell in Lane's *Structuralism*, pp. 389–410.

One does not have to rely on inference alone, however, to discover what the import of structuralism might be for the historian's work. Roland Barthes, in an essay on "Historical Discourse," raises the question (and answers it negatively) whether there is any real difference between factual and imaginary narrative, between fiction and history. He insists that there are no linguistic features which are peculiar to one or the other of these two literary types, since the historian is just as personally present in his writing as is the fiction writer, even though the former may feign noninvolvement and act as though he were an "objective subject."[63] The historian's tactic of writing only assertive statements, rather than dealing with what did not happen or what might have happened, is akin to the repressive stance of psychotic or schizophrenic discourse.[64] The historian's linking of fact and meaning is an act of illusion, even of self-delusion, since "'fact' can only exist linguistically, as a term in a discourse, yet we behave as if it were a simple reproduction of something on another plane of existence altogether, some extrastructural 'reality.'" Or again, "Historical discourse does not follow reality, it only signifies it;[65] it asserts at every moment: *this happened*, but the meaning conveyed is only that someone is making an assertion." History is no more than a "reality effect," a "secularized reliquary," "the present sign of a dead thing." Barthes concludes his biopsy—or autopsy—with the pronouncement: "Historical narrative is dying; from now on the touchstone of history is not so much reality as intelligibility."[66]

Lévi-Strauss himself sounds not quite so lugubrious in his assessment of the place of history in social analysis. Writing on "History and Anthropology,"[67] he takes to task Malinowski and

63. R. Barthes, in ibid., pp. 145, 148.

64. Barthes, in ibid., p. 153.

65. "Signify" is a technical term for structuralists, drawn from F. de Saussure, who in language analysis differentiates between the verbal sign (= signifier) and what is signified. Between them is no intrinsic rapport and hence no stable relationship.

66. Barthes, in Lane, *Structuralism*, pp. 154, 155.

67. Claude Lévi-Strauss, *Structural Anthropology* (New York: Basic Books, 1963), 1: 27.

his followers, who spurn the inductive method in favor of isolated studies of phenomena but who nevertheless make procla-
mations based on intuitions. In Lévi-Strauss's opinion, "A little
history . . . is better than no history at all."[68] He goes on to com-
mend the work of ethnographers and historians, whose aim is
"to enlarge a specific experience to the dimensions of a more
general one, which thereby becomes accessible *as experience* to
men of another century or another epoch." To do their work
effectively, they must possess the qualities of skill, precision, a
sympathetic approach, and objectivity, although their output
differs significantly: "History organizes its data in relation to
conscious expressions of life, while anthropology proceeds by
examining its unconscious foundations."[69] Tracing the diachronic structures is indispensable to historical work, because
"by showing institutions in the process of transformation, history alone makes it possible to abstract the structure which underlies the many manifestations and remains permanent
throughout a succession of events." The historian's work, according to Lévi-Strauss, is merely preparatory to the major enterprise: anthropology. Thus, "If the anthropologist brings to
analysis of social phenomena the same scrupulous attention as
the historian, it is in order to eliminate, by a kind of backward
course, all that they owe to the historical process and to conscious thought. . . . His goal is to grasp, beyond the conscious
and shifting images which men hold, the complete range of unconscious possibilities."

More is at stake here than a kind of intellectual status, as though
historians could take part only in the preliminaries but never in
the main event. More serious is the ontological distinction between the allegedly ephemeral, phenomenal realm in which historians may legitimately work, and the universal, noumenal realm
where the anthropologist of this persuasion operates.

Throughout these reductionist enterprises we have surveyed,
from the rise of the history-of-religions method down to con-

68. Ibid., 1:12.
69. Ibid., p. 18.

temporary structuralism, there is a terror-stricken flight from history, an anxious retreat into a changeless, universal realm of the unconscious or the intuitive. Critics might note that such an internal realm is by definition inaccessible to critical analysis or empirical demonstration. What eludes us T. S. Eliot described in "The Dry Salvages":

> Men's curiosity searches past and future
> And clings to that dimension. But to
> Apprehend the point of intersection of
> The timeless with time, is an occupation
> For the saint—

If not for the saint, at least for the historian. The choice is not between the historicist's foolishly confident reconstruction of cause-and-effect historical past "as it really happened" on the one hand, and retreat into a realm of theoretical fancy, a kind of Cloud of Unknowing on the other. What seems called for is to take with full seriousness the announced aims of the structuralists, but to eschew both their assumptions and their procedures.

HISTORY AS THE TRANSFORMATION OF STRUCTURES

The one structuralist who makes more nearly adequate provision for assessing the transformations that take place in historical process is Jean Piaget. Although he develops a dialectical system of thought, it is fundamentally different from that of Lévi-Strauss, whose "binary opposition" consists of two juxtaposed abstractions, which are supposed to be "deep structures," and therefore "real" in a way that phenomena which reflect the binary opposition are not. For Piaget, however, the dialectic is between the *structure* as a system of transformations and *construction* which is continually in process. "There *is* no 'form as such' or 'content as such,' but each element . . . is always simultaneously form to the content it subsumes and content for some higher form."[70] The visual image Piaget calls forth is not that of

70. Jean Piaget, *Structuralism*, ed. and trans. Chaninah Maschler (New York: Harper, 1970), p. 35.

oscillation of a charge between two poles, but a spiral of human knowledge, in which the radius increases as the spiral rises. Simplicity is a sign of weakness of any theory.[71] He rejects the notion that mathematics can be reduced to logic and that logic can be exhaustively formalized.[72] And he denounces the goal of Chomsky and others of reducing mathematics and logic to linguistics, and limiting the entire life of the mind to speech, since he sees in this falling back on a fixed, innate scheme an attempt to avoid both history and the notion of transcendent essences. The model for the study of human intelligence to which Piaget makes repeated reference is drawn from the field of biology: C. H. Waddington's study of the interaction between the gene complex and the environment in the course of embryological development "involves a kinetic equilibration whereby deviations from certain necessary paths of development are compensated for." The genes respond to the environment in such a way that 'selection' operates, not on the gene complex as such, but on these responses. Waddington pictures "the relationship between the organism and its environment as a cybernetic loop such that the organism selects its environment while being conditioned by it." Piaget declares that this process is to be discerned, not only in the development of the individual organism, nor in the population alone, but in the whole complex of milieu and genetic pool.[73]

What this means specifically for human history is that, unlike animals who can alter themselves only by changing their species, human beings can transform themselves by transforming the world and can structure themselves by constructing structures. To study history, therefore, is to examine the outcome of interactions between the subject and his environment—biologically, personally, socially. Piaget notes the lament of Godelier that so much work remains to be done on the relations between historic structures and their transformations. The question which confronts the inquirer about human history is why some structures

71. Ibid., p. 34.
72. Ibid., p. 32, in dependence on Godel's proof, note 11.
73. Ibid., p. 50.

among the range of possibilities dominate. Piaget concludes, "Not until contemporary structural analysis has perfected its methods by studying historical and genetic transformations will it be able to furnish the answer."[74]

In spite of the warnings about the fallacies of Lévi-Strauss's method and the challenges represented by Piaget's own more profound and responsible brand of structuralism, exegesis of ancient texts is currently being carried out by some scholars dependent upon Lévi-Strauss with results that devotees may find charming but others will deplore. F. Bovon, in the introduction to a collection of programmatic essays on "Structural Analysis and Biblical Exegesis," calls structuralism a "scientific method which can aid exegesis by orienting it toward synchrony instead of diachrony and . . . provide distance from the text."[75] The distance from the text is set forward as the preferred alternative to the traditionally dominant approach of inquiring about the author, his thought, and the contextual influences which have shaped his genius. The text alone is the proper focus, Bovon insists. The pretentiousness of this program might be more easily accepted if the results, as evidenced by his actual exegesis of the Gospels, included in his study, were not so banal, trivial, and artificial.

In one example of structuralist exegesis—Jean Starobinski's analysis of the miracles in Mark 5—the clue to the exegetical task is derived from a statement preceding the pericope about the parables in Mark 4:10–13, where the disciples are privately informed that to them alone has been granted understanding of the mystery of the Kingdom of God. Although the text actually says that it is the outsiders who will hear Jesus' teachings as "parables"—implying a lack of comprehension[76]—Starobinski wants to interpret everything parabolically. He is fond of parables, which he apparently equates with allegory, and thus proceeds to interpret not only the parables but the miracle stories

74. Ibid., pp. 126–27.
75. F. Bovon, ed., *Analyse structurale et exégèse biblique* (Neuchâtel: Delachaux et Niestlé, 1971), p. 2.
76. Cf. J. Jeremias's theory that "parable" here is equivalent to "enigma"— *The Parables of Jesus*, trans. S. H. Hooke (London: SCM Press, 1954).

as well along allegorical lines. The spirit of David F. Strauss has
not departed from among us. In the story of the Gerasene demoniac, the falling of the pigs into the lake is a figure for the
fall of the rebellious spirits into the abyss. The life of demoniac
among the tombs is a symbol of alienation. The story is to be
read on the spiritual rather than the literal level: "At the same
time that this moral signification of the story of the demoniac is
revealed, one senses that the historicity of the narrative is dissi-
pated. It is no longer an episode of the earthly ministry of Jesus,
a moment from his life in time: it is a timeless victory to which
every individual is able to appeal."[77]

The retreat from time and history represented by this sort of
structuralist exegesis has attracted a voluble following in the
current biblical hermeneutical scene.[78] The dominant historical
methods, however, continue to be those directly influenced by
the history-of-religions school in the later nineteenth and the
first half of the twentieth century. It is to a representative group
of these leading history-of-religions scholars that we now turn
our attention.

ANACHRONISTIC RECONSTRUCTION OF
THE SOCIOHISTORICAL CONTEXT

Most of the basic questions raised in the pre-1950 period by historians of Christian origins (Jesus or Paul? Palestinian or Hellenistic Christianity? Kingdom of God or church?) were posed
earlier by scholars from the history-of-religions school. These
issues continue to dominate the field of inquiry today. Largely
unacknowledged is a set of assumptions, historical and literary,
on the basis of which answers to these historical dilemmas have
been advanced and historical reconstruction has been carried
on. Representative figures may be examined briefly to see what
concrete forms these investigations and proposals have taken.

77. Bovon, *Analyse*, p. 88.
78. Representative of this trend are the journal *Semeia* and the writings of
such scholars as J. D. Crossan and Daniel Patte.

The climate for this enterprise was in part established by, in part reflected in, the work of nonbiblical scholars, and of authors and literary critics. The powerful impact of the late classical and Renaissance traditions on such figures as Goethe in Germany, Walter Pater in England, and Ernst Renan in France contributed to the flourishing of the Romantic mood, with a high esteem for the aesthetic and intellectual values of the ancient pagan world.

Erwin Rohde's *Psyche: The Cult of Souls and Belief in Immortality among the Greeks*, the first part of which was published in 1890, traces the development and continuities of this aspect of Greek religion from Homer down to Hellenistic and early Roman times. In the concluding pages he reports with thinly disguised distaste the effect of the triumph of Christianity over Greek religious tradition, showing how the latter penetrated the former. He concludes: "The outward embodiment of Hellas is gone; its spirit is imperishable. Nothing that has once been alive in the spiritual life of man can ever perish entirely; it has achieved a new form of existence in the consciousness of mankind—an immortality of its own."[79]

In the same decade Rohde's survey appeared, Paul Wendland (1864–1915) published his *Die hellenistisch-römische Kultur*, in which he pointed to the nineteenth century as an epoch when the humanistic traditions of ancient Greece, and particularly the universalizing modification of these traditions in Hellenistic times, exerted a powerful intellectual influence in Germany.[80] The pervasive presence of syncretism and Gnosticism at the opening of the Roman imperial period deeply influenced the Hellenistic-Roman culture, including diaspora Judaism (with minimal evi-

79. E. Rohde, *Psyche: The Cult of Souls and Belief in Immortality among the Greeks*, English trans. W. B. Hillis (London: K. Paul, Trench, Trubner and Co., 1925; New York: Harcourt, Brace and Co., 1925). The first complete edition was published in 1893, with eight editions by 1920. Ibid., p. 549.

80. Paul Wendland, *Die hellenistisch-römische Kultur in ihren Beziehungen zu Judentum und Christentum. Die urchristlichen Literaturformen* (Handbuch zum Neuen Testament Vol. I, Part II), 2d and 3d eds. (Tübingen: J. C. B. Mohr, Paul Siebeck, 1912), pp. 6–11.

dence of effects on Palestinian Judaism), and hence affected
Gentile Christianity.[81] Wendland seems not in the least intimi-
dated by the fact that nearly all the evidence on which he draws
comes from the Antonine period or much later. But by extrap-
olating backwards, he assumes the earlier existence of Gnosticism and of other religious phenomena which can be documented only from considerably later times. Wendland insists,
however—and this point was to reappear in one form or another among most of his successors in the history-of-religions
school—that the message of Jesus had no relationship to Hellenism and was not influenced by the cultural forces which dominated Graeco-Roman culture in his time.[82] On the other hand,
Wendland turned to Lucian of Samosata and Philostratus for
parallels to the miracle tradition which the Gospels and other
early Christian tradition link with Jesus. For Wendland there are
no differences between pagan and Christian miracle-faith, and
the Christians built up that aspect of their tradition as a resource
to aid them in the religious competition of the era.[83]

Although Franz Cumont (1868–1947) was careful to present
his evidence for the spread of oriental religion in the Roman
world as predominantly a phenomenon of the second and subsequent centuries, and therefore as a movement concurrent with
the spread of Christianity within, and its adaptation to, Roman
culture,[84] German scholars continued to read the post-second-
century developments back into the pre-Christian period and to
ignore, or at least to minimize, any changes that took place within
these religious traditions over the centuries from Alexander to
Constantine. Drawing on the Hermetic literature, on the apocryphal New Testament, on Gnostic writings, and on Plutarch,
Plotinus, Apuleius, Philostratus—all from the second or third,
or even later, centuries—Richard Reitzenstein (1861–1931) constructed a Gnostic redeemer model which he claimed antedated

81. Ibid., pp. 163–87.
82. Ibid., pp. 212–13.
83. Ibid., pp. 218–19.
84. Franz Cumont, *The Oriental Religions in Roman Paganism* (New York: Dover,
1911, 1956). See especially chap. 2, "Why the Oriental Religions Spread," pp.
20–43.

and was incorporated into the early Christian portraits and theological representations of Jesus.[85] Not only did his reconstruction ignore basic differences within the Gnostic documents, but he drew heavily on Iranian material which has since been shown to be far too late to have influenced nascent Christianity.[86] In his effort to document his thesis from the writings of Philo of Alexandria, Reitzenstein had to acknowledge that the crucial technical language of the Gnostic documents—which are known to be centuries later than Philo—was missing. He assumed that Philo had this material before him, however, but that his misunderstanding of them was such that, "by giving them a linguistically elegant paraphrase he transformed them into meaninglessness."[87]

On the subject of miracle, Reitzenstein blandly used *magic* and *miracle* interchangeably and pointed to Apollonius of Tyana as the model of the *theios anthropos*, as though that were a term of fixed, unchanging signification for a miracle-worker. Recent research has shown that the phrase and its equivalent, *theios aner*, had importantly different meanings in earlier literature than they did in Philostratus's *Life of Apollonius of Tyana*, and that the later use of the term was simply not in existence as a pre-Christian paradigm on which Christians could model their pictures of Jesus and the Apostles.[88] Furthermore, the goal of the magical formulae preserved in the Magical Papyri is predominantly not mystical union but the achievement of pragmatic goals such as rendering an enemy helpless, recovering a lost item, escaping a

85. Richard Reitzenstein, *Hellenistic Mystery Religions: Their Basic Ideas and Significances*, trans. John E. Steely (Pittsburgh: Pickwick Press, 1978), pp. 3–105.

86. Carsten Colpe has offered a detailed and devastating criticism of Reitzenstein's hypothesis in *Die religionsgeschichtliche Schule. Darstellung und Kritik ihres Bildes vom gnostischen Erlösermythus (FRLANT*, n.f. 60), (Göttingen: Vandenhoeck und Ruprecht, 1961).

87. Reitzenstein, *Hellenistic Mystery Religions*, n. 100.

88. Cf. D. L. Tiede, *The Charismatic Figure as Miracle Worker* (Missoula, Mont.: Scholars Press, 1972). Carl R. Holladay, *Theios Aner in Hellenistic-Judaism: A Critique of the Use of This Category in New Testament Christology* (Missoula, Mont.: Scholars Press, 1972). See my treatment of this in *JBL* 93 (1973): 402–422, and in the article, "Divine Man," in *Interpreter's Dictionary of the Bible*, supplemental volume, ed. K. Crim (Nashville: Abingdon Press, 1976).

curse. The transfiguration narrative in the Gospels is not an account of apotheosis or new birth, as Reitzenstein assumed, but an experience of proleptic vindication by God in the face of one's enemies, as may be seen in certain strands of Jewish Merkabah mysticism and in apocalyptic writings such as Daniel 10.[89] In short, the models of redeemer figures advanced by Reitzenstein and accepted universally by his immediate followers are tissues of anachronisms and unfounded guesswork. Yet subsequent scholarship continues to accept these theories as though the case had validly been made.

Another enduringly influential work employing this form of the history-of-religions method was Wilhelm Bousset's *Kyrios-Christos*, in which the writer traced the development of the concept of Jesus as the Christ from the primitive Palestinian Christian community to the christological formulations of Irenaeus. Bousset (1865–1920) assumed a complete discontinuity between Palestinian Judaism—which was the historical context for Jesus and his teaching—and diaspora Judaism, which was thoroughly Hellenized.[90] Jesus was initially linked with the eschatological figure of the Son of Man, but the church gradually—and thoroughly—transformed that model for his redemptive role into the figure of the present redeemer epitomized in the title *kyrios*. Three factors from the Graeco-Roman culture that contributed to the more complete christology were (1) the cult of the ruler-savior; (2) the dying-and-rising savior of the mystery cults; (3) Primal Man, as in Iranian religion.[91] That the imagery and the

89. Ithmar Gruenwald, "Apocalyptic and Merkavah Mysticism", in *Arbeiten zur Geschichte des antiken Judentums und des Urchristentums*, vol. 14 (Leiden: Brill, 1980). Also discussed in my *Community of the New Age: Studies in Mark's Gospel* (Macon: Mercer University Press, repr. 1983).

90. Wilhelm Bousett, *Kyrios-Christos, A History of the Belief in Christ from the Beginnings of Christianity to Irenaeus* (New York and Nashville: Abingdon Press, 1970), p. 13. The pervasive influence of Hellenistic thought and expression on Jews in Palestine has been abundantly demonstrated by Saul Liebermann in *Greek in Jewish Palestine* (New York: Jewish Theological Seminary, 1942) and *Hellenism in Jewish Palestine* (New York: Jewish Theological Seminary, 1962).

91. Bousett, *Kyrios-Christos*, pp. 138–200.

aspirations (both personal and social) which these terms and titles represent in the post-Hadrianic Roman world powerfully influenced the reformulation of the Christian message and especially of its christology can scarcely be denied. But that these features were present in the culture of the early empire simply lacks proof. Missing from Bousset's theorizing is adequate appreciation for the fact that religious institutions such as the Isis and Asklepios cults were not unalterably fixed in the first century, but, like early Christianity itself, were in process of transformation throughout the period covered by Bousset's work. The specifics of these changes will be presented below in chapters 2 and 3.

On the question of miracle tradition in the Gospels, Bousset did not deny that Jesus performed healings, but he asserted that this feature has been added to the oldest Jesus material (which consisted solely of teachings).[92] The secondary nature of the miracle stories can be detected by literary analysis and betrays the influence of Old Testament miracle stories and legends linked with the Hellenistic miracle-working divinities.[93] The objective in importing this material into the Jesus tradition was to enable Christianity to compete more effectively with the pagan religions, which had their own accounts of miracles. For Bousset, the real Jesus stands above this supernaturalism and sensationalism, just as he stands apart from the whole subsequent development of Christianity.[94]

Significantly, the introduction to the reissue of Bousset's work was written by Rudolf Bultmann (1884–1976), who affirmed the major theses of *Kyrios-Christos*: (1) that it was the cultic model of "kyrios" which in the Hellenistic church replaced the eschatological Son of Man of Palestinian Christianity; (2) that these two branches of Christianity are completely separate and are to be "clearly distinguished"; (3) that it was Hellenistic Christianity (= non-Palestinian) which was involved "with the thought world and conceptualizations of pagan Hellenism."[95] Bultmann's two

92. Ibid., p. 100.
93. Ibid., p. 98.
94. Ibid., pp. 101–103.

points of mild dissent from Bousset were that the latter gives insufficient attention to theology (preferring to concentrate on religion) and that there is inadequate consideration of Pauline themes other than Christology.[96] Yet the basic assumptions and methods with which Bousset operated stand unchallenged by Bultmann. There is no recognition that miracle functions very differently in certain stages of Hellenistic culture than in others, that the piety of the mysteries changed significantly during the period under scrutiny, that what is distinctive about Gnosticism in the second and subsequent centuries is missing from the older documents that are adduced by Bousset as evidence for pre-Christian gnosis, and above all, that Palestinian Judaism itself was profoundly affected by Hellenization from at least the second century B.C. onward. To a distressing extent, however, the Bousset-Bultmann assumptions are even today taken as axioms by those carrying on historical research, rather than being fundamentally reexamined in light of more recent research and the discovery of new documents.

The full range of no longer valid assumptions upon which Bultmann based his work is epitomized in his little book *Primitive Christianity in Its Contemporary Setting*.[97] But in his *Theology of the New Testament*, as well as in his *Jesus and the Word*, he betrayed his reductionist strategy, according to which the real Jesus announced the Kingdom of God, not as an epoch impending in the future, but as a possibility for human existence present in every moment of faithful decision for the will of God. The essence of Paul and the Gospel of John were similarly seen by Bultmann to be an ancient statement of existentialism's reduction of human responsibility to the individual's call to decision in the midst of the crises of life.

---

95. Ibid., p. 13. This false distinction between Palestinian and Hellenistic Judaism has been effectively countered by Martin Hengel in *Judaism and Hellenism*, 2 vols. (Philadelphia: Fortress, 1974).

96. Ibid., pp. 7–9.

97. R. Bultmann, *Primitive Christianity in Its Contemporary Setting*, trans. R. H. Fuller (New York: Meridian, 1956).

The history of the history-of-religions method, therefore, can be seen to have two foci: methodologically, there is *the comparative method*, by which the development of Christianity is accounted for by pointing out parallels in concepts and institutions discoverable in other religions of the broad period ranging from Alexander to Augustine. What is important is similarity of certain features; ignored, or at least seriously underestimated, is the fact that these religious phenomena themselves underwent change and adaptation through those centuries. By dealing with sweeping categories like "Hellenism" or "Palestinian Judaism," generalizations are arrived at, with inadequate attention given to the assumptions and the world-view associated with any particular phenomenon.

The other focus is on an antecedently arrived-at reductionistic *essence*. Having decided on grounds external to the evidence and prior to assessment of it what are the basic elements—whether a theological system, a mode of piety, a view of universal humanity, a theory about the human mind—the aim of these studies is to demonstrate the centrality of these essential ingredients or features. What is called for in reaction to these pervasive methodological fallacies, and in the name of responsible historical method, is what Turretini was reaching for two and a half centuries ago: "One must put oneself into the times and into the surroundings of the sacred writers"—or, one might add, of any ancient writer—"and one must see what concepts could arise in the souls of those who lived at that time."[98] That undertaking requires deliberate consideration of method and strategy if the historian is to enter the life-world of an ancient writer or of his community, analyzing not only what is said but what is left unspoken. It is to the sketching of such an enterprise that we turn in the next chapter.

98. Turretini, *Concerning the Method* (n. 16 above). Details in Kümmel, *New Testament*, p. 59.

CHAPTER TWO

Personal Identity and World-Construction

In every epoch the historical and hermeneutical approaches to earlier tradition are fundamentally affected by the cultural context of the interpreter-historian. This is not a modern phenomenon, but may be seen in such diverse instances as Plotinus's reworking of the Platonic tradition, Philo's and the Alexandrine Fathers' allegorical treatment of Scripture, or the appropriation of the Exodus imagery in early America both by colonists in search of freedom and by blacks seeking escape from slavery in the Promised Land. W. G. Kümmel has amply demonstrated this practice in his history of New Testament interpretation,[1] and we have seen it at work in chapter 1 in the post-Enlightenment period, during which hermeneutics was—as it continues to be— dominated by empiricist, Kantian, Hegelian, or related systems of thought. The dominant philosophical bases of operation for historical criticism have been empiricism or some form of idealistic reductionism, as we have noted. Rather than examine religious phenomena in their uniqueness, against the background of their distinctive historical context, the generalizations that historical critics offered were made on the basis of common human experience (so Frazer) or of formal criteria, whether philosophical (as in F. C. Baur and A. Harnack) or literary (as in Bultmann and Dibelius). The differences in life-world which lie behind the external similarities of historical documents and which therefore profoundly influence the ways in which religious factors—such as miracle—function, were almost wholly ignored in the rise of historical criticism.

1. W. G. Kümmel, *The New Testament: The History of the Investigation of Its Problems*, trans. S. M. Gilmour and H. C. Kee (Nashville: Abingdon, 1972).

MAX WEBER'S CONTRIBUTION TO HISTORICAL METHOD

The failure to take adequately into consideration the life-world of the recorder of events is an irony in the twentieth-century development of historical criticism. Ever since the attention of biblical scholars turned to literary genre, whether in Hebrew or early Christian literature, a term widely used—and presumably integral to the analytical process carried out by form-critics—has been *Sitz-im-Leben* (literally, "situation in life"). In the form-critical study of the Gospels, for example, both Dibelius and Bultmann wrote often of the importance of correlating literary form with the life-situation in which the form was used. Neither, however, dealt with the social setting in anything more than a superficial manner; both resorted to simplistic categories for classifying by an abstract *Sitz-im-Leben*, such as Palestinian/Hellenistic, or kerygmatic/didactic.

The irony lies in the fact that during the years when historical critics were employing the sociological term *Sitz-im-Leben* a seminal thinker was addressing himself to historical questions about the origins and growth of religions by the methods of sociological analysis: Max Weber's pioneering studies of religious leaders and religious community structures continue to stand as a too rarely tapped resource that could contribute directly and substantively to the historian's task in both its analytical and constructive dimensions. Weber produced an enormous corpus of scholarly writings, much of which is still widely read in translation in English and other languages. What impact, we may ask, did Weber's work have, and what value might it yet have for historical study of religion in the Roman world? It is significant that in the more than 500 pages and 500 footnotes of Kümmel's history of New Testament interpretation, for example, the name of Weber never appears. The irony is increased by the fact that, not only was Weber working on historical issues identical with those of his colleagues in the theological faculties, but also he was planning to write a history of early Christianity, similar in scope and method to his studies of the religions of China, India, and ancient Judaism. Although he never undertook that project, the methods he developed and the concepts he formulated had and may still have great importance for the interpretation of religion in the period of our concern.

Even though there are some signs that the rich resources offered in Weber's writings *are* being drawn upon for the reconstruction of primitive Christianity,[2] recent studies which seek to build on Weber's insight are limited in their results, since these are offered for the most part on data concerning strictly social features of the early church. They devote inadequate attention to the questions of aims and methods that should give structure and direction to the interpretive undertaking. When, therefore, we ask ourselves what are the contributions that Max Weber's work may yet make to the task of interpreting religious phenomena in the first centuries of our era, we shall propose answers in four different categories: (1) methodological, (2) conceptual, (3) epistemological, (4) hermeneutical. Let us examine these in sequence, offering first a description in Weber's own terms of aspects of his thought under each, and then exploring how his insights and methods, whether directly or in subsequent development, may contribute to the historical study of religion in the Roman period.

Methodologically, Weber's major contribution was in the development and refinement of his notion of ideal types. As Karl Jaspers has correctly noted,[3] Weber did not set out to be a philosopher of history in the tradition of Hegel, nor to be largely a narrator like Ranke, nor a portrait-painter of great figures like Burckhardt, nor did he vainly suppose he could write a history

2. The significance of Weber for historical study of the ancient world is apparent in the area of classical studies, especially in the work of Ramsay MacMullen, *Roman Social Relations* (New Haven: Yale University Press, 1974, 1976); also his *Enemies of the Roman Order* (Cambridge: Harvard University Press, 1966). In the field of Christian origins the use of Weber's insights is explicit in John G. Gager, *Kingdom and Community* (Englewood Cliffs, N.J.: Prentice-Hall, 1975); also E. A. Judge, *Social Patterns of Christian Groups in the First Century* (London: Tyndale Press, 1960); and in Germany, Gerd Theissen, *Urchristliche Wundergeschichten* (Gütersloh: Gerd Mohn, 1974), and *Sociology of Early Palestinian Christianity* (Eng. trans.), (Philadelphia: Fortress Press, 1978).

3. Karl Jaspers, *Three Essays: Leonardo, Descartes, Max Weber*, trans. R. Manheim (New York: Harcourt Brace and World, 1964), pp. 236–40.

of the world, either in detail or in grandiose schemata. His aim, impressive though it was in scope, was comparison: to see how phenomena in various times and cultures produce similar developments, while at the same time recognizing that contrasts appear when, from among the range of possibilities, different results emerge. As Gerth and Mills note, Weber's ideal type was an attempt to construct a logically precise conception of reality rather than the positing of an inexorable ideal force in the Hegelian tradition.[4] Weber's own description of this method is unambiguous: "The ideal type is a conceptual construct which is neither a historical reality nor even the 'true' reality. . . . It has the significance of a purely ideal limiting concept with which the real situation or action is compared and surveyed for the explication of certain of its significant components . . . the function of the ideal type is an attempt to analyze historically unique configurations of their individual components by means of genetic concepts."[5] Weber warned against identifying historical reality with the types, against using the types as procrustean beds in which historical data must be forced to lie, and against hypostasizing the types into the 'real' forces behind the events of history.[6] Weber's critics seriously misread him when they assert that his use of the ideal types is nonhistorical, or as one writer put it, the types are "unitary and systematic frames that admit of no development" or "isolated and almost impenetrable geometric forms."[7] Karl Jaspers accurately asserts that for Weber the ideal types "are not reality itself, but technical instruments by which to approach reality." They are not classes of phenomena but formal patterns by means of which we measure reality in order to discern the degree to which reality does or does not conform to

4. Max Weber, *From Max Weber: Essays in Sociology*, trans. and ed. with intro. by H. H. Gerth and C. Wright Mills (New York: Oxford University Press, 1946, 1971), p. 59.

5. Weber, *Methodology of the Social Sciences*, trans. and ed. E. A. Shils and H. A. Finch (New York: Free Press, 1949), p. 93.

6. Ibid., pp. 94–98.

7. Carlo Antoni, *From History to Sociology—The Transition in German Historical Thinking*, trans. Hayden V. White (Detroit: Wayne State University Press, 1959), p. 161.

them. They are neither the ultimate goal of investigation nor the laws of historical process, but means by which to gain the clearest awareness of the specific characteristics of the human reality in question.[8]

Probably the best-known concept investigated and analyzed by Weber is that of the charismatic leader, although he readily acknowledges that he did not coin the term. His familiar depiction of the charismatic is that of a natural leader, lacking official credentials or formal training, who arises in times of psychic, physical, economic, ethical, religious, or political distress. His gifts of body and spirit are believed to be supernatural in origin. The charismatic lacks a financial base or social status in the fixed order of society. He has neither abstract code nor the means of adjudication of disputes; law derives rather from the leader's personal graces and strengths, or specifically by oracle or prophetic insight. Although the original source of his authority is seen to be supernatural, it can become institutionalized and thus serves as the basis for his legitimate successors, though the mode of transmission varies with the historical situation.[9]

S. N. Eisenstadt, in the introduction to his edition of Weber's *On Charisma and Institution Building*,[10] makes the important point that in Weber's thinking charismatic and institutional aspects of society were closely interrelated, contrary to the charge brought against him by some of his critics and the careless use of his concepts made by others. His major concern was for the process of institution building, of social transformation, and of cultural creativity flowing out of this process. In describing the charismatic as prophet, Weber differentiated between the ethical prophet, who preaches obedience as an ethical duty, and the exemplary prophet, who summons his hearers to follow him in order to achieve salvation. If the charismatic leader makes use of discipline, its effects may survive his passing, but the charisma

8. Jaspers, *Three Essays*, p. 260.

9. Weber, *From Max Weber* (Gerth and Mills), pp. 245–50.

10. S. N. Eisenstadt, edited and with an introduction to Max Weber's thought, *On Charisma and Institution Building* (Chicago: University of Chicago Press, 1968), xix; 263, 266.

itself becomes routinized so that the values it promulgated may be preserved as tradition or in a rationally socialized form.

In addition to the appeal of his personal authority, the prophet conveys to his hearers the conviction that there is a coherent meaning in the life of mankind and the world, in both its social and its cosmic dimensions. But that notion brings us to Weber's *epistemological* contribution: namely, his conception of the "image of the World," by which he meant a systematized and rational view of the world. On the basis of the world-image, for example, one could know from what and for what deliverance might be awaited—which might range from bodily impurity to radical evil, or enslavement in an astrologically determined universe, or imprisonment in the finite, or deliverance from the cycle of rebirths. The system, Weber noted, might be more or less rational, more or less carefully thought out by intellectuals, even while resting on irrational presuppositions, which have simply been accepted as given and incorporated into the image of the world. The earlier unitary views of the world tended to yield either to rational systems of cognition or of world mastery, or to mysticism.

Weber was careful to point out, however, that the specifics of a religious world-view are not a simple function of the social situation or stratum of society which serves as the characteristic bearer of that view. There is no causal link between a social stratum and an ideology, nor does its religion merely reflect the ideal interest-situation of a stratum. Rather, the outlook inherent in a religious ethic, for example, "receives its stamp primarily from religious sources, and, first of all, from its annunciation and its promise."[11] Thus Weber sought to avoid the charge of his critics that religion was reducible to or caused by social factors. Instead he aimed to show that the network of assumptions about reality and about the place of human beings within the world—both in present plight and in ultimate deliverance—was the constitutive base for identity among those whose community shared any given world-view. Viewed methodologically, Weber's effort to show the links between a prevailing psychological state, an act of percep-

11. Weber, *From Max Weber*, pp. 280–81.

tion, and the meaning of a phenomenon—and to do so with full acknowledgment of the historical situation within which the perception–meaning process is taking place—anticipated the rise of what is now known as sociology-of-knowledge. That development, as we shall see, required assists from Husserl and Alfred Schutz, and later from Luckmann and Berger.

Hermeneutically, Weber stood in the tradition of Wilhelm Dilthey, as Talcott Parsons recognized and as, more recently, H. P. Rickman insists. The materials from the Dilthey corpus which Rickman has organized and edited in his *Pattern and Meaning in History*,[12] show that not only Weber's concept of *Verstehen* (that is, "grasp" or "understanding"), but also his view of the life-world derive from Dilthey. With an obvious take-off on Kant, Dilthey called his hermeneutical enterprise, "A Critique of Historical Reason." Noting how the individual is involved in the interactions of society because its various systems intersect in one's life, he describes the effort of the mind to determine the systematic meaning of the world which links these converging factors. He declares, "The task can only be accomplished if the individual processes, which work together in the creation of this system, can be sorted out and it can be shown what part each of them plays, firstly in the construction of the historical course of events in the mind-affected world and secondly, in the discovery of its systematic nature."[13] Already hinting at the specific terms that Max Scheler and others were later to use in their hermeneutical projects, Dilthey describes an interpretive enterprise that was to be developed by both Weber and Scheler, "Understanding is the rediscovery of the I in the Thou; the mind rediscovers itself at ever higher levels of interconnectedness; the sameness of the mind in the I and the Thou and in every subject of a community, in every system of culture, and, finally in the totality of mind and universal history, makes the working together of the different processes in human studies possible."[14]

12. Wilhelm Dilthey, *Pattern and Meaning in History*, ed. and intro. H. P. Rickman (New York: Harper, 1961, 1962), pp. 18, 107.

13. Ibid., p. 67.

14. Ibid., pp. 67–68.

Vast as was the range of Weber's research, he set himself to a far more modest enterprise than did Dilthey and made no claim to universal inclusiveness. Dilthey rejected the notion that meaning derives from a metaphysical or any other structure outside of life itself and thereby defined his position over against Hegel or Marx. He was careful to stress the importance of the parts to the whole of life, of the individual's identity in relation to the community. The pattern of meaning in life is not shaped by ineluctable causal forces, either: "There is only a loose progression from the presupposition to what follows it; what is new does not formally follow from the presupposition; it is rather that understanding passes from something already grasped to something new which can be understood through it. The inner relationship lies in the possibility of reproduction and empathy."[15] In these lines are the seeds of the problems and the approaches to their solution that were to occupy Weber throughout his career: the relative significance of the individual and of society in social change; how innovation occurs; how religious factors contribute to the shaping of the economic order, or why it was only in Protestantism that capitalism arose. Rickman, in showing how Dilthey distanced himself from both reification of such entities as classes, ages, or nations and from radical restriction of history to the actions of individuals, offers a useful summary of those aspects of Dilthey's hermeneutics which were to be developed and refined by Weber: "He certainly believed that, as a matter of empirical fact, individuals stood in certain relationships to each other, were affected by common factors, strove for common goals and shared a common stock of ideas and that these and similar facts were most conveniently and most precisely referred to by assertions with such logical constructions as nations, ages or classes as their subjects."[16] Obviously, both Weber's ideal-types and his notion of world-image shared by a com-

15. Ibid., p. 107. For a fuller account of Dilthey's contribution on *Verstehen*, see Talcott Parsons's *Structure of Social Action* (Boston: Beacon, 1949), pp. 483–84. On Weber's concept of "Understanding," see also Reinhard Bendix, *Max Weber: An Intellectual Portrait* (Garden City, N.Y.: Doubleday, 1960).

16. Dilthey, *Pattern*, p. 36.

munity were anticipated in Dilthey's work, as was his *Nachdenken* strategy for the interpretive task.

PHENOMENOLOGY AND THE RECOVERY OF THE LIFE-WORLD

The potential of this range of Weber's insights and methodological procedures for facilitating and enriching the work of the historian of religion has been heightened by the impact of his thought on philosophers and social scientists during his lifetime and subsequently. In his brilliant monograph on Edmund Husserl, Maurice Natanson[17] demonstrates how Husserl's phenomenology at crucial points is a working out of themes from Weber. And the phenomenological sociology of Alfred Schutz, whom Husserl sought to bring to Freiburg just before his death and before Schutz's flight to America, has been recognized as manifesting deep influences from both Weber and Husserl. By drawing on insights and methods of Husserl, Schutz[18] was able to refine and develop Weber's topology, his concepts of social dynamics, the relationship between the individual and society, the image of the world (or life-world, as the phenomenologists called it), and above all, the hermeneutical goal of understanding meaning-in-history. We shall assess this contribution as it bears on the task of historical reconstruction, organizing our material around the four themes already enunciated: methodological, conceptual, epistemological, hermeneutical.

1. Methodological

Weber's method of analysis of phenomena across cultures by means of ideal types we have already noted, just as we have described briefly the efforts of the history-of-religions school to interpret the historical aspects of one religion by the use of so-called parallels from another cultural setting. Superficially, the two enterprises look alike, yet at least two serious fallacies lie

17. Maurice A. Natanson, *Edmund Husserl: Philosopher of Infinite Tasks* (Evanston, Ill.: Northwestern University Press, 1973), pp. 112, 179 ff., 184.

18. Alfred Schutz, *On Phenomenology and Social Relations*, ed. and intro. H. R. Wagner (Chicago: University of Chicago Press, 1970), p. 1.

concealed in the history-of-religions tactic. The first is the assumption by the history-of-religions school that surface resemblances in cross-cultural phenomena assure that there is fundamental kinship. The second is that the emergence of a phenomenon superficially similar to that in an earlier culture enables the historian to determine the historical cause of its later manifestation. By way of illustration, in classical Greek texts the devotees of a savior-god share a cup of mystic ecstasy; in the New Testament, the devotees of a savior-god share bread and wine—which proves *ex hypothesi* that the Christians have borrowed their sacrament from Hellenistic culture. Or again in John's Gospel, Jesus speaks in the first-person singular and recites his titles and his benefactions in precisely the same way as does Isis in her aretalogies: "I am the light of the world: he that follows me shall not walk in darkness."[19] Does this imply that the early Christians engaged in conscious borrowing or cultural imitation? Did the Isis-Wisdom tradition *cause* Johannine revelatory speeches? The history-of-religions answer would be yes. The venerable fallacy post hoc, ergo propter hoc has not weakened with age, at least among those whom Samuel Sandmel felicitously, if a bit sarcastically, described as stricken with "parallelomania."[20]

Weber's typological ground rules should have been more carefully observed. In addition to his warnings that ideal-types are not historical realities but heuristic instruments, he noted that "the goal of ideal-typical concept construction is always to make clearly explicit, not the class or average character, but rather *the unique, individual character of cultural phenomena* [emphasis mine]. Even when one is dealing with developmental sequences by means of ideal types, the danger is to be avoided of confusing them with reality." Or again Weber declares that constructing the ideal-type "is no more than a means for explicitly and validly imputing an historical event to its real causes while eliminating those which on the basis of our present knowledge seem impossible."[21]

19. See chap. 4 below.
20. Samuel Sandmel, *JBL* 81 (1962): 1–13.
21. Weber, *Methodology*, pp. 101–02.

In current and traditional practice among historians of religion, the identification of a roughly analogous phenomenon in a culture contemporary with, prior to, or even later than the first and early second century is seized upon as providing the historical explanation for what was occurring in the nascent Christian movement. This strategy is evident in popular works on miracle,[22] in which the Greek Magical Papyri, dating mostly from the third and fourth centuries of our era, are appealed to as explanations for "what really happened" in the New Testament accounts of Jesus and the Apostles. Other scholars have claimed to expose the historical base of the gospel tradition by reasoning back from the accounts of itinerant tricksters in the later-second-century A.D. satirical narratives of Lucian of Samosata. The warning of Weber about mistaking ideal-types for reality and his plea for making clear "the unique individual character of cultural phenomena" have both been ignored.

2. Conceptual

No single concept employed by Weber in his sociology of religion has been more widely used by historians of Christianity than his bipolar scheme of charismatic leadership and institutionalization. As an early-twentieth-century historian suggested, Jesus announced the coming of the Kingdom of God; what came was the church.[23] That implicit value judgment has been continued down to the present by Bultmann and his school. In his popular Jesus book, Bultmann portrayed Jesus as an eschatological prophet whose aim was to call his hearers to radical obedience to God, an attitude and response which Jesus himself exemplified, as we noted earlier. Break with family, with gainful occupation, with national aspiration, with subservience to the

22. Morton Smith, *Jesus the Magician* (New York: Harper, 1978), p. 197; John M. Hull, *Hellenistic Magic and the Synoptic Tradition* (London: SCM, 1974).

23. Alfred Firmin Loisy, *The Gospel and the Church* (1903) (repr. Philadelphia: Fortress Press, 1976); *The Birth of the Christian Religion*, trans. L. P. Jacks (London, 1948: repr. New York: University Books, 1962), p. 166. Loisy offers a psychological and sociological reconstruction of the historical development from Jesus' proclamation of the end of the age to the emergence of the church, esp. pp. 89–119.

political power and the religious establishment—all these characteristics of Jesus' life conform precisely with Weber's ideal type, the charismatic leader. As already noted, Bultmann's rationalistic conditioning gets in the way, however, of his acknowledging, with Weber, that an essential feature of the prophet's role is the performance of miracles. Bultmann prefers to assign that aspect of the tradition to later Hellenistic influences, not because the evidence unambiguously points that way, but because his philosophical leanings incline him to admire the existential encounter with radical decision, whereas he finds intellectual embarrassment in a "real" Jesus who expelled demons and healed the sick.

But the distortion of the Weberian ideal-type is not at an end. Bultmann regards as central to the New Testament only those writings which show that their writers—from Bultmann's point of view—understood and transmitted faithfully the essence of Jesus' call to decision. Each was concerned with individual confrontation with the divine demand; none had a place for the church as institution. By the second century, however—according to the Bultmannian reconstruction—the gospel of radical obedience had been abandoned in favor of an organizational drive whose interests were chain of command, ritual and doctrinal conformity, and good public relations. In short, the New Testament period ends in what Bultmann and his student, Ernst Käsemann, call Early Catholicism.[24] Although they do not overtly employ the charismatic-institutional polarity, it seems implicit in their reconstruction.

The irony is that, as S. N. Eisenstadt pointed out in his introduction to Weber's *On Charisma and Institution Building*, not only were these themes interrelated in Weber's thought, but also his major concern was for institution building, for social transformation, for cultural creativity.[25] These processes involve crystallization, continuity, and change of major types of institutions; they demonstrate the limits of transforming existing institu-

---

24. Ernst Käsemann, "Paul and Early Catholicism," in *New Testament Questions of Today* (Philadelphia: Fortress Press, 1970), pp. 236–51.

25. Eisenstadt, in Weber, *On Charisma*, pp. xvii–xix, xxxix.

tional and cultural complexes, as well as the stages in building new ones. Of central interest to Weber was "the continuous tension between . . . the constrictive and the creative aspects of institutions and social organizations." Although charisma is inherently anti-institutional and antinomian, it does not necessarily lose its power with the passage of time. It can be transmitted, as we have noted, by office, by kinship, or by heredity.[26] On the other hand, Weber described ideal-types of leadership at the institutional stage as well: those who can set up broad orientation, establish new norms, articulate new goals, and implement them both administratively and by rallying support. The utility of these ideal-types of leadership and of social dynamics has yet to be investigated seriously, much less to be exploited by historians of early Christianity.

3. Epistemological

In their introduction to a set of Weber's essays, Gerth and Mills remark that his correlation of world-images and social conditions paves the way for, or perhaps launches, the intellectual enterprise that has come to be known as sociology-of-knowledge.[27] This aspect of Weber's work needs to be examined from at least two different perspectives: how the formulation of the world-image (or life-world) takes place in a religious movement; and how recognition of this factor may aid in understanding the history of a religion.

Weber saw this world-construction as a primary task of the prophet: "To the prophet, both the life of man and the world, both social and cosmic events, have certain systematic and coherent meaning. To this meaning the conduct of mankind must be oriented if it is to bring salvation, for only in relation to this meaning does life obtain a unified and significant pattern." Yet once such a charismatic's reorganization of the symbolic and cognitive order (together with the sociostructural counterparts) has become institutionalized, the system begins to change. In the case of ethics, for example, Weber wrote that although a reli-

26. Weber, *From Max Weber*, pp. 245–48.
27. Ibid., p. 64.

gious ethic receives its stamp initially from religious sources, frequently the very next generation reinterprets those claims and promises in a fundamental fashion.[28] "Such reinterpretations adjust the revelation to the needs of the religious community." He went on to observe that, even when a change in the socially decisive strata of the community occurs and exerts a decisive impact, the basic type of religion continues to have far-reaching influence on the life-conduct of its adherents, however diverse their stratification may be.

The implications of this for the historian of religion, including those concerned with the origins of Christianity, are apparent. The religious phenomena cannot be analyzed without serious attention to the system of "symbolic and cognitive order" as well as the social setting in which the religion functioned. But further, it is not sufficient to reconstruct "*the* Christian worldview," or even multiple static entities such as historical critics' artificial constructs like "Palestinian Christianity" and "Hellenistic Christianity." Careful analytical attention must be paid to the process of transformation of the various forms of Christian community reflected in the New Testament, including full accommodation for how their life-world changed in the changing circumstances of their epoch.

Acknowledging his debt to both Husserl and Weber, Alfred Schutz has provided a concise description of the "world" from the perspective of sociology-of-knowledge:

> The social world into which one is born and within which one has had to find his or her bearings is experienced as a tight-knit web of social relationships, of systems of signs and symbols with their particular structure of meaning, of institutional forms of social organizations, of systems, of status and prestige, etc. The meaning of all these elements of the social world in all its diversity and stratification, as well as the pattern of the texture itself, is, by those living within it, "taken for granted." They consider it to be the socially accepted way of life for the members and the appropriate means for coming to terms with things. This social world is perpetuated by ancestors, teachers, and authorities, and is deemed

28. Ibid., p. 269.

adequate for action and understanding, and as a guide for problem-solving and other forms of action. It is assumed that the traditions should be transmitted whether we understand their origins or not. Through the tradition one learns to define the environment, what to take for granted, what are the typical constructions and solutions.[29]

The chief medium for communicating this life-world is the vocabulary and syntax of language. In naming things and events, in typifications and generalizations, are conveyed the relevance system within a linguistic in-group. These define the subjective meaning the group has for its members and the social roles and statuses of each. Schutz then observes that this description of a shared life-world and its social dimensions is true of both existential groups and voluntary groups, although in the latter case the system must be learned and appropriated. Here is a factor of profound importance for historical reconstruction of early Christianity: persons were being converted to the new faith from a variety of social worlds. Even after conversion, they did not fully abandon the taken-for-granted aspects of their past. Schutz's discussion of in-groups and out-groups is directly relevant to the break between various types of Christians and various types of Jews. The fact that they were employing common language and common concepts does not mean that they were operating on identical assumptions. Careful investigation must be undertaken to decipher what each meant by the language used, what were their central myths, how their processes of rationalization and institutionalization differed from each other.[30] Schutz does not provide the answers, but he makes the historian aware of neglected or unrecognized issues and problems.

4. Hermeneutical

After sketching out various patterns of world-abnegation as found by him in major religious systems, Weber offers a remark which is appropriate for describing the interpretive usefulness of his sociological method as a whole, offered here in my paraphrase: The constructed scheme . . . only serves the purpose of offering

29. Schutz, *On Phenomenology*, pp. 82, 96.
30. Ibid., p. 82.

an ideal-typical means of orientation. It does not teach a philosophy of its own. The theoretically constructed types of conflicting 'life orders' are merely intended to show that at certain points such and such internal conflicts are possible and adequate. These 'spheres of value' can appear in reality and in historically important ways—and they have. Such constructions make it possible to determine the typological locus of a historical phenomenon. They enable us to see if, in particular traits or in total character, the phenomenon approximates one of our constructions, to determine the degrees of approximation of the historical phenomenon to the theoretically constructed type. To this extent, the construction is merely a technical aid which facilitates a more lucid arrangement and terminology.[31]

When Husserl called for *epoché* (that is, for withholding assent to the natural attitude toward the world), he was demanding that the historian bracket his own historical conditioning. As Natanson has expressed it, "In phenomenological reduction the bracketing of history means rendering either naïve believing or self-conscious analysis explicit to reflection; thereby one is prepared for phenomenological inquiry by which one can trace out and reconstruct the path of originary constitution by which the life-world took shape."[32] Natanson observes that Schutz saw as his central task the systematic exploration of the everyday social world. In pursuing that goal he developed a conception of social action based on Max Weber, according to which man's action in the world can be understood when one asks, not what it means to the observer, but what it meant to the actor. Employing the term and the basic insight of Dilthey, Schutz conceives of *Verstehen* as the means through which human beings respond to other human beings' intentions. That can be achieved only when the interpreter enters the life-world of the other.

PERSONAL IDENTITY AND THE SOCIAL PERCEPTION OF REALITY

Although Weber's brilliant insights were essential preparation for the rise of sociology-of-knowledge, with its attention to the

31. Weber, *From Max Weber*, pp. 323–24.
32. Natanson, *Husserl*, pp. 70–71; 107–13.

life-world in which a phenomenon appeared and in light of which it is to be interpreted, his own historical analysis of religion focused chiefly on the dialectic between charismatic leadership and institutionalization. It has remained for others, therefore, to develop his methodological proposals in such a way as to take more fully into account the social dimensions of religion. Careful attention to the interrelation between personal identity and group identity in human experience is essential in historical interpretation, since the individual can achieve his or her sense of meaning and identity only in the context of a social group, whether ethnic, hereditary, or voluntary. This illuminating approach to the study of religion through personal identity has been laid out most effectively by Hans J. Mol in a work which bears the significant title *Identity and the Sacred*.[33] The analytical method he advances offers important possibilities for the study of religion, ancient and modern, so as to take seriously the context of religious documents while avoiding the pitfalls of reductionism, rationalism, and idealization. Yet it builds directly and consciously on the foundations laid down by Max Weber.

Mol defines religion as "the sacralization of identity." By identity he means the basic drive, common to chickens, tree-shrews, baboons, gorillas, and human beings,[34] to establish and defend a place to exist, the right to survive, and a viable role in relation to others. Among humans, there is a vast range of symbolic locations of identity—among others, sex and celibacy, war and peace, nationalism and psychoanalysis, reason and escape through drugs—beyond those of class and property, as the Marxists would have it.[35]

Closely linked with the factor of identity is that of integration, by which a person seeks to gain or maintain both meaning and stability in life. The symbol systems that provide the basis for identity and integration, according to Mol, "acquire the same taken-for-granted, stable, eternal quality which on the level of instinctive behavior was acquired by the consolidation of new

33. Hans Mol, *Identity and the Sacred* (New York: Free Press, 1977).
34. Ibid., pp. 1–2.
35. Ibid., p. 2.

genetic materials."[36] He notes that what is sacralized may not be generally regarded as sacred in the traditional sense, but its "sacral" value and function become evident when they provide the center and mainstay for personal identity. In his sense of the term, "the sacred" is as apparent in the attitudes and actions of a committed Marxist as in those of a dedicated Catholic, a charismatic, or a Klansman.

Personal identity should not be equated with individual identity, however. The social pathology of our era is nowhere more evident than in the tired cliché "Do your own thing." As a consequence of the undermining of group identity and social stability in the name of individual self-fulfillment, anxiety and alienation are increased and intensified, in the present era or in any other. In our own culture, pathological substitutes or compensations for authentic personal identity are endemic: drugs, sadism, "trashing," and a return to witchcraft or the occult. Conversely, political, social, or religious movements which provide a firm sense of integration, purpose, and identity—such as the Unification Church, Synanon, various forms of Jesus People—thrive, not in spite of, but because of a failure of the larger society to furnish identity or integrating centers for life. So powerful is the integrative force of such groups that even when the original reason for the start of the movement wanes or is discredited, as has frequently happened with millenarian groups whose date set for the Second Coming proved to be erroneous,[37] the cult survives, because (as Mol explains) "the latent provision of identity was more important than the overt focus of the group."[38]

The social features we have been sketching are perhaps most clearly evident among members of cults or sects, which Mol describes as "enclaves of disenchantment and alienation." Revamp-

36. Ibid., p. 5.

37. On millenarian groups, see Leon Festinger et al., *When Prophecy Fails* (Minneapolis: University of Minnesota Press, 1956); K. O. L. Burridge, *New Heaven, New Earth* (New York: Schocken Books, 1969); Norman R. Cohn, *The Pursuit of the Millennium*, 2d ed. (New York: Harper, 1961); Bryan R. Wilson, *Magic and the Millennium* (New York: Harper, 1973).

38. Mol, *Identity*, p. 167.

ing Ernst Troeltsch's classic distinction between church and sect, he observes that "churches sacralize identities that are essentially congruous with and congenial to the social whole," while sects are a response to a sense of powerlessness, disorder, and unpredictability concerning the world and its future.[39] The sect offers a promise of radical change, new identity, vindication of the faithful, and the ultimate triumph of justice and peace. Just as "sacred" serves as an appropriate way of characterizing a worldview that is not traditionally religious, so the roles of "church" and "sect" are to be found in movements that are not formally religious. As we shall see, the conditions of anomie and of cosmic anxiety characterized life in the early Roman world to a remarkable and previously unprecedented degree. Sectarian features were to be expected, therefore, both within the explicitly religious establishment and outside the traditionally religious sphere.

Returning to the broader question of sacralization as the basis for personal identity, we may ask how—in sociological terms— it actually takes place. Mol sets forth four operations that characterize the sacralization process: objectification, commitment, myth, and ritual.[40] We must examine each of these in some detail, especially as they relate to the processes of identity and integration. In doing so, we move from theoretical generalization to specific instances of the social conditions during the period of our inquiry, from Alexander to the Antonine epoch. In setting out the details, however, we have added a category not included in Mol's theoretical discussion—namely, responsibility. As we shall see, this dimension of religion has ties to what Mol calls "commitment" as well as to ritual, but it differs from both and is as substantive an indicator of the life-world of the adherent to a religion as is any of the four factors listed by Mol.

VOLUNTARY PARTICIPATION AND HOSTILE POWERS

According to Mol's identity theory of religion, once the construction of the sacred cosmos has been completed or adopted,

39. Ibid., p. 169.
40. Mol's expansion of these four themes occupies the last four chapters of his book, pp. 202–61.

the individual who has achieved identity in relation to that world has thereby expressed commitment to its view of reality, its values, and its obligations. An important consequence of the breaking up of indigenous populations and cultures under the impact, first of Hellenization and then of extension of Roman imperial power and administration, was the rapid increase of the voluntaristic element in religion. With the hold of tradition and ethnic heritage broken by the new mobility, men and women felt free to choose new forms of religious identity that better served their felt needs. Conversion—which was appropriately chosen by A. D. Nock for the title of his masterful study, "The Old and New in Religion from Alexander the Great to Augustine of Hippo"[41]—became a common feature of religious life, with persons engaged in open quests and proponents working to gain converts.

Essential to the conversion process were the twin functions of myth and ritual. Myth is here understood as the story of the dealings of the gods with the cosmos and with human beings and their destiny. When a story is adopted as one's own, then that myth becomes an essential ground of identity. Ritual is the public, or visible, group-means by which one enacts a commitment to the story of the gods, which has become "our story." The potency of these dimensions of religion is apparent in a wide range of cultures and ethnic backgrounds. From the first century B.C., for example, these two factors as mode of identity are to be found in Cicero, who in spite of his skepticism about direct intervention of the gods, insisted on performance of the civil cult. But they also appear in the first-century A.D. Qumran community, whose meal of bread and wine expressed their adherents' confidence in the imminent revelation of the messianic priest and king who would usher in the new age and vindicate them as the true people of the New Covenant.

The modes of responsibility required by participation in the sacral group varied widely, of course. In some instances, such as the imperial cult, taking part in the periodic rites was sufficient in itself. But for voluntary groups, a wide range of responsibili-

41. A. D. Nock, *Conversion* (London: Oxford University Press [1933], 1961).

ties was operative. For example, celibacy seems to have been required for those who waited at Qumran for eschatological deliverance. Hasidic Jewish groups took literally the injunction of the Psalmist (Psa 1) that the faithful were to meditate on the Law day and night, with the result that prayer and study of the Law were a never-ending process. In the second century of our era devotees of the healing divinities, such as Asklepios and Isis, took up residence near the shrines in order to be on hand for visions and benefactions, and to share in the ceremonies required. In the Gospels, as we shall see, there was an obligation laid on the followers of Jesus to evangelize and to carry forward the ministry of exorcisms and healings launched by Jesus. What is paramount in millenarian movements is divine deliverance in the age to come, not how to cope from day to day.[42] Even the disappointment of millennial hopes will not destroy a movement, but will lead it merely to adjust its expectations.[43] Martin Hengel has shown how the Hasidism of the second century B.C. was transformed into a range of Jewish sects by the beginning of our era.[44]

On the other hand, to those for whom coping with present problems is more important than discovering ultimate meaning, there was available another possible resource, magic. The relationship of magic to religion in the Roman period will be discussed more fully below (chap. 6), but here some general observations may be useful. Although anthropologists are not in agreement as to whether magic can be sharply differentiated from religion, there is a kind of useful, consensual opinion about magic—namely, that religion involves communication with beings, while magic consists in manipulation of forces.[45] Both seek ends that are not attainable by human efforts and hence call on forces or beings outside the realm of the ordinary. Where communication dominates, is religion: where operation of forces prevails,

    42. Mol, *Identity*, p. 181.

    43. Cf. H. C. Kee, *Christian Origins*, p. 174, n. 21.

    44. Martin Hengel, *Judaism and Hellenism*, 2 vols. (Philadelphia: Fortress Press, 1974), pp. 78–83, 175–247.

    45. Lucy Mair, *An Introduction to Social Anthropology* (Oxford: Clarendon Press, 1972), pp. 225–29.

is magic. In his *General Theory of Magic*, M. Mauss, after tracing the great range of practices and instruments used in connection with magic, observes that in the effort to coerce actions or alter conditions, "Certain formulas . . . are used over and over again, without rhyme or reason and end up by becoming unintelligible."[46] The essential feature is not intelligibility but efficacy. Religion, on the other hand, relies on the presence and action of differentiated spiritual beings or intermediaries.[47] The Greek Magical Papyri, which date from late Hellenistic times down to the fourth century, show that the efficacy of magic depends on recitation of multiple divine names, on the forcefulness of the order given to the gods, and—above all—on the proper use of technique. Proper chronology, recipes, and prescriptions for magical foods and rituals must be observed. Often the formula consists of nonsense words or syllables.[48] The individualistic and coercive aspects of magic are evident in *PGM* XIII.788–89:

> Enter my mind and my thoughts for all the time of my life and perform for me all the wishes of my soul. For you are I and I am you. Whatever I say must come to be, for I have your name as the sole phylactery in my heart, and no fleshly thing will move against me by means of a curse, nor shall any spirit attack me, no demons, no ghost, no evil power of Hades. By your name, which I have in my soul and which I invoke, there shall come to be for me in every way good things, good upon good, thoroughly, unconditionally you shall grant me health, salvation, welfare, glory, good repute, vic-

46. M. Mauss, *General Theory of Magic*, trans. R. Brain (London, Boston: Routledge and Kegan Paul, 1972), pp. 27–58.

47. Ibid., pp. 85, 136. Judith Willer, in *The Social Determination of Knowledge* (Englewood Cliffs, N.J.: Prentice-Hall, 1971), has offered a perceptive criticism of M. Malinowski's *Magic, Science and Religion* (Garden City, N.Y.: Doubleday, 1948, 1954). She sees as the chief feature of magic that it is empirical: Because *A* is followed by *B*, *A* is the cause of *B*, so that knowledge remains at the level of the immediately observable. Religious knowledge, on the other hand, combines rational connection of concept to concept with the abstract connection of concept to the observable (pp. 26–29). Her distinction is useful, although unduly neat and intellectualistic. In ancient documents, the two phenomena mingle and at times merge. Nevertheless, the life-world assumed by each can be differentiated and ought to be in typological fashion.

48. In *PGM* XIII.21 there are 49 consecutive letters of nonsense.

tory, strength, contentment. Cast a spell on the eyes of all who oppose me.[49]

Against the background of this mode of historical analysis, based as it is on the process of social and cultural change, what changing patterns of world-view are evident among pagans, Jews, and Christians in the centuries before and after the birth of Christ which are the focus of our interest? In what follows in this chapter I have sketched—in a preliminary manner—some of the ways in which various groups within this period perceived the movement of history and their own place within that process.

THE PROMISE OF ORDER AND THE EXPERIENCE OF ANXIETY

The mixture of anxiety and voluntarism which characterized the culture into which nascent Christianity grew was in large part launched by the impact of Alexander, whose efforts to unify the human race paradoxically heightened awareness of differences and of the range of options among which one must choose. Generalizations about religious phenomena at this period are tempting but historically dubious. Full allowance must be made for diversity.

The theoretical notion of One World, which Alexander the Great is alleged to have absorbed from his tutor Aristotle, was attractive in its simplicity and its conceptual beauty. Bringing it to pass was quite another matter, as both Alexander and his fiercely combative successors discovered. By the turn of our era, Augustus's imperial goal of unifying the Roman territories was difficult of accomplishment, not only militarily and culturally, but in terms of human resistance at the personal level as well. In Rome itself, the forms of the Republic, based as they were primarily on the shared authority of the landed gentry, were ostensibly retained when Octavian became the first among equals, but in fact there was a real erosion of the power of the senate and a corresponding concentration on the one who outwitted

---

49. *Papyri Graecae Magicae: Die griechischen Zauberpapyrus*, ed. Karl Priesendanz (1938); 2d ed. by Albert Henrichs (Stuttgart: Teubner, 1973).

his competitors and became Augustus. The struggles between the senate and the principate, and among rival claimants to that seat of authority, began before Augustus's seizure of control, and reached an unsavoury climax in the years A.D. 68–69, when five men claimed the imperial power, from the time of Nero's death to the ascension to power of Vespasian. The more prominent the role one played in the power struggle of this era, the greater was one's personal jeopardy, in spite of the outward signs of imperial peace and relative prosperity.[50]

In Greece, both within the city-state of the mainland and in the Greek cities and lands of Asia Minor, social and political traditions were likewise undermined or even overturned by the imperial power of Rome. The democratic institutions continued to have only severely limited authority and could at any moment be overridden by Rome. The important decisions concerning their own destiny, their social and economic life, were not made by the Greeks. Alexandria, which had from the onset of the Hellenistic age been the political and cultural center of Egypt, had lost its autonomy with respect to both politics and culture. The older centers of Egyptian life and religion were also affected by the transfer of power away from the capital city. Policies of expansion in the developing provinces brought both inviting opportunity and unceasing threat, by reason of uprising or invasion. Soldiers and bureaucrats were forced to move from place to place, with the resultant loss of roots and of personal allegiance or even identity. The increasingly mobile population of the early empire transferred to new locations ancient gods, as is especially evident in Ostia, the port of Rome. There shrines of foreign gods have been found, in addition to those dedicated to the emperors and to the traditional Roman divinities (Vulcan, Jupiter, Juno, Minerva, Castor and Pollux, Venus, Ceres, Hercules, Silvanus, Mars, Neptune) and the deified personifications (Spēs, Fortuna, Liber, Pater, Pater Tiberinus). The newcomers included temples or shrines of Syrian gods (Jupiter Heliopoli-

50. M. L. Clarke, *The Roman Mind: Studies in the History of Thought from Cicero to Marcus Aurelius* (Cambridge: Harvard University Press, 1960), p. 127.

tanus, Jupiter Dolichenus), of the Magna Mater, of Mithras, and of Isis, Sarapis, and Bubastis.[51] The period when these cults were at their height was during the second and third centuries of our era. Once ensconced in Italy, these deities attracted a wide following of the indigenous population rather than chiefly serving expatriates longing for the gods of the distant homeland. The ground of the appeal of these Eastern divinities, as we shall see (chaps. 3 and 4) lay in their accessibility to their worshipers and in the directness of their benefactions, of which a most common form was the miracle of healing.

The official Roman religion continued to exercise an astonishing hold on the ruling class and on many intellectuals throughout the first three centuries of the empire's existence. This is not wholly surprising, since the empire provided people like Cicero with the framework of power and meaning within which they lived. The preservation of the symbolic and cultic world which was believed to be indispensable for maintaining the empire was of supreme importance to them, however incompatible the cult might seem to us to be with their intellectual station and pursuits. Although on philosophical grounds Cicero was skeptical about the gods, he had one of the characters in his *De natura deorum* declare:

> I will always defend, and have always defended, the traditional Roman religious opinions, rites and ceremonies, and nothing that anyone, learned or unlearned, says will move me from the views I have inherited from our forefathers about the worship of the immortal gods. . . . I have never held that any branch of traditional Roman religion should be despised, and am persuaded that Romulus by establishing the *auspices* and the *numen* by instituting our sacred rites, laid the foundations of our state, which could never have been so great as it is if the favor of the immortal gods had not been ensured.[52]

Similarly, well down into the second century, Marcus Aurelius was faithful in honoring the Roman deities, on the assumption

    51. L. Ross Taylor, *The Cults of Ostia: Greek and Roman Gods—Imperial Cult—Oriental Gods* (Chicago: Ares Publishers, [1913], 1976).
    52. Cicero *De Natura Deorum* 3.5 f., cf. Clarke, *Roman Mind*, p. 60.

that the ritual was necessary for the survival of the state and the cohesion of its people.[53] The argument for the restoration of the civic cult by Augustus was that neglect of the civic gods was the cause of the civil wars, and that resumption of their appropriate honors would assure the peace and prosperity of the state. In the *Aeneid*, Vergil lent eloquent support to this point of view when he depicted the time of Augustus as the true Golden Age, the fulfillment of the destiny of the Roman people determined by the will of Jupiter.[54] To neglect or to undermine the official cult of the Roman gods, therefore, was an act against the state.[55] To be an "atheist" was forbidden, since atheism was perceived to be disbelief in, and hence dishonor toward, the civic gods.[56]

For many, perhaps most of all those who were alienated from imperial power, what the imperial cult failed to offer was intellectual or emotional appeal, or the extension of any assurance of personal identity. Once the initial optimism over the establishment of the principate, as voiced by Vergil, had faded, a mixture of cynicism and abstract theorizing about the ideal king set in, the latter under Stoic influence.[57] Only with the advent of the Antonines did peace and freedom become a real possibility for the majority of the populace. Prior to that, political freedom was an empty hope; the most that could be gained was personal tranquillity through philosophy. And even at the climax of the Antonine period, Marcus Aurelius himself found peace only through meditation and the inner light of reason. The end of the Flavian epoch and the coming of the Antonines did, however, again make credible for a time the notion of a beneficent destiny.[58] When that confidence faded once again, as it did in the period of the Severi, anxiety prevailed.

53. Michael Grant, "The Gospel of Self-reliance," in *The Climax of Rome: The Final Achievements of the Ancient World A.D. 161–337* (London: Weidenfeld and Nicolson, 1968).

54. Clarke, *Roman Mind*, p. 80.

55. Ramsay MacMullen, in *Enemies of the Roman Order*, notes that Rome tolerated cultural and religious diversity so long as it did not foster disloyalty to Rome (p. 221).

56. Ibid., p. 156.

57. Clarke, *Roman Mind*, pp. 102–06.

58. Ibid., p. 121.

THE JEWISH QUEST FOR POLITICAL AND PERSONAL IDENTITY

In chapters 3 and 4, and again in chapter 8, we shall note how the breakdown of social and political security had led many Romans—leaders and subjects—to turn to divinities who promised personal salvation. To perceive the dynamics of social tensions and change which underlie the early Christian literature, however, it is essential to note the specific impact on Judaism—the matrix from which Christianity grew—of that people's loss of political autonomy as well as of any prospect of regaining it. The unity of the Jewish people had been shattered as a consequence of the failure of the Maccabean leadership in the late second and first centuries B.C. The semblance of national independence which Jews had gained under the Maccabees was irretrievably lost a century later.

The experience of exile in Babylon in the sixth century B.C. had left the remnants of the nation Israel leaderless and had deprived them of a sense of destiny. All that they could be sure of was that their hopes of political independence had been demolished. The prophecy of Amos was apparently fulfilled: "They shall fall, and never rise again" (Am 8:14). Even when the Persian authorities had authorized the nation's return to its own land, most remained behind in the Land between the Rivers, and those who went back to Palestine in the mid-fifth century with memories of earlier splendor thought the rebuilt temple looked like nothing (Hg 2:3) compared with the fabled splendors of Solomon's glittering edifice. The leadership of the people was in the hands of priests and interpreters of the Law. There was no king and no certain kingly line, and no claimant appeared for nearly three centuries. Living under political domination by the Persians, then by the Ptolemies and finally by the Seleucids, the Jews enjoyed a high degree of freedom until Antiochus IV Epiphanes polluted the sanctuary in Jerusalem with an image of himself and required that all his subjects participate in divine honors to him as a god in their midst. That demand, linked as it was with his own inherent political weakness, became the occasion for a revolt under the leadership of the sons of Mattathias (1 Mc).

The initial joy of the Jews at the recovery of a degree of political autonomy—as a client state of the Seleucids, with their own priest-ruler—is reflected powerfully in 1 Maccabees. There is a clear sense that the era of ancient Israel has been recovered, with God acting directly ("God himself will crush the enemy before us," 3:22) or through a heavenly agent ("through God's angel," 7:41). Prayers are uttered for God to "shut up the enemy in the camp" or to "strike them down with the sword" (4:30–33). The Maccabees had strong pragmatic inclinations, however, so that while insisting on full obedience to the Law and on the maintenance of the separateness of Israel from "the heathen," the leaders entered into nonaggression pacts with the Romans (1 Mc 8: 1–32 12: 1–4) and with Spartans (12 : 5–23) and even sent troops to aid the Seleucid rulers when it was to Israel's advantage to do so. Although the sons of Mattathias, as hereditary priests, had no valid claim to the royal title, they functioned as monarchs. Simon was high priest and general forever, or "until a true prophet should appear"—an obvious reference to Deuteronomy 18:18, which was widely understood in this era to be a prediction of the advent of an eschatological prophet, as was the case in the Dead Sea community. The life-world implicit in this document is one in which human initiative on the part of those who obey God's Law will be matched by divine support or even intervention. The enemy is very much of this world: a blasphemous monarch on a pagan throne, his troops sent to enforce his perverted will. The remedy is direct action, including military initiative and strategic alliances with pagan powers. The goal is peace and prosperity (14:11–14), in words which echo the pre-exilic prophets: "Each one under his vine and fig tree" (Mi 4:4; Zec 3:10).

With the accession to power of Aristobulus at the end of the second century and the adoption by the Jewish rulers of the title of "king," the secularization of the Maccabean heirs was thorough and obvious, with the result that groups which earlier had supported the ruling family now opposed it. Rather than trying to establish a political counterforce, however, they developed a new life-world, with a new focus for the destiny of the Jewish people as a community of the obedient, rather than as an autonomous national state.[59] The Pharisees, who defined themselves thus, became a largely quietistic group, devoted to the study of the Law and to an appropriation of it in the present as a means to achieving a life of righteousness and obedience. Their non-political stance was rewarded by the Romans after A.D. 70, when they were the one segment of Judaism that was encouraged to assume a role of religious leadership, following the destruction of the Jerusalem temple and the scattering of both the militant nationalists and the priests.

Another form of piety that seems to have emerged in the days of disillusionment with the Maccabees was that of the Essenes,[60] who withdrew totally from their coreligionists and took up life in the desert, awaiting the final divine intervention that would defeat the enemies of God, vindicate his obedient people (i.e., themselves), and establish them as the true and faithful priest-hood, presiding over the proper worship of God in Jerusalem.

Both Pharisees and Essenes had a modified dualistic view of the world: God was the ultimate source of authority and would finally bring to fulfillment his plan for the creation, but his adversary (Satan), or Belial, had for the present usurped control and was at work in the world through his agents to thwart God's purposes and harass his people. Other than the broad conviction about God's providential care of his own and the confidence in eschatological vindication, they seem not to have expected divine intervention in the present state of affairs. The factor of miracle is a minor one in Pharisaic traditions. For example, Paul Fiebig's classical study of Jewish miracle stories[61] lists only nine individual stories from the rabbinic tradition prior to the Fall of

59. This basic transition has been traced and documented brilliantly by Jacob Neusner in his *From Politics to Piety: The Emergence of Pharisaic Judaism* (Englewood Cliffs, N.J.: Prentice-Hall, 1973). Comprehensive amassing of the evidence for the Pharisees in their earlier period is in process of a multivolume publication by Neusner, *The Rabbinic Traditions about the Pharisees before 70 A.D.* (Leiden: Brill, 1971).

60. It is here assumed that the Dead Sea community is either identical with the Essenes or a wing of the group.

61. Paul Fiebig, *Die jüdische Wundergeschichten* (Tübingen: Mohr, 1911), pp. 1–28.

Jerusalem. Although they vary in subject matter—ranging from a miraculous supply of rain and bread, through healings and an exorcism, to divine protection of God's approved interpreter of the Law—in every case, the miracle is a sign to the faithful of divine attestation or vindication against enemies. The qualities of the one in whose behalf or through whom the miracle is performed include persistence, perception, and personal piety. Apart from these exemplary virtues, the miracle has no larger function, and in the one instance where a link with the role of prophet is suggested, that interpretation is forthwith rejected.[62] While the existence of the demonic powers is assumed, there is a quiet confidence that God is in ultimate control and will reward fidelity to his Law. Miracle is regarded as a public guarantee of that confidence.

A world-view akin to those of the Pharisees and the Essenes, and yet divergent at many important points, was that of the persons and groups which produced the Jewish apocalypses of the Maccabean and early Roman period. Probably the oldest of the surviving apocalypses, and perhaps the prototype of the genre, is the Book of Daniel. Written after the Seleucid desecration of the Jerusalem temple (as reflected in the desolating sacrilege of Daniel 9:27 and the sarcastic allusion to Antiochus IV Epiphanes as "the little horn with eyes like a man, and a mouth speaking great things"; Dn 7:8), Daniel sees the demonic forces at work through the pagan civil authorities. Military or political resistance is useless; the only hope is to endure the hostility, to remain obedient unto death if necessary, in confidence that God will vindicate the faithful in the New Age, which is about to dawn. All the world powers are instruments of Satan; all will go down to defeat; all will be superseded by the Reign of God, which will be administered through "the saints of the Most High," to whom God will assign vicegerency in his behalf (Dn 7:27). God may act in the present to deliver from martyrdom those who stand firm in their refusal to violate his statutes, even under the decrees of earthly monarchs, whether the issue is offering honors to a hu-

---

62. The story is Hanina ben Dosa's healing of the son of R. Gamaliel II. Hanina knows his prayer has been heard because it felt fluent on his tongue.

man ruler, the prohibition of prayer to the God of Israel, or the refusal to eat unclean food (Dn 1–6). God may intervene to deliver the faithful, but his will can also triumph through suffering and death, and the ultimate outcome will be the exaltation of his own obedient people. Through mystical transport into the presence of God, the faithful can, in the present, gain assurance of their future vindication (Dn 10:1–19).

Later apocalypses elaborate details or present variants on this picture. The Similitudes of Enoch and the Apocalypse of Ezra picture the Man, or the Son of Man, as the instrument of God through whom his enemies are overcome and his purpose for his people achieved. Others present two figures—an Anointed King and an Anointed Priest—as the dyarchy through whom his reign is established (Testaments of the Twelve Patriarchs: Zechariah 1–8; Scroll of the Rule, appendix 1, 2:17–18). In all the documents of this type, the focus is not on political freedom in the present but on divine vindication in a New Age, when the covenant promises are fulfilled from the side of God and his people. There is at best resignation to injustice, but there is no despair about the ultimate future of the creation: it will be renewed, and God's purpose in having brought it and his people into being will in the near future be accomplished. The duality is not between the material world and a realm of the spirit, but between the present age of conflict and disobedience, as a consequence of evil powers having temporarily wrested control of the universe, and the future when God's rule will be triumphant and his people will come into their own.

The last of the Jewish world-views to be sketched is one that may have been unique to its exponent, but which probably represented the outlook of a segment of Jews characterized by a blend of pragmatism and secular values. In Josephus's *Jewish Wars* we have vivid accounts of events in which the author sees God at work in the destiny of his people, and at one point he is explicit about his views on this subject. He makes an absolute distinction between authentic portents, which he attributes to God, and the fraudulent promises of miraculous deliverance uttered by those whom he terms false prophets, charlatans, swindlers.

In the *Jewish Wars*, Josephus describes two false prophets who led a gullible crowd of followers out into the desert—numbering thirty thousand in one instance, according to Josephus (2.258–60)—on the promise that God would intervene in their behalf, freeing the city and them from the Roman armies. (The analogy with the deliverance of Israel from the Egyptians by God in the desert as reported in Exodus is evident.) But in this instance, the Romans killed or imprisoned the misguided followers of the prophets. A similar fate awaited those who, on instruction from another false prophet, gathered in the temple court, expecting a "sign of deliverance" from God (6.285).

As we shall see in detail in chapter 6, Josephus does believe both in portents and in divine pronouncements. These, the leaders of the Jews, as well as the masses of the people, had chosen to ignore.[63] He describes in detail the extraordinary astronomical signs and miscarriages of nature,[64] as well as direct indications of the destruction of the temple.[65] All these unusual occurrences he regarded as divine pointers to the way of salvation. Those who failed to read them properly were doomed to destruction for their folly.[66] We shall see that this outlook on history has its closest analogue among the Roman historians who were Josephus's somewhat younger contemporaries, Tacitus and Suetonius, or who drew on sources contemporary with him, such as Dio Cassius.

ARE THE GODS IN CONTROL?

The importance attached by these historians to portents and oracles anticipating events of major national significance is apparent in the treatise of Cicero, *De divinatione*, written about 45 B.C. There Cicero lays out the argument of one Quintus on behalf of divination: it has ample precedent among ancient civilizations, including the establishment of the Sibylline oracles in early Roman times and among philosophers as well. Just as one

63. *Wars* 6.285.
64. Ibid., 6.289–95.
65. Ibid., 6.293–95.
66. Ibid., 6.300–10.

can use medicine and herbs without understanding why they are efficacious, so one can judge on the basis of results that divination through oracles and dreams does give accurate predictions of the future and should therefore be respected. Indeed, for the gods who determine the future to withhold knowledge of it from human beings would demonstrate a lack of love.[67] A rational dimension of the argument for divination draws attention to the fact that continuing human observation begets a fund of knowledge on the basis of which accurate prognoses can be made. Quintus's case concludes with two claims that are directly relevant for our line of inquiry: (1) examples may be adduced for the gods having given divine warnings to political and philosophical leaders in the past; (2) since events unfold in a predetermined order, the seer can correctly read the signs of the impending changes, either by external means (entrails, lightning, other celestial phenomena) or by internal inspiration.[68]

Cicero's point of view is not wholly consistent, however, and stands in sharp contrast to the faith in portents and divination evident in Josephus and the Roman historians. He acknowledges that extrapolations can be made on the basis of intelligent observation, through reason and experience, but thinks that conjectures based on interpretation of dreams give evidence of the interpreter's sagacity rather than proving any causal link between dreams and events. On the theological issue, he asks why the gods do not communicate directly, and why they rely instead on the uncertain and contradictory interpretation of dreams. Divination is a superstition and should be rooted out, but he ruefully observes that it has taken advantage of human weakness, is widespread among the nations, and has cast its spell over the minds of nearly the entire human race.[69] Cicero wants to affirm that the universe operates by natural laws, and that religion—including rites and ceremonies—ought to be continued to preserve the stability of the state and the sanctity of law. Yet in the course of his argument he gives evidence of the contem-

67. Cicero *De Divinatione* 1.1–38.
68. Ibid., 2.64, 70.
69. Ibid., 2.72.

porary overwhelming faith in divination, and especially in divine portents, as a way of foreseeing and preparing for the future.

In Book 1 of his *Histories*, Tacitus presents details of the prodigies that occurred during the period of the multiple emperors, such as warnings through thunderbolts, heavy rain,[70] and animals giving birth to strange young. The reports that Vitellius's troops were approaching Rome were presaged by the following signs: the reins of the chariot fell from Victory's hands in the vestibule of the Capitol; a statue of Julius on the Island of the Tiber turned from west to east on a bright, calm day; the Tiber overflowed at Rome, causing vast destruction in the lower part of the city and blocking Otho's military advance.[71] On the other hand, good omens pointed to the prosperity of Vespasian and Titus, including favorable readings of entrails and of movements of the stars. The priest of a shrine on Mount Carmel in Judaea foretold that Vespasian's plans and achievements would receive divine support.

A unique feature of the Roman historians' accounts of the imperial period is to be found in the reports of Tacitus, as well as Suetonius and Dio Cassius, about Vespasian's experiences in Alexandria prior to his return to Rome and accession to the principate. The sources describe the cures effected by or through Vespasian: a blind man had his eyesight restored by the application of spittle; a crippled hand was cured when Vespasian stepped on it.[72] It is tempting to generalize on the basis of this literary evidence and to conclude that miracle-working of this sort was commonly associated with divinely endowed human beings of this period. But a precaution against that easy inference is established, not only by its uniqueness in the literature, but also and more importantly by the fact that the healing stories are linked directly with the god Sarapis. It was in his temple that Vespasian was staying at the time the healings took place; it was a devotee of Sarapis who received his sight.[73] Tacitus under-

70. Tacitus *Histories* 1.3, 18.
71. Ibid., 1.86.
72. Ibid., 4.81; Suetonius, *Lives of the Caesars,* Vespasian, 7; Dio Cassius, bk. 65, sec. 271.
73. Tacitus *Histories* 4.81–82.

scores this fundamental connection by recounting at this point in his narrative the story of the founding of the Sarapis cult under Ptolemy Soter (306–283 B.C.) who, through an extended process of dreams and oracular consultations, arranged for the transfer of the god from Sinope to Alexandria. The god showed his eagerness for the relocation by making the voyage in two days.[74]

With this single exception, the prodigies reported by both Suetonius and Dio Cassius concern signs that presage the accession to power of one of the emperors or portents of the violent end of his reign. The ambivalence of the rulers concerning astrology is apparent, some favoring it, others prohibiting it. Features shared with Josephus are the miraculous opening and closing of doors as cosmic reminders of historical transitions.[75] Tacitus mentions the very same portents that preceded the destruction of Jerusalem as those given by Josephus.[76] Dio Cassius, in describing the signs of divine sanction for Octavian's designation as emperor, uses language identical to that of Josephus to describe the predictive supernatural power at work, *to daimonion* and to characterize the signs themselves, *to theion proesēmanen*.[77] Idiosyncratic is Suetonius's fondness for recounting the wonders that occurred during the infancy and childhood of Augustus—which is what we might expect to appear in the romance-oriented literary atmosphere of the turn of the second century. Significantly, Dio Cassius reports that magic was resorted to in order to cure Hadrian of various ailments, but that Marcus Aurelius, after first gaining relief in battle through the aid of Egyptian magicians, decided to refuse magical assistance and turned instead to invoke the help of the Christian God, who helpfully dispatched a thunderbolt against the enemy and sent a rainshower to refresh the Roman troops. Yet the dominant stance toward the miraculous in the historians of the first and second centuries is that the gods send signs attesting chosen leaders and forewarning of major changes in the power structure.

74. Ibid., 4.83–84.
75. Suetonius *Julius* 71; Dio Cassius 61.35; 63.185, 233.
76. Tacitus *Histories* 5.13.
77. Dio Cassius, bk. 42; cf. Josephus *Wars* 300–10.

Personal Identity and World-Construction   **77**

In the period between the rise of Alexander's successors and the ascendancy of the Antonines, however, many persons were far more concerned about their own personal needs and destiny than about the fate of the incumbent political power—though in fact the two issues were not unrelated. Those in pursuit of personal fulfillment turned from the gods of the state to those divinities who promised personal benefactions, both in matters of health and in sense of purpose. We move now to an analysis of the development of the cults of two of these beneficent deities: Asklepios (chap. 3) and Isis (chap. 4).

CHAPTER THREE

Asklepios the Healer

From the era of Homer down to the reign of Constantine, the preeminent figure linked with healing in the ancient world is Asklepios. He appears throughout these centuries not only as the agent of divine cures but also as the founder of the medical profession. The witnesses to the healing god-physician throughout these many centuries have been assembled by E. J. and L. Edelstein,[1] although since publication of their volume in 1945 other inscriptional evidence has come to light as well. Since Asklepios appears in these materials as a human being with therapeutic skills, as a hero, and as a god, attempts to trace the development of this figure have not produced definitive results.[2] My procedure will rely entirely on extant texts and inscriptions, eschewing extrapolations and conjectures. The evidence is set forth in chronological sequence, but attention will be paid to the changing cultural and social contexts in which this material originated.

THE ORIGINS OF ASKLEPIOS

In the *Iliad*, Homer's description of the ships and their leaders assembling for the attack on Troy includes the following details:

1. E. J. Edelstein and L. Edelstein, eds., *Asclepios: Testimonies* (Baltimore: Johns Hopkins University Press, 1945).

2. W. A. Jayne, in *The Healing Gods of Ancient Civilizations* (New Haven: Yale University Press, 1925), suggests five stages: Asklepios (1) as mortal Thessalian physician; (2) as heroized after death; (3) as designated son of Apollo and healing god at Epidauros; (4) as a demigod and hero at Athens; (5) as Aesculapius, the great healing-god at Rome. C. Kerenyi, in *Asklepios: Archetypal Image of the Physician's Existence* (New York: Pantheon/Bollingen Foundation, 1959), pp. xiii–xviii, wants to reject the divinization of a hero-physician from Thessaly, supposing rather that Homer has passed over in silence an older cult. Kerenyi suggests a development of the Asklepios cult (parallel to that of Dionysus) which was linked with Apollo and based originally at Delphi, and which expressed the same birth-in-death motif as did the cult of Dionysus.

> They who held Trikke and the terraced place of Ithame
> and Oichalia, the city of Oichalian Eurytos, of these
> in turn the leaders were two sons of Asklepios, good
> healers both themselves, Podaleiros and Machaon.[3]

The implication is obvious: Asklepios is renowned as a healer, and has transmitted this skill and reputation to his two sons. There is no hint that father or offspring are of other than human origins, since the sons take their place among the all-too-human venturers about to attack Troy.

By the time of Pindar, however, there is an elaborate legend recounting the schemes and plots of the gods and goddesses associated with the birth of Asklepios. Before Phlegyas (Coronis) gave birth to Asklepios, she was fatally wounded by arrows of Artemis for having consorted with Apollo and thereby conceiving his child even though she was wedded to another man. Unable to deceive Zeus as to the paternity of the child, Coronis was placed on a funeral pyre, to which Apollo came and there delivered his child from the dying mother. Then the god gave the child "to the Magnesian Centaur to teach it how to heal mortal men of painful maladies."[4] The healing techniques used by Asklepios in Pindar's description include potions, even surgery, but also incantations and unspecified ways by which "those whosoever came suffering from the scores of nature, or with bodies wasting away from summer's heat or winter's cold, he loosed and delivered divers of them from diverse pains."[5] There is no hint of ritual, of petitions addressed to a god, of dreams or visions, of nocturnal incubations. The moral of the ode is drawn by Pindar from the inappropriate attempt of Asklepios to bring someone back from the dead, which resulted in both healer and restored one being struck down by a lightning bolt from Zeus. The story ends with the solemn warning to seek only what is appropriate to mortals: "Seek not, my soul, the life of the immortals; but enjoy to the full the resources that are within thy

---

3. *Iliad*, 2.728–33, trans. Richmond Lattimore (Chicago: University of Chicago Press, 1951, 1961).

4. Pindar, *Third Pythian Ode*, lines 15–45, trans. Sir John Sandys, Loeb Classical Library, (London: Heinemann, 1915).

5. Ibid., lines 46–50.

reach."[6] Asklepios, then, is depicted as an extraordinarily endowed human being who is free to exercise his healing gifts to the full but must be aware of his human limitations.

In the *Protagoras*, Plato refers to Hippocrates as a Coan, an Asklepiad, and as a trainer of medical students. W. H. S. Jones rejects the notion that an Asklepiad was a priest of Asklepios or a member of a guild bound by the Hippocratic oath, but suggests that it is "at least possible that the Asklepiads were a clan of hereditary physicians, who claimed to be descended from Asklepios." Assuming that they were basically a hereditary family group, though with the possibility of inclusion of non-kin by adoption, the term could have come to be a general designation of medical practitioners.[7] A likely analogy could be seen in the use of "Homeridae" for poets tracing their descent from Homer.

In "Ancient Medicine" Hippocrates seeks to develop what we might more nearly call a scientific view of medical technique. He respects ancient tradition and insists that it must be taken into account but urges reliance on careful observation of the human condition and on experimentation which can lead to generalizations, especially in the realm of diet and abstinences. Conversely, he rejects simple solutions such as prescribing opposites: heat for cold, cooked meat for someone made ill by eating raw meat. His theories rest on analysis of the humors, their relative strengths and intensity, and on bodily structures (shapes and spaces). Clearly Hippocrates was trying to develop principles that correlated the physical conditions of the organism with its health.[8] At the end of the fifth century B.C., therefore, one important strand of the Asklepios tradition was seeking to develop principles of healing along empirical, rational, experimental lines. And that outlook will run concurrently with the others that we shall be tracing below.

Aristophanes, a contemporary of Hippocrates, included in his *Plutus* a deliciously satirical account of a visit to the shrine of Asklepios at Piraeus which the narrator, Cario, made in the

6. Ibid., lines 55–63.
7. *Hippocrates*, Loeb Classical Library, (London: Heinemann, 1923), 1.xliv.
8. Ibid., 13, 22.

company of the god Plutus and an Athenian politician, Neo-
clides.⁹ After a bath in the sea, Cario entered the sacred precincts with his companions. Loaves and other oblations were on
the altar, including a well-baked cake. All bedded down for the
night in the Abaton, where, after putting out the lights, the sac-
ristan ordered them to remain quiet no matter what noise they
heard. After watching the priest carry off in his own knapsack
all the edibles from the altar, Cario took advantage of the darkness to try to help himself to the porridge that an elderly woman
pilgrim had brought with her, pleasant odors of which drifted
toward him, but the woman pulled her porridge under the bed-
clothes with her. At the solemn climax of the incubation vigil
when the god approached, Cario farted. The god was not fazed
by the noise or the odor, but his accompanying daughter, Jaso,
blushed and held her nose. Cario depicts Asklepios as an apoth-
ecary, complete with mortar, pestle, and box. He prepared a
plaster of hot spices and vinegar, which he placed on the ailing
eyes of Neoclides, whereupon the latter ran amok in pain until
he could be calmed. Plutus's healing required a different technique: Asklepios's daughter, Panacea, covered his head with a
scarlet cloth, after which two serpents appeared from the sacred
part of the temple, crept under the cloth, and licked Plutus's
eyes, whereupon he was promptly healed as well. Then the god
disappeared and the serpents withdrew to their sacred recesses
of the temple.

Although the story is told in a mocking tone, it probably reflects accurately what was known, or claimed, to occur in the
epiphanies of Asklepios, either in his own bodily form or through
his symbolic agents, the serpents. The assumptions of the suppliants at the shrines of Asklepios in the early fourth century
are clear: an ailing person came with appropriate offerings and
with solemn expectations. If the god was favorable, healing would
occur, either by some simple medicament or by direct action of
the god or his surrogates. Apart from the attendant priests and
assistants at the shrine, there is no indication of a cult group,
nor of any ongoing ritual or cult in which the beneficiaries par-

9. Aristophanes *Plutus*, act 3, scene 2.

ticipated. It was enough for the keepers of the shrine that the ailing brought gifts; it was enough for the sick that they—or at least some of them—went away cured. It was a simple quid pro quo transaction. As we shall see when we turn to the testimonies from Epidauros from the Hellenistic period, the same general features of the Asklepios cult are evident.

Before examining the inscriptional material from Epidauros, we must consider how, in the early third century, and therefore before the impact of Hellenistic culture on Rome, Asklepios was brought to that city. The story is recounted by both Livy and Ovid,[10] though their versions differ in some details. Although the year 292 B.C. had been one of blessing in many ways, a great misfortune befell both the city and the surrounding countryside when a severe plague struck. Oracles were consulted as to how to remedy this calamity—Livy says the "Books" (presumably Sibylline oracles); Ovid says the Delphic oracle—and the advice was to bring Asklepios from Epidauros to Rome. The reluctance of the council of Epidauros to agree to this request from the Roman emissaries was overcome by the appearance of the god, who said he would accompany the delegation back to Rome. A serpent from the temple—Ovid says it was golden—slithered aboard the ship carrying the image of the god and ordered a brief detour to the island of Antium, to enable him to honor his father, Apollo.[11] As the ship sailed up the Tiber, which was lined with devotees of Asklepios, sacrifices, incense, and perfumes were offered up on altars erected for the occasion, all of which was carefully observed by the serpent, who had climbed the mast and was looking about for an appropriate place for his new abode. He found it on the Island of the Tiber, went ashore there, resuming his heavenly (rather than his chthonic) form. A temple was erected on the spot in his honor. An end was brought to the woes of the Roman people now that this bearer of health had taken up residence among them.

Although the site later became a hospital and continues as

10. Livy *From the Founding of the City* 10.47; 11; Ovid *Metamorphoses* 15.625–744.

11. Ovid *Metamorphoses* 15.715.

such down to the present day, there is no indication in the Latin
sources of the extent to which the medical technique side of the
Asklepios tradition was fostered there, or whether it functioned
merely as a shrine where healings occurred through incubation
and the therapeutic effects of snakes and epiphanies. The
prominence of the serpent image of the god in both accounts
suggests that divine ministrations dominated over the techniques of physicians. Even allowing for hyperbole on the part of
Ovid, the god's arrival was not the launching of his cult in Rome
but a climactic public recognition and sanction of an existing,
broadly based cult of the healing god.

ASKLEPIOS AS MEDICAL AND CULT HEALER

Ancient and modern descriptions of Greece devote long sections to the complex of buildings and associated structures at
the shrine of Asklepios outside the city of Epidauros. Pausanias,
writing in the middle of the second century A.D., details, not
only what was visible in his time, but also provides specific information about which of the facilities had only recently been constructed. As we shall see, there were important changes taking
place in the Asklepios cult in the Antonine era, which are concretely demonstrated in the then new buildings.

Pausanias's *Description of Greece* is arranged along geographical
lines, beginning with Attica and ending with Phocis. Shrines of
Asklepios are mentioned in all ten books of the *Description*, which
obviously attests their presence throughout Greece. But equally
clear is that by Hellenistic times the chief center of devotion to
Asklepios had moved from Trikka to Epidauros. Pausanias has
a variant of Pindar's legend of the birth of the god; in the new
version, Coronis, while pregnant with Apollo's child, was brought
by her father, Phlegyas, on a journey to spy out the land in the
Peloponnesus. She gave birth to Asklepios and exposed him on
a mountain near Epidauros, where he was given milk by a goat
and guarded by a dog. The herdsman who owned these helpful
beasts was warned away from touching the child by flashes of
lightning that surrounded him. As the child grew, word spread
"over every land and sea" that Asklepios, son of Apollo, was

discovering everything necessary to heal the sick. Other legends
are mentioned by Pausanias, but the ultimate argument that Asklepios was born in that vicinity is that other sanctuaries traced
their origin to Epidauros and that the festival honoring the god
was called Epidauria. The Delphic oracle put it succinctly:

> O Asklepios, born to bestow great joy upon mortals
> Pledge of the mutual love I [i.e., Apollo] enjoyed with Phlegyas'
>   daughter,
> Lovely Coronis, who bore thee in rugged Epidauros.[12]

The sacred grove was surrounded on all sides by boundary
markers. No birth or death could take place within the holy area,
and all offerings had to be consumed within the grounds. The
image of the god was chryselephantine and pictured the god as
seated, grasping a staff with one hand and with his other hand
above the head of a serpent. A dog was lying by his side. The
linking of the god with a serpent and a dog is to be found on
fourth-century B.C. coins, as well. Prominent among the buildings Pausanias describes is a circular structure, known as the
tholos; within it stood slabs (*stelae*), on which were inscribed the
names of those who had been healed, the nature of their diseases, and the details of their cures. The facilities had been enlarged in Pausanias's own time through the generosity of "a Roman senator, Antoninus"—presumably, Antoninus Pius (138–
61). In addition to various baths and auxiliary temples, there
was a new residence in which women could be delivered of children and the sick might die "without sin,"[13] located adjacent to
the sacred precincts but outside the territory where births and
deaths were prohibited.

Systematic excavation and analysis of the site were carried out
in the nineteenth century, and the results have remarkably confirmed, but also significantly supplemented, Pausanias's report.
By combining the evidence from the remains with the ancient
testimonies, it is possible to reconstruct with assurance the functions that the various facilities had within the Asklepion. The

12. Pausanias *Description of Greece* 2.26.1–27.6.
13. Ibid., 2.27.6.

tholos, a circular structure with forty columns in peristyle arrangement, had a plain wall with a single doorway. In the basement there is a triple circuit of walls penetrated by doors; hence, it is not a labyrinth, since moving about is simple. Rather, the circles and openings were a way of making available to numbers of people simultaneously the waters of the sacred springs, for washing and for refreshment.[14] From Pausanias we can infer that springs or wells were a regular feature of shrines of Asklepios.

The pilgrims were required to spend the night within the shrine, so that they might receive communications from the god, either directly by an epiphany or indirectly through dreams, or by an intermediary in the form of a dog or snake. It is easy to imagine the vigil of the suppliants, lying in the total darkness of the *abaton*, listening for the padding of the feet of the priests or the sacred dogs, or the nearly noiseless slithering of the sacred snakes. It seems likely that the lower recesses of the *tholos* could also have served as the abode of the serpents, who shared chthonic origins with the waters from the sacred springs. And, of course, the serpent was believed to be the visible form of Asklepios himself.[15]

Although one may be grateful to Rudolf Herzog for having edited and published the *Iamata* preserved on the tablets at Epidauros,[16] his commentary and introduction manifest a regrettable, almost pathetic, effort to find some features of the cult that can be deemed credible or comprehensible from the perspective of modern medical science. More serious is Herzog's lumping together evidence from these plaques, which date from

---

14. A. Defrasse and H. LeChat, *Epidaure: Restauration et description des principaux monuments du sanctuaire d'Asclépios* (Paris: Librairies Imprimerie Reuniés, 1895), pp. 96–127. A similar interpretation of the *tholos* is offered by Charles Diehl, in *Excursions in Greece to Recently Excavated Sites of Classical Interest* (London: Greuel, 1893), p. 33.

15. Alison Burford, *The Greek Temple Builders at Epidauros* (Liverpool: Liverpool University Press, 1969), pp. 19–20.

16. Rudolf Herzog, *Die Wunderheilungen von Epidauros: Ein Beitrag zur Geschichte der Medizin und der Religion* (*Philologus*, suppl. Bd. 22, Heft 3) (Leipzig, 1931).

around 300 B.C., with inscriptions and texts from the mid- to late second century A.D. Further, Herzog has failed to allow for the full implications of a basic split in the Asklepios tradition: one that stressed divine intervention, as at Epidauros; the other that relied on medical technique. In several of the testimonies from late-fourth-century Epidauros the god appears in a dream and performs some sort of therapeutic action. Some may be as violent as cutting off a head, while others are as gentle as drawing a disease out of the victim (an epileptic) by applying a ring to the nose. Not only is there no hint in the accounts of healing that a medical procedure was actually followed, but in the excavations there was no trace of surgical equipment. At Cos, on the other hand, where Asklepios was linked with the developing medical school tradition, were found an operating theater, with all its instruments and apparatus, levers of all kinds and beams to help reset dislocated bones, knives, trephines and instruments for cutting the uvula, as well as sick-rooms and facilities for apothecaries.[17] By contrast, at Epidauros, the healings were wholly matters of divine operation.

The accounts of healings at Epidauros are given in compact, stylized form: the name and place of origin of the suppliant; the nature of the ailment or problem; the divine action at the shrine; the successful result. In nearly every case there is a sacred sleep, a vision, a dream; through these the god speaks and accomplishes the desired result. The ailments listed include facial and mouth injuries, dumbness, stones (kidney or gall), extended pregnancies, leeches, baldness, dropsy, tumor, lice, worms, headaches, infertility, tuberculosis, and other unspecified bodily diseases. Most common are injured or disfigured limbs, wounds from weapons, and blindness. Only occasionally is there a touch of humor, as when a young pilgrim, on being asked what he would offer the god in exchange for a cure, suggests "knucklebones" (i.e., a gambling device), which elicits from Asklepios laughter as well as the remedy for his difficulty. Other problems solved by the beneficent god include the mending of a broken cup, the recovery of a lost child and of lost treasure. Uniformly

17. Diehl, *Excursions*, p. 339.

characteristic of these testimonies from the Hellenistic period are a brief diagnosis, a divine manifestation, and a speedy cure. There is no hint of extended ritual before or after the cure, and nothing of a cultic group of followers. There is no suggestion that the healing had any meaning outside of itself; it is not a pointer to a spiritual transformation or a promise of anything transcendent. In Hellenistic times, the Asklepion at Epidauros was an out-patient clinic, where the god worked directly to meet the needs of those who came to him in need of his aid. The single exception to these general observations about the testimonies from Epidauros collected by Herzog is the stelae of M. Julius Apellas. But that document dates from about 160 A.D. and fits well with the evidence about the Asklepios cult of that time, which has been preserved in literary and inscriptional form from Pergamum, and which will be analyzed below. First, however, we must examine the medical strand of the Asklepios tradition.

We have had occasion to note that Asklepios was linked both with Hippocrates and with the medical school located on Cos, near Rhodes. Galen (A.D. 130–201), one of the most important figures in the history of medicine, was born and received his basic education at Pergamum, which in addition to being a major medical center of the empire, was the seat of an Asklepion which rivaled in prestige that of Epidauros. Among cities where he extended his studies was Smyrna, likewise the setting for both a renowned shrine of Asklepios and a medical school.

It is with Hippocrates and the experimental practice of medicine rather than with the Asklepios tradition that Galen associated himself.[18] He was severely critical of one Asclepiades, a physician of the first century B.C., but on grounds of basic differences in medical theory, rather than objections to his seeking cures through incubation and dreams, as in the mystical Asklepios tradition.[19] Galen's opinions are based on confidence in the human organism to restore itself (a principle he derives from Hippocrates), but especially on direct experimental observation

18. Galen, *On the Natural Faculties*, 1.2; 1.13, where Galen commends Hippocrates for joining philosophy and medicine.
19. Ibid., 1.13, 14, 16.

of the ways in which the organs of the human body function. His treatise "On the Natural Faculties" defines the two factors that effect the growth and nutrition of living organisms: *physis*, which functions in both plants and animals, and *psychē*, which functions in animals and human beings only. All change within the organisms is the result of the operation of these forces. Galen then seeks to show how the bodily humors and individual organs operate in sickness and in health. His detailed knowledge of physiology is impressive, in spite of the fact that his theories about humors are obsolete. His creative combination of experimental inquiry and philosophical insight is admirable, but it places him and his approach to medicine in a world removed from that of the mood and methods that characterized the shrines of Asklepios in Galen's time,[20] even though his approach to health and that of the priests and devotees at the shrines both claimed to be in the true tradition of the ancient god of healing.

ASKLEPIOS AS BENEFACTOR AND PERSONAL GUIDE

The substantive shift away from the no-nonsense, direct cures of the Hellenistic period is apparent in the Apellas inscription from Epidauros, which dates from about A.D. 160. To convey the atmosphere of the shrine and the mood of those who frequented it, we quote the inscription in toto:[21]

> I, M. Julius Apellas, was sent forth by the god, since I fell sick often and was stricken with indigestion. On the journey to Aegina, not much happened to me. When I arrived at the sanctuary, it happened that my head was covered for two days during which there were torrents of rain. Cheese and bread were brought to me, celery and lettuce. I bathed alone without help; was forced to run; lemon rinds to take; soaked in water; at the ἄκοαι in the bath I

20. Kerenyi, *Asklepios: Archetypal Image*, notes that when the medical center at Cos was at its height—in the second centuryA.D.—there was no shrine there. Instead, the physicians seem to have called themselves Asklepiads, i.e., descendants of the son of Apollo, whose name was linked with a sacred cypress grove on the island (pp. 51–55).

21. *IG* 4² Syll. 3.1170; reproduced in R. Herzog, *Wunderheilungen*, pp. 43–45 (my translation).

rubbed myself on the wall; went for a stroll on the high road; swinging; smeared myself with dust; went walking barefoot; at the bath, poured wine over myself before entering the hot water; bathed alone and gave the bath-master an Attic drachma; made common offering to Asklepioa, to Epion, to the Eleusinian goddess; took milk with honey. I used the oil and the headache was gone. I gargled with cold water against a sore throat, since this was another reason that I had turned to the god. The same remedy for swollen tonsils. I had occasion to write this out. With grateful heart and having become well, I took leave.

The contrasts with the *Iamata* of Hellenistic times are striking: although the god is given ultimate credit for the cure, the therapy seems to have been largely self-administered. There is no mention of the sacred sleep or dream-visions. Rather, there are baths and strolls, presumably extending over a period of many days. The ailments are multiple; to heal them there is no lick by the tongue of a snake or a dog. The beneficiary is grateful for the improvement in his health, but there is no miraculous healing at a stroke. Significant, however, is the clear implication that the course of Apellas's life is under the guidance of the god. It is a factor which figures importantly in the evidence from Pergamum in the same period that Apellas was overcoming his maladies at Epidauros with the aid of the god.

Pergamum, Smyrna, and Ephesus were the leading cities of Asia Minor in the second century of our era. In the epoch of the Attalids (approximately a century ending with the death of Attalos III in 133 B.C.), Pergamum had been the capital city. With its commanding location on a hilltop, the impressive monuments on its acropolis, and its tradition for learning—Mark Antony reportedly took 200,000 volumes from its library as a gift for Cleopatra—its religious significance had been enhanced when Attalos established, or gave state support to, the cult of Asklepios there.[22] Yet it was to Smyrna, which had excelled Pergamum in beauty and intellectual repute as a center for the sophists since the first century B.C., that one Aelius Aristides migrated from his ancestral home in Mysia to the north.

22. André Boulanger, *Aelius Aristide et la sophistique dans la Province d'Asie au IIᵉ siècle de notre ère* (Paris: Boccard, 1923), pp. 16–17.

The son of a moderately wealthy landowner, Aristides had been cared for from his birth about 117 B.C. by a beloved nurse, Philomena. He probably attended the lower schools in Smyrna and then was sent to study rhetoric with Alexander, one of the most highly regarded teachers of his day, whom he was later to meet again in Rome. The lectures he heard were on Plato, Homer, and Pindar. It has been inferred from the extended quotations in Aristides' writings from historians, poets, and playwrights, as well as philosophers and biographers, that the school regimen included a heavy demand for memorization.[23] His education was capped by study at Athens with Herodes Atticus, who was not only an outstanding orator but also a major benefactor of the city. Following a sightseeing journey and a stay in Smyrna, the death of his father led Aristides to travel to Egypt, apparently in quest of improved health and of some sort of religious life-orientation. From that time on, Sarapis was the name he chose to invoke as the supreme god of the universe. Other divine names designated for Aristides other sacred aspects or functions, but he never attempted to integrate them into the Greek family of gods and goddesses. Sarapis remained for him the ultimate manifestation of divine power and wisdom. For personal and professional needs, however, it was Asklepios who came to dominate Aristides' private and public life.

In 143 B.C. Aristides set out to make his fortune as a rhetor in Rome, but illness, which had stricken him before departure, grew worse en route. Mingled disease and disappointment drove him back to his native coasts within the year. Unable to recover his strength through Sarapis, he visited the shrine of Asklepios at Smyrna, and a dream-vision he received there was the turning-point in his life, since the god became not only the source of his health—or bestower of periods of relative recovery—but also the guiding force in all his travels and career decisions. He shortly began the first of a series of extended stays in Pergamum, where the central focus of his life was Asklepios.

The cult of Asklepios in Pergamum, in spite of initial royal patronage, seems to have become an enterprise involving pri-

---

23. C. A. Behr, *Aelius Aristides and the Sacred Tales* (Amsterdam: Hakkert, 1968), pp. 11–13.

vate individuals. Earlier on, there were public festivals. The image of the god appeared on coins; a hereditary priesthood honoring him was established, but with the passing of Attalos III, who reigned 138–133 B.C., the cult receded in public interest. Such inscriptions honoring Asklepios as have been found from this period are individual testimonies, not unlike those from Hellenistic Epidauros. All this changed, however, beginning under the Flavians and reaching a climax under the Antonines.[24] Habicht has drawn attention to a passage from Martial in which is reported a gift of an expensive mirror to Asklepios by one Flavius Earinus, eunuch and favorite of Domitian. Asklepios is called "the Pergamene god," and Habicht observes, "With these verses the Pergamene Asklepios becomes at home in Roman literature and in higher society." The god's image appears once again on coins; citizenship, together with the forename "Flavius," is awarded to the priest of Asklepios at Pergamum. By the first quarter of the second century the god is sought out for aid and honored for his benefactions by prominent members of Roman society.[25] Our most abundant documentation for this comes from the *Sacred Discourses* of Aelius Aristides, but the architectural additions to and enrichment of the shrine in Pergamum attest that Aristides was by no means unique for his era in his devotion to the son of Apollo and Coronis.

The basic plan for the grandiose expansion of the sanctuary complex was begun under Hadrian and carried out by Antoninus Pius. Added to the shrine proper were baths, a theater, and a gymnasium, and the residential quarters were enlarged. Statues of the imperial family were erected in the sacred courts, and the numbers of dedicatory inscriptions increased vastly. It is probably no exaggeration to say, with Habicht, that Asklepios had become "the precise new center of public life" in Pergamum.[26] The symbolism of the round temple of Zeus-Asklepios-Soter, with its vast dome as indicator of the cosmic rule of the

24. The history of the Asklepios cult at Pergamum has been traced succinctly but in sufficient detail by Christian Habicht, in *Die Inschriften des Asklepions* (Altertumer von Pergamon. Bd. 8.3. Deutsches Archäologisches Institut) (Berlin: W. de Gruyter, 1969), pp. 1–20.

25. Ibid., p. 8.

26. Ibid., pp. 8–9.

god, was the prototype for others in subsequent centuries, both
in the East (Hagia Sophia) and in the West (the Roman Pantheon). The syncretistic and unifying thrust of this symbol was
made explicit through the equation of Asklepios with Zeus and
through the dedication of five altars at Pergamum to all the gods
and goddesses. The dedicatory inscription of the cupola temple
shows that the theoretical uniting of the gods was a concept fostered by an elite, intellectual and social, but a fundamental shift
in the Asklepios piety had occurred. No longer do the inscriptions testify to healing miracles accomplished by Asklepios in
behalf of individuals. These are mentioned in our major literary
source, Aristides, but in a context which manifests a basically
different outlook from that implied by the Epidauros inscriptions. This change is confirmed by the Lex Sacra,[27] which mentions therapy and provides ground rules for incubation, but which
is chiefly concerned with the experience of salvation rather than
with the remedy for an ailment.

The most common feature of the inscriptions for the Antonine period is the mention of the dedicatory gift, accompanied
of course by the name of the donor. Those responsible for the
dedications include senators, members of the equestrian order,
and others linked with the imperial establishment, as well as
persons with Roman names (presumably newcomers to Pergamum). Aristides mentions by name the rhetors, sophists, and
philosophers who were there and who seem to have shared his

27. Michael Wörrle, "Die Lex Sacra von der Hallenstrasse" (*Inv* 1965, 20), in
Habicht, *Inschriften*, pp. 167–90. After describing the sacrifices that are to be
offered to various gods (Zeus Apotropaius, Zeus Meilichios, Artemis Prothyroia,
Ge), instruction is given to "offer to Asklepios on the altar a suckling pig and
place the right thigh and the entrails on the sacrificial table. Into the offering he
should throw three obols. At evening he should lay out three cakes with nine
knobs . . . of which two are to be placed on the altars for Tyche and Mnemosyne,
and one in the incubation chamber for Themis." To enter the chamber one must
be pure from sexual relations and from other forms of pollution (goat meat,
cheese, etc.). "The incubane shall place the wreath and return to the couch."
Further instructions deal with offerings of food and money, with special regulations for "compensation for healing," though earlier the law speaks more generally of "whoever makes a petition to the god" without specifying the nature of
the request.

devotion to Asklepios. Poetry was recited at the shrine and dec-
lamations were uttered there. Clearly, one of the clienteles appealed to by Pergamene Asklepios was that of the economic and
cultural elite, to whom the god offered the meaning of their
lives, not merely a cure for a disease or disability. Let us examine
Aelius Aristides as the chief witness to this piety which, at the
height of the Roman Empire's political power and internal stability, found solace in divine intervention and mystical meaning
for personal fulfillment.

ASKLEPIOS AS SAVIOR: AELIUS ARISTIDES

As we have noted, Aristides came to his position of devotion to
and dependence on the Pergamene Asklepios by a route which
was theologically and geographically roundabout. The first great
change in his outlook on life came in Egypt, in the temple of
Sarapis. And that deity continued to exercise an important influence on him throughout the period covered in the *Sacred Discourses* and presumably throughout his life. We have noted that
it was the failure of his debut as a rhetorician in Rome that
brought him back to the Ionian coast, sick and despairing, in
144. A dream of Asklepios at Smyrna transformed his life—
both his health and his rhetorical skills—and led him to take up
residence within easy access of the shrine of the god at Pergamum. Unlike the Asklepion at Epidauros, that at Pergamum had
no *abaton* and no dormitory within the precincts. We learn from
the discourses that Aristides resided in the living quarters of a
priest or temple warden named Asclepiacus (II.35).[28]

Aristides' favorite epithet for the god is Savior (I.2; IV.4), by
which he means far more than one who delivers him from sickness. That deliverance does take place to some extent, but more
important is the divine power granted him by which he can fulfill his role as rhetorician. His life is divinely preserved, and his
place in heaven is assured through the benefactions of the god

28. The references in our text are to the *Sacred Discourses* by number (I–VI)
and line, in arabic numbers. The edition used is that of C. A. Behr, Loeb Classical Library (Cambridge: Harvard University Press, 1973).

in his behalf. Meanwhile, he finds opportunity for and spectacular success in the exercise of his god-given capability as an orator. The overarching term by which he identifies the god who
makes all this possible is *Soter*. When that god is thought of in
his cosmic sovereignty, he may be designated as Sarapis, though
the latter is linked with Zeus.[29] When, however, Aristides is describing the god who is near and beneficent, it is Asklepios.

Just as his interest in Asklepios arose out of Aristides' many
and protracted ailments, so a continuing feature of his relationship to the god is as divine healer. Unlike the earlier stage of the
Asklepios cult, in which visits to the shrine seem to have been
brief, and cures—when they occurred—were instant and devoid of thaumaturgic technique, at Pergamum the line between
medical and miraculous cures cannot be so sharply drawn. Most
frequently mentioned are curative baths,[30] occasionally in mud.[31]
Other cures include gargling and purgation.[32] There is at the
same time a pervasive denigration of the medical profession,
and an acknowledgment on the part of the physicians of the
superiority of Asklepios's direct actions and instructions to the
standard medical processes.[33] Studies of Roman medicine have
rightly observed that Aristides does have knowledge of medical
technique in his era, but he moves from this intellectual approach to basic human needs to a "mystical, all-encompassing
solution"[34] which his devotion to Asklepios provided.

Clearly, healing was not the major benefit of association with
the god. The illnesses provided the occasion for enjoying his

29. *Sacr. Disc.* III.48. Inscriptions from the third century A.D. link Asklepios
with Sarapis, Isis, Hygeia, and Poseidon as well as with Zeus: in nos. 713 and 161
from L. Vidman, *Sylloge inscriptionum religionis Isiacae et Sarapiacae* (Berlin: de
Gruyter, 1969).

30. *Sacr. Disc.* I.7; II.72; V.29.

31. Ibid., II.51–72.

32. Ibid., V.1–10; IV.5–7.

33. Ibid., I.57, 62; II.5, 69; III.8, 16–20.

34. John Scarborough, *Roman Medicine* (London: Thames and Hudson, 1969),
pp. 107–08. Scarborough refers disapprovingly to E. R. Dodds's characterization
of Aristides as a "brainsick noodle with a religious sentiment," in *Pagan and Christian in an Age of Anxiety* (Cambridge: Cambridge University Press, 1965), p. 43,
n. 3.

benefactions, with the result that there was no hurry to be cured. It is estimated that Aristides remained in Pergamum, associated with the Asklepion there, for at least five years.[35] He points out that he submitted to the god as to a doctor, and did in silence whatever Asklepios wished.[36] After having been ill for ten years, he had been ordered to engage in an elaborate series of intestinal purgations and induced vomiting. The chief benefit, however, was not restoration of health but mystical transport:

> It was all not only like an initiation into a mystery, since the rituals were so strange and divine, but there was also something marvelous and unaccustomed. For at the same time there was gladness, and joy, and a cheerfulness of spirit and body, and again, as it were, an incredulity if it will ever be possible to see the day when one will see himself free from such great troubles, and in addition, a fear that some one of the usual things will again befall and harm one's hopes about the whole. Thus was my state of mind, and my return took place with such great happiness and at the same time anguish.[37]

The inclination of others to discuss their ailments and cures left Aristides with mixed feelings, since he considered the guidance of the god of greater importance than health: "For it is strange that both I and another would recount whatever cure he gave to my body even at home, but to pass by in silence those things which at the same time raised my body, strengthened my soul, and increased the glory of my rhetorical career."[38] The divine shepherding was pervasive, Aristides claimed: "Thus the God directed us in many things, giving us signs as to what should be done, and having us obedient, if ever any other man was obedient to the god."[39]

Before turning to the matter of the bearing of Aristides' mystical visions on his career, it may be useful to trace some of the other dimensions of his mysticism. Central to his religious ex-

---

35. Boulanger, *Aelius Aristide*, pp. 135–36.
36. *Sacr. Disc.* I.4.
37. Ibid., IV.6–7.
38. Ibid., V.36.
39. Ibid., VI.1.

perience are dreams.[40] But dreams also reinforce his role as orator. In a dream a philosopher told him that he surpassed even Demosthenes in dignity, "so that not even the philosophers scorn you." The god himself set his seal to this when Aristides was in a waking state. When he began rehearsing on the night following the dream and without revealing that his rhetorical skill had been granted him, his hearers, on "hearing my words for the first time, especially approved of their dignity, and this caused them much excitement."[41] The ability to write hymns for Apollo and Asklepios was granted to him through dreams; some of them he could recall by memory from the dreams.[42] He dreamed that in the midst of a rhetorical contest he besought Asklepios: "Lord Asklepios, if I excel in rhetoric and excel much, grant me health and cause the envious to burst."[43] On another occasion, while planning a journey to Smyrna, he dreamed of a passage from Aristophanes' *The Clouds*, which deterred him from making the trip and saved him from some nasty weather.

Not only through dreams, but also directly, the god appeared to Aristides, providing him with meaning and purpose in life, capacity to fulfill his role as rhetor, assurance of his destiny, and explanations for the preservation of his life. The healing of Aristides had occurred in public view by the river, and was accompanied by a manifestation of the god. The mystical experience transformed his attitude, furnishing him with "certain inexplicable high spirits" and assuring him that he "was wholly with the god."[44] When Aristides was in deep grief following the death of a beloved household servant who had reared him, Isis and Sarapis, as well as Asklepios, appeared to him following his sacrifice of geese to Isis. The two gods are described by him as "marvelous in beauty and magnitude, and in some way like one another."[45] Following this was the aforementioned epiphany of

40. Ibid., I.3; III.25; IV.54–56, 85–87, 89; V.11–16, 42–46.
41. Ibid., IV.19–20.
42. Ibid., IV.41.
43. Ibid., IV.68–69.
44. Ibid., II.20–24.
45. Ibid., III.45–46.

Sarapis as the sovereign of the three-storied universe.[46] Visions of Athena and Asklepios are also reported.[47]

Perhaps the most elaborate epiphany story in the *Sacred Discourses* depicts a series of visions that Aristides had that pointed to the divine source of his eloquence and therefore of his career as an orator. In the Temple of Olympian Zeus he had a vision of himself crowned with a crown of gold in recognition of his superiority as an orator, and he was hailed by the divine voice as "invincible in rhetoric." In the Temple of Asklepios, however, he discovered a monument honoring jointly Aristides and Alexander the Great. He wrote that he "rejoiced and conjectured that we both had reached the top of our profession, he in military and I in rhetorical power." At this point the other devotees of the god were told to leave the shrine, but Aristides was ordered to remain. An epiphany of Asklepios followed. When Aristides greeted him as "The One," the god replied, "*Su ei*" ("you are [it]"), which is tantamount to identifying the god with his devotee. To that divine acclaim Aristides responded: "For me this remark, Lord Asklepios, was greater than human life, and every disease was less than this, every grace was less than this. This made me able and willing to live."

Then the divine logos was uttered pertaining to his rhetoric as well as to his communion with the god. He was told that it was fitting for his mind to be changed from its present condition, that having been changed it would become superior, and that on becoming superior he would associate with the divine. As a token of this new relationship, he was given the name Theodoros, since all he had was "the gift of god." That vision was confirmed by a dream, through which he learned that the Mother of the gods regarded him as Theodoros.[48] In his divinely transformed life he was granted visions of the god himself, and associated with Sophocles and Aeschylus, as well as other great rhetorical and literary figures.[49]

46. Ibid., III.48.
47. Ibid., II.39.
48. Ibid., IV.48–54.
49. Ibid., IV.55–57.

The consequence of these epiphanies was to transform Aristides' rhetorical skills. Even though symptoms of illness over-
took him as he was preparing for a rhetorical contest, he was
filled with increasing strength and lightness as he proceeded with
his preparations. His dazzled audience realized that there was
no one in the oratorical field who could be compared with him.[50]
Others began to dream about him, while in his own dreams he
"heard many things which excelled in purity of style and were
gloriously beyond" the rhetorical models by which he had been
trained. His technical skills continued to improve, including
mastery of ex tempore style and learning speeches word-for-
word, as was recognized fully by others. All this accomplishment
and recognition made him realize that Asklepios had greater
plans for him than personal salvation alone, that he was destined for unparalleled greatness as an orator.[51] Similarly, the god
enabled him to write hymns and poetry. One of his songs was so
effective as to cure a cough.[52]

Furthermore, the outpouring of divine gifts gave him the capacity to discern portents, as when he refused to sail from Delos
on one occasion because of his intimations of an impending storm.
After the storm—which would have destroyed the ship—had
passed, Aristides himself was hailed as benefactor and savior.[53]
The gods communicated to Aristides in a variety of other ways.
Following severe earthquakes in Asia Minor, he had sacrificed
an ox to Zeus at Smyrna, in the course of which a shining star
darted through the agora, which was understood to be a sanc-
tioning of the offering. Advised to make an offering at the Temple
of Olympian Zeus, Aristides did so and learned that his estate
had been saved from destruction by the earthquake.[54] Stories of
rescue from storms at sea[55] are reminiscent of that theme in the
popular romances of the period, such as Xenophon of Ephesus's

50. Ibid., IV.22–23, 62.
51. Ibid., IV.22–29.
52. Ibid., IV.38. In IV.4 we hear about Aristides writing a song to Asklepios
as savior as he traveled along in a chariot.
53. Ibid., IV.32–37.
54. Ibid., III.38–43.
55. Ibid., II.65–68.

Ephesiaca. Even the fact that Aristides survived the severe shock of prescribed baths in icy-cold water is understood by him to be a sign of miraculous preservation.[56]

One of the most astonishing portents reported by Aristides is said to have occurred during the illness and death of a child of his foster-sister. After having sent a doctor to her, he dreamed that he had immolated an animal, and on inspecting it, found that it bore the name "Deliverer." On inquiring of a seer what this might mean, Aristides was told that it was merely the result of the climate, stars, and such things. Convinced of the seer's unbelief, and encouraged by oracles which had been recorded before the girl died, Aristides learned that her entrails were inscribed with a description of her problem, and that the oracles had mentioned his name, describing him as Sosimenes ("safe-abiding"). From this he inferred that her soul and body, as well as that of her brother, had been given vicariously for him.[57]

The outcome of this divine enablement of Aristides was that he was widely recognized by the populace as extraordinarily gifted and that he drew throngs whenever he presented one of his orations. An Egyptian had announced well in advance his own rhetorical display at the Odeon but drew only seventeen listeners, while on an hour's notice, Aristides addressed a frenzied, packed crowd in the Council Chamber.[58] At Smyrna, following a dreary speech by the local custodian, Aristides held forth for hours, at the end of which the crowd demanded that he continue immediately with a second discourse. The listeners were the more astonished to learn that Asklepios had forewarned Aristides of the extra exertion he would be forced to produce and had counseled him to eat ahead of time.[59] The populace sought to have Aristides assume public offices, from which he managed to have himself excused through exercise of his oratorical skills before the emperor (Antoninus Pius).[60] The emperors Marcus and Verus extended honors to Aristides which he

56. Ibid., III.38–40.
57. Ibid., V.22–23.
58. Ibid., V.32–34.
59. Ibid., V.39.
60. Ibid., IV.71–77.

perceived in a dream to be "marvelous and unsurpassable," in that he "alone was granted everything, and no one else had even a small part of these honors." He added that the emperors were grateful for the privilege of having known such a man as he.[61]

Aristides' fifth discourse ends with a kind of transfiguration story, in which he recounts a dream that while a student at Athens, a servant of one of his comrades had linked him with Plato, and that he had accepted an offering of eggs and presented them at an altar which turned out to be that of a temple of Plato. Aristides observed that it was proper to honor the gods with temples while celebrating famous men with books. But later, as he turned toward the Acropolis, a shaft of light touched his hair, which his youthful companion took for a sign of glory. Aristides' imagination thereupon led him to think that he was ascending and descending ladders—apparently in mystical communion.

The suggestion of a rational explanation for this divine illumination, without denying its supernatural meaning, is in keeping with Aristides' efforts—wholly unsuccessful—to sound modest about his own achievements. Persuaded as he was that his skills were the gift of Asklepios, he seemed to suppose that speaking of his accomplishments in superlative terms would serve only to glorify the god through whom these benefactions came. He seemed genuinely to believe that he was free from pride.[62] The glowing estimate of him by his fellow-rhetor Quadratus, who had recently been appointed governor of Asia, was so filled with praise for Aristides that for him to recount it "would seem to be boastfulness . . . because of the excessive praise which was involved." In any case, the honors accorded him by other men paled in comparison with the honors he had received from the gods.[63]

Fortunately for the historian, insight into Aristides' view of the gods, of medicine, of healing, and of his own life is provided not only by inference from the somewhat loose-jointed *Sacred Discourses*, but also directly and explicitly from a discourse of his,

61. Ibid., I.46.
62. Ibid., V.38.
63. Ibid., IV.63–67.

"In Defense of Oratory."[64] As C. A. Behr points out in his introduction to this work, Aristides claimed to have direct knowledge of the gods. This came to him through his experience of ailments which the physicians could neither name nor cure. Like others who frequented the shrines of Asklepios and Sarapis, he laid no claim to mastery of a technique in his field of rhetoric, but rejoiced rather in the concern of the gods for him and other human beings and in his and his colleagues being saved through dreams. He acknowledges that he must use a rational argument (*logos*) and rhetorical technique even while making the argument for divine communication through the irrational medium of dreams and visions.[65]

Aristides comments directly that he considers medicine to be merely the practice of probabilities. If only the doctors could come to understand the physical state or constitution of human beings, "they would not be so inferior to the god who holds Epidauros." Instead, they can do no more than generalize on the basis of experience, conjecturing what will be best for the ailing, in spite of the fact that human nature is so various that such generalizations can never be complete or accurate.[66]

In his own case, his delicate constitution had limited his public appearances as an orator, but his condition had also led him to seek aid directly from the god, who became "the leader and patron of his life and speech."[67] Aristides declared the "scorn of art"—that is, of cultivation of technique—as "the beginning of taking refuge with the gods." Speaking on the basis of one who participated regularly in incubation at the Asklepion (or elsewhere, perhaps, since he did not reside in the temple), he describes the importance of dreams: "We employ dreams, not knowing in advance of the evening what we are going to see, and we know what we must do to be saved (*sōthēnai*), although we are in ignorance up to that minute in which the benefit (*agathon*) has come from the gods." He raises and answers the ques-

64. *Aelius Aristides*, "In Defence of Oratory," Loeb Classical Library (Cambridge: Harvard University Press, 1973), ed. and trans. C. A. Behr.

65. Introduction, *Aristides*, ed. C. A. Behr, p. 72.

66. *Aristides*, Behr, secs. 149–56.

67. Ibid., secs. 427–37.

tion: "So do dreams cause a concern for man to be attributed to the gods, or does the gods' care for mankind cause mankind to be saved through dreams? I think the latter."[68]

It might seem very strange to modern rationalist eyes that a man of the learning, wealth, and sophistication of Aristides, one so highly regarded by his contemporaries and sought after for leading roles in government and public life,[69] could be so totally dependent on dreams and visions for the progress of his career. And yet Aristides was by no means an oddity for his time. G. W. Bowersock has described him as one of those who "brilliantly mirror the world" in which he, and other sophists, flourished.[70] The range of cities linked with the sophists—including Byblos, Gadara, Tyre, and Tarsus—attests the pervasiveness of their influence and the broad base of their appeal throughout the originally diverse segments of the Roman Empire at this, the height of its extent and the peak of its cohesiveness. As Bowersock notes, the sophists were "almost always from the notable and wealthy families," and many others contributed enormously to the restoration and enhancement of the Greek cities and monuments, as Herodes Atticus did so splendidly in Athens.[71] Aristides is unique, therefore, only in the abundance of his work that has been preserved and in the depth of insight into a life-world that his *Discourses* and other essays display. In him we have a rich and accurate portrait of his era,[72] including the outlook of wealthy

68. Ibid., secs. 67–71.

69. One of Aristides' persistent problems, especially in the years covered by the *Sacred Discourses*, was the pressure from the populace and from the rulers for him to assume public functions: i.e., Severus's nomination of him as the leading citizen of the province; his selection for the priesthood, as tax-collector, as Prytanis, and as member of the provincial assembly (*Sacr. Disc.* 4.71–104). Clearly the people and the governing authorities wanted to exploit for public benefit both his eloquence and his considerable personal fortune. However, his pleas of piety and of preoccupation with divine things were persuasive; the authorities excused him from serving.

70. G. W. Bowersock, *Greek Sophists in the Roman Empire* (Oxford: Clarendon, 1969), p. 1.

71. Ibid., pp. 23–24.

72. M. Rostovtzeff, in *The Social and Economic History of the Roman Empire* (Oxford: Oxford University Press, 1926, 1966²), p. 130, sees in Aristides' enco-

intellectuals on the question of the gods' involvement in human life.

A similar picture of the mid-second-century culture may be drawn from Artemidorus's *Oneirocritica*, a miscellany of reports of dreams through which deity is manifested in human existence. As E. Le Blant has noted, the cast of characters "in this bizarre collection" (as he characterizes it) includes "rich and poor, ingénues and slaves, athletes, comedians, courtesans, lovers, travellers, hunters, artists, workers, priests, lawyers, doctors," all of whom "pass before our eyes" in their search for "clarification of the doubts which the phantoms of the night have inspired in them."[73] Although in this collection of material there is a preoccupation with death that is different from the salvific outlook of Aristides, both authors are one in their assumption that knowledge of self, the gods, and the future is conveyed preeminently through dreams. The traditional gods are both the symbols and the media through which this knowledge is conveyed to the seekers.[74] They come as deliverers from peril, but also as messengers of death. Complementing the more explicitly religious features of these dreams is a preoccupation with mass entertainment—theater, mime, gladiators, acrobats, fighters, athletes—as well as with crucifixion and martyrdom.[75]

In the Antonine era Asklepios, and the Greek pantheon of which he is a leading figure, were no longer regarded as primarily agents of divine assistance to be turned to in time of need, in response to specific crises, as was the case at Epidauros in the Hellenistic age. Rather, Asklepios was a god concerned with the

mium from Rome "a masterpiece of thoughtful and sound political analysis," which superbly illustrates the political, social, and economic aspects of the empire of his era.

73. Artemidore: "De quoi on revait dans le monde romain, au temps de Marc Auréle," in *Mémoires de l'Institut National de France, Académie des Inscriptions et Belles-Lettres* (Paris, 1909), 36: 18.

74. The gods who appear in the dreams reported by Artemidorus include Bacchus, Cerberus, Mercury, Diana, and the Dioscuri. Ironically, Asklepios's entrance into the house of a sick person was not regarded as a visit for healing purposes but as a forewarning of death (Le Blant, "Artemidore," p. 27).

75. Ibid., pp. 25–26.

wider range of human needs, anxieties, and aspirations, throughout this life and on into the life beyond. He was transformed from divine friend-in-need to a cosmic savior. His shrines were no longer out-patient clinics, but something like the spas of nineteenth- and early-twentieth-century Europe and America, where the wealthy went to enjoy bad health and to find comfort in sharing their ideas and their accomplishments with others of like background and persuasion.

This picture of the transformation of the Asklepion at Pergamum and of the cult that flourished there is confirmed by the evidence from both inscriptions and nonliterary sources.

As Christian Habicht has observed, it was during the reigns of Domitian and Trajan that the expansion and embellishment of the shrine at Pergamum resulted in its eclipsing every other Asklepion in the Roman world.[76] As the "outstanding healing establishment of the whole empire," it came to be included among the wonders of the world. Why this enormous surge of interest in and veneration of Asklepios? Because the Olympian deities had come to be regarded as of little interest, as arbitrary and impersonal, while Asklepios—together with Isis and Sarapis— were directly concerned with the total welfare of the faithful and with the course of their lives and the fulfillment of their destinies. It is probably not an exaggeration to describe Asklepios in the Antonine period as the precise new center of public life.[77] The symbol of the god's cosmic triumph is to be seen in the construction of the gigantic round shrine in which the compassionate healer of the Hellenistic era was now honored as Zeus-Asklepios-Soter, whose universal authority was symbolized by the vast cupola, under which his devotees gathered in his honor.[78]

---

76. Habicht, *Inschriften*, p. 6.

77. Trajan built an arcade in the vicinity of the Asklepion; Hadrian further enriched the area architecturally, including the placing of statues there and of inscriptions honoring the imperial family, thereby linking them with Asklepios. A theater and an amphitheater, as well as gymnasium, baths, and residential quarters, were also constructed. From this point on, dedicatory inscriptions flourished —no longer primarily as testimonies to healing but as attestations of Asklepios's power as Savior (Habicht, pp. 8–10).

78. Ibid., pp. 11–12.

CHAPTER FOUR

Isis

There is no figure in the study of religion in the ancient world—and perhaps in the entire scope of history of religion—whose role is more widespread in time and space and undergoes more marked transformations than that of Isis. An action of hers that appears in the oldest texts (which date back to the fourth millennium B.C.), and that seems to have been an act of respect for the dead, became in Hellenistic and Roman times the center of an elaborate myth and set her forth as a primary agent of miracle. These basic changes provide us with a prime example of the transformation of structures, so that we shall trace her history in greater detail and over a longer period of time than we have done with our other examples. The cast of characters remains the same; the drama alters substantively.

THE ANCIENT ORIGINS OF THE ISIS CULT

In the "Memphite Theology," first published in usable form by J. H. Breasted[1] and now dated to the first dynasty (3100 B.C.),[2] the central figures are Osiris and his son Horus. The latter is the ascendant king; the former is his dead father, whose powers and position Horus assumes. Historians have long observed that the physical situation and circumstances of Egypt were fundamental to the shaping of the world-view that prevailed in this land as far back as it can be documented. Protected from invad-

---

1. J. H. Breasted describes earlier attempts to read the text and his own interpretation of it in *The Development of Religion and Thought in Ancient Egypt* (New York: Scribner, 1912), p. 46, n. 1.

2. Henri Frankfort, *Kingship and the Gods: A Study of Ancient Near Eastern Religion as the Integration of Society and Nature* (Chicago: University of Chicago Press, 1948), pp. 24–35. Discussion of the date is on page 352, note i, where Kurt Sethe's argument on philological grounds is adopted.

ers by desert on both sides, and richly endowed with fertile land by the inundations of the Nile, the outstanding feature of the life-world in Egypt was stability. As Henri Frankfort described it, "A cosmic order was once and for all established at the time of creation. This order might occasionally be disturbed, for the forces of chaos were merely subdued, not annihilated. Nevertheless, revolts against the established order were bound to remain mere ripples upon the surface."[3] The agent of cosmic order was the king, who was considered divine. His godhead was not a quality acquired by ritual or assigned at his coronation. As Frankfort says, "His coronation was not an apotheosis but an epiphany."[4]

The king is described in the Memphite text as having been generated by Ptah:

> There came into being as the heart and there came into being as the tongue (something in the form of Atum). The mighty Great One is Ptah, who transmitted [life to all the gods], as well as to their *ka's* through his heart, by which Horus became Ptah, and through his tongue, by which Thoth became Ptah.[5]

The heart as the seat of thought and the tongue as instrument of expression combine to achieve the act of creation. The king is not only the creation of Ptah, the supreme god, but is also identical with him in his royal power. The major task of the divine king is to enable the people of the Two Lands of Egypt to live in prosperity:

> The Great Sea, which rejoices the heart of the gods, which is in the House of Ptah, the mistress of all life, is the Granary of the God, through which the sustenance of the Two Lands is prepared, because of the fact that Osiris drowned in his water, while Isis and Nephthys watched. They saw him and were distressed at him. Horus commanded Isis and Nephthys repeatedly that they lay hold on Osiris and prevent his drowning. They turned their heads in time and they brought him to the land. He entered the mysterious portals in the lands of eternity in the steps of him who shines forth

---

3. Ibid., p. 4.
4. Ibid., p. 5.
5. J. B. Pritchard, ed., *Ancient Near Eastern Texts*, 2d ed. (Princeton: Princeton University Press, 1955), p. 5, line 53, trans. John A. Wilson.

on the horizon, on the ways of Re in the Great Seat. . . . Thus Osiris came to be in the "House of the Sovereign: on the north side of this land which he had reached. His son Horus appeared as King of Upper Egypt and appeared as King of Lower Egypt, in the embrace of his father Osiris, together with the gods who were in front of him and behind him."[6]

Thus the sovereign roles are assigned to Ptah, Osiris, and Horus. The latter both restores Osiris to life and allows his father to move on to the realm of the blessed dead. The visible, regnant ruler is Horus—now and forever. By contrast, at this early period the role of Isis is modest, though essential to the narrative of the myth. The rescue of Osiris accomplished by the sisters seems not to have occurred to them on their own until they were urged to undertake it by Horus. The implication is that they might have watched the floating Osiris, responding only with feelings of distress, had not Horus "commanded [them] repeatedly" to keep the god from drowning. Once that vital chore was performed, they disappear from the narrative. Indeed, as Frankfort points out, it is perhaps too strong to render this verb describing Osiris's condition as "drowning," since his condition is paradoxical: his floating in the water is a state of seeming death and yet is the means of the fecundity of the land and the sustenance of its populace.[7]

In the text under consideration the lifting up of the body of Osiris is the counterpart of the ritual act of the pouring out of the water of the Nile as a symbol of revitalization through the divine potency. The guarantee that that line of power will not be broken lies in the endless succession of former Horuses (become Osirises in death) by new Horuses, sons of Osiris. As mother of Horus, Isis's role is represented as passive. As one who, when urged, turns her head toward Osiris afloat on the Nile, her function is merely auxiliary. Although Osiris begets Horus by Isis, she rates no fuller mention than to be identified as "mother of Horus,"[8] except in much later texts. The characterization of Isis

6. Ibid., pp. 5–6.
7. Frankfort, *Kingship*, p. 30.
8. Pritchard, *Ancient Texts*. Two texts from Thut-mose III (1490–36) mention Isis: once as protectress of the king, together with Nephthys; once as (implicitly) the mother of Horus (p. 446). Frankfort proposes that in the early pe-

as compassionate does come through at times in the older texts, as when she and her sister weep for their brother and embalm his body to prevent its decay.[9]

It is Horus who takes major responsibility for preserving the body of the dead Osiris—which is to say that the new king accomplishes the embalming of his predecessor as a guarantee of the stability of the realm. A Pyramid Utterance expresses this sentiment: "Horus collects for thee thy limbs that he may put thee together without any lack in thee." It is he who prepares Osiris for ascent to and acceptance among the gods.[10] In other texts, Nut is pictured as welcoming him and providing a place for him in the celestial regions.[11] No comparable role is assigned to Isis. The closest we come is the passing reference, in a text reminding Osiris of how much Horus has done and continues to do for him, that "Isis and Nephthys have healed thee."[12] Not surprisingly, it is these two themes of compassion and healing which will be selected and greatly elaborated in the later stages of the Isis myth. Meanwhile, however, other roles are assigned to the Mother of Horus.

ISIS AS AGENT OF ORDER

A charming text from the nineteenth dynasty[13] (1350–1200 B.C.) portrays Isis as schemer and exorcist. Described as "more discerning than a million of the noble dead," Isis undertook to learn the secret name of Re, in order that she might have access to the power latent in it. Re is depicted as going for a stroll, much like Yahweh enjoying an evening walk in the Garden of Eden (Gen-

---

riod Isis was regarded as the deified throne (*Kingship*, pp. 43–44). But as he acknowledges, in the Memphite theology the Great Seat of Horus is Memphis itself (p. 43), and as the bearer of Horus, the mother figure Isis plays only a supporting role (p. 44).

 9. *Pyramid Text* 2144–45; 1257. Other texts give credit for this pious act to Anubis.

 10. *Pyramid Text* 635.

 11. *Pyramid Text* 1345.

 12. *Pyramid Text* Utterance 364.

 13. Wilson, Pritchard, *Ancient Texts*, pp. 12–14.

esis 3), to survey his own handiwork: the cosmos that he had created. Showing signs of senility, Re drools as he ambles about. Isis finds the saliva lying on the ground and combines it with earth to fashion a snake, which then comes alive. As Re passes, it bites him. He is wracked by fever and pain but also tormented by his inability to find an antidote for the poisonous bite. The other gods are summoned in order to determine what it was that bit him.

Isis generously offers assistance, but she asks one thing in return: that he reveal to her his secret name. After going through so much suffering, he seemingly decides to grant her request and tells her that his name in the morning is Khepri, at noon is Re, and in the evening is Atum. This information is useless in overcoming the poison of the snake, so Isis returns to tell him that he has not indeed revealed his true secret name. Re then agrees to disclose it, but only on condition that Isis will tell it to Horus and swear him to secrecy. The narrative then reports, "The great god divulged his name to Isis, the Great of Magic." Thereupon, Isis was successful in overcoming the malevolent power of the serpent she had formed. The success was effected "through the speech of Isis the Great, the Mistress of the Gods, who knows Re (by) his own name." Then there follow directions as to how her achievement may be matched through the use of her exorcistic formula—which, curiously, is never actually disclosed—with the added instructions that the image of Horus should be painted on the hand of the victim or on a linen strip to be placed around the throat. The process may be further "worked up with beer or wine" drunk by the person bitten. Even in her role as magician, therefore, Isis is to some degree dependent on Horus, who remains the ultimate source of power.

A drama depicting the succession of the king, dating from 2000 B.C. in its present form but very likely incorporating elements from as early as the First Dynasty (3000 B.C.), includes stage directions and instructions to the actors for what seems to have been a performance on royal barges on the Nile. Its ritual character, therefore, is unmistakable.[14] The climaxes, not sur-

14. Summarized in Frankfort, *Kingship*, pp. 126–39.

prisingly, are the coronation of Horus and the embalming of Osiris. Running throughout the drama are references to barley and other grains, as symbols of the life-sustaining power of the god-king, providing for his people in the Lands of the Nile. The relationship between the two gods is seen in the mutual embrace by which the divine power of kingship is transferred from father to son, which is then celebrated by a great meal. Pyramid Texts confirm this signification of the embrace:

> O Osiris, this is Horus within thine arms.
> He will support thee.
> There is further transfiguration for him with thee
> In thy name "He of the Horizon from which Re goes forth."
> Thou hast closed thine arms around him, round him;
> He will not go away from thee
> Horus does not allow thee to be ill.
> Horus has put thy enemy under thy feet,
> And thou livest again.[15]

How does Isis figure in this ritual drama of the orderly transfer of power? The stage directions note that, in preparation for the meal, bread and beer are brought. Osiris provides the bread; Isis provides the beer. Obviously these are not marginal features, since the directions also note that in order to supply the bread, Osiris has been "Put into the earth." Accordingly, he is bewailed. The cycle of planting grain and its seeming death leading to new life, as well as the process of fermentation of the grain for beer, which generates new vitality, are clearly central to the whole ritual pattern of renewal. Isis, alas, is identified in all this simply as "Mistress of the House"—a kind of barmaid who furnishes the beer for the festivities.[16]

ISIS AS INSTRUMENT OF JUSTICE

As early as the middle of the second millennium B.C., texts attest the personification of the divine mind (Sia)—that is, of the power

15. *Pyramid Texts* 636–37. Quoted in translation of H. Frankfort, *Kingship*, p. 135.

16. Frankfort, *Kingship*, p. 136.

to effect what the mind conceives and the divine mouth declares (Hu), and of the ordered purpose which is thereby achieved (Ma'at):[17] "Authoritative Utterance is in thy mouth. Understanding is in thy heart. Thy speech is the shrine of truth." Here the kinship is evident with the outlook expressed in the Memphite Theology which describes the act of creation as the efficacious work of the heart and tongue of Atum.[18] What happens when these three factors are not functioning is vividly portrayed in the lament of Ipuwer, which probably originated in the period between the Old and Middle Kingdoms (2300–2050 B.C.). After describing how crime has taken over, agriculture has been abandoned, taxes go unpaid, houses fall down, and social roles are reversed, Ipuwer laments that there is no one in charge, no one who avails himself of the instruments of order which are available to the responsible ruler: "But there is no pilot in their hour. Where is he today? Is he then sleeping? Behold the glory thereof cannot be seen. . . . Yet Authority (Hu), Perception (Sia), and Justice (Ma'at) are with thee."[19]

The world-view implicit in this text and related documents is one in which the mind (or heart) of the god conceives an ordered creation and an ordered society resident within that world; the creation and guidance of that order are effected by the authoritative utterance of the god; the triumph over chaos and the cosmic order which is thereby established—or in chaotic times, is in need of restoration—is Ma'at, the embodiment of justice, the right ordering of all creation, including human, personal, and corporate existence. Her role is not merely ethical, as her name Justice might imply, but social, political, and cosmic as well. By analogy with the traditions of ancient Israel, where Wisdom is both the instrument of creation (Proverbs 8) and the voice of common sense (Proverbs 6), the wisdom literature of ancient Egypt includes both features. "The Instruction of Ani" from the Twenty-First or Twenty-Second Dynasty (1000–700 B.C.), for example, counsels against wanton women, garrulousness, and

17. Ibid., p. 51.
18. Wilson, *Ancient Texts*, pp. 5, 11, 53–54.
19. Ibid., p. xii, 5:443.

confiding in strangers.[20] But personified as Ma'at, wisdom in
Egyptian tradition is the embodiment not of practical good sense
but of cosmic design and divinely maintained order.

In a document dating from the Fifth Dynasty (2450 B.C.) there
is an appeal to heed the words of one's ancestors, who had
hearkened to the gods, in order "that strife may be banished
from the people and the Two Lands may serve thee."[21] In "The
Instruction of the Vizier Ptah-Hotep," which goes back at least
to the Middle Kingdom (second millennium B.C.) and is perhaps
much older, the declaration is made, "Justice (Ma'at) is great,
and its appropriateness is lasting, since the time of him who made
it." There follows a series of items of advice for specific roles,
such as serving as a private emissary, succeeding a more renowned person in an official post, rearing a son, exercising official authority. In every case, the overall goal is the achievement
of peace and order, while the personal goal is length of days.[22]

A document from the reign of Thut-Mose III (1490–1436 B.C.)
expresses a similar outlook. In the autobiography of the vizier,
Rekh-mi-Re, there is a description of his appointment to office.
In the process of his installation he experienced a kind of mystical transformation: "My abilities were not as they had been:
my yesterday's nature had altered itself, since I had come forth
in the accoutrements of the vizier, having been promoted to be
Prophet of Ma'at." In the document the king then expresses
confidence that the vizier will act in accordance with the royal
"heart," in spite of the many decisions to be made in his office.
In phrases anticipating W. S. Gilbert's lament about the unhappy lot of the policeman, the king observes, "Decisions are
many, without limit to them, and the judging of cases never falls
off." But he adds the earnest hope, "Would that thou mightest
act in conformance with what I may say! Then Ma'at will rest in
her place," which is later explained to mean that the vizier's
"produce" will be "the carrying out of justice."[23]

20. Ibid., pp. 420–21.
21. Ibid., p. 442.
22. Ibid., p. 414.
23. Ibid., p. 213.

Ma'at, therefore, is both the concept of order and the capacity to effect and maintain it. As such she shares in the very life of the gods, as attested in a Hymn to Amon as the Sole God (from the Nineteenth Dynasty, ca. 1300 B.C.): "Thy Mother is Truth, O Amon. To thee she belongs uniquely, and she came forth from thee (already) inclined to rage and burn up them that attack thee. Truth is more unique, O Ammon, than anyone that exists."[24] Apart from the genealogical difficulty of how Ma'at can be both mother and offspring of Amon, the point is clear that the reign of the divine king is dominated before and after by her who embodies truth, justice and order.

From about the same epoch comes another text describing even more broadly the role of Ma'at in maintenance of order and human prosperity under the divine king:

> I (the king) come to thee. I bring to thee Ma'at.
> Thou livest by her. Thus rejoicest in her,
> thou art perfect by her, thou unitest by her,
> thou givest by her, thou restest upon her.
> Thou placest by her, thou givest food by her,
> thou art powerful by her, thou art stable by her,
> thou art adorned with her, thou risest by her,
> thou shinest by her, thou . . . by her.
> She overthrows thine enemies,
> thy heart is delighted when thou seest her.
> Those who are in thy chapel are rejoicing
> when they see Ma'at in thy suite.
> Distress disappears, disorder is driven away,
> all gods are at peace.[25]

Her work is not the violation of natural law, as a post-Enlightenment thinker might depict miracle, nor is it the performance of an extraordinary act. Rather, her task is to sustain the orderly progress of the creation and of humanity's place within it.

In the Hellenistic period, a significant shift in this outlook oc-

24. Ibid., p. 371.
25. Translated in Helmer Ringgren, *Word and Wisdom* (Lund: Ohlsson, 1947), p. 481.

curred. The role of Ma'at was transferred to Isis. The clearest and most extensive evidence for this shift is to be found in Diodorus Siculus's *Library of History*, Book 1. He asserts that the two gods whom the ancient Egyptians venerated since "ages ago" were the Sun and the Moon—namely, Osiris and Isis. After noting Osiris's identity with Dionysus, he explains that Isis's name means "ancient," "because her birth was everlasting and ancient." She is linked with the cow-goddess of Egypt—Hathor, though Diodorus does not mention the name—as her horns resemble the crescent shape of the moon.[26]

This divine pair "regulates the entire universe, giving both nourishment and increase to all things." Diodorus then proceeds to outline the cycle of the seasons, which they regulate, and the physical elements of the universe, which they furnish: "So it is out of the sun and the moon that the whole physical body of the universe is made complete." The names the Greeks give their gods are nothing more than ways to articulate the powers of the universe which derive from Osiris and Isis.

Of the two, Isis is clearly the more powerful. Diodorus links her with Demeter, whom she resembles more than any other goddess.[27] And it was only by marrying Isis that Osiris was able to gain the kingship. It was she, with a slight assist from Osiris, who led the human race to abandon cannibalism and who set the pattern for agriculture, especially how to grow and harvest grain. More importantly, it is Isis who is seen to have established justice in human society:

> Isis also established laws . . . in accordance with which people regularly dispense justice to one another and are led to refrain through fear of punishment from illegal violence and insolence; and it is for this reason also that the early Greeks gave Demeter the name Thesmophorus, acknowledging in this way that she had first established laws.

In striking contrast with the subsidiary role that Isis played in the older myth and literature, Diodorus reports that after Osiris

26. Diodorus Siculus *Library* 1.1–4, trans. C. H. Oldfather, Loeb Classical Library, (New York: Putnam, 1933).

27. Ibid., 1.13.4–5.

had succeeded in establishing order in Egypt, he "turned over supreme power to Isis his wife."[28] Once Osiris had completed his instruction of the Egyptians in agriculture and viniculture, he devoted himself to the education of the entire human race.

Fascinated as he was by Hermes, "who was endowed with unusual ingenuity for devising things capable of improving the social life of man," Diodorus declared that it was Hermes who should be given credit for inventing the alphabet and language, for ritual ordinances appropriate for honoring the gods, for knowledge of the harmony of the stars as well as of music, and for developing principles of interpretation, to which he gave his name, hermeneutics.[29] Having benefited from Hermes' counsel, Osiris, on surrendering power to Isis, placed him at her side so that she in her regal role might benefit from his knowledge and prudence.[30] In token of her supreme authority, she was endowed with the names of other deities: Demeter, Thesmophorus, Selene, Hera.[31] We shall have occasion to note how the names assigned to her multiplied on down into the Roman period. A recurrent aspect of her role as described in Diodorus's time is that of orderer. In the Hymn of Isidorus, from early first century B.C. in Egypt, it is she who establishes laws, transmits knowledge of skills, and makes possible knowledge of the nature of all things. The aretalogy of Isis reported by Diodorus describes her as queen of every region, instructed by Hermes, and "whatever I have established as laws, no one is able to destroy."[32] That motif is repeated in the later Isis inscriptions from Kyme, Ios, and Saloniki as well.[33] Concrete evidence of her devotion to law is noted by Diodorus in her having broken with the Egyptian custom—regarded as scandalous by other peoples—of marriage

28. Ibid., 1.17.3.
29. Ibid., 1.15.9–16.2.
30. Ibid., 1.17.3.
31. Ibid., 1.25.1.
32. Ibid., 1.27.3.
33. Texts available in W. Peek in parallel alignment, *Der Isishymnus von Andros und verwandte Texte* (Berlin: Weidmann, 1930): the Ios inscription (2d–3d cent. A.D.); the Kyme inscription (1st–2d cent. A.D.). The text from Saloniki in *ZPE 10* (Bonn, 1973), p. 45.

between brother and sister. Although she had been married to her brother Osiris, when he died she vowed never to marry again. Her virtue was rewarded, Diodorus tells us, by her being granted "greater power and honor than the king."[34] Her benefactions, enumerated on the stele, include her having first discovered fruits for mankind and her founding of the city of Bubastis.[35] One of the few surviving links between this text and the ancient myths is that she is also called "wife and sister of Osiris . . . mother of king Horus."[36]

ISIS AND THE MAINTENANCE OF LAW

The heavy emphasis on law and order in the description of Isis in this period is surely linked with the earlier role of Ma'at, though it is also strongly influenced by Stoicism in this period, with its assumptions about universal law and the harmony of the heavenly bodies. The Stoic notion of rulership seems also to have influenced the portrayal of Isis, in that stress falls not merely on stability and peace, as it does in the Ma'at texts, but also and preeminently on the divine purpose working itself out through the divinely ordained rulers. It is to the political dimensions of this idea that we turn before examining the other important role of Isis the Benefactress, healer of human ills. Françoise Dunand has noted that the efforts of the Hellenistic rulers of Egypt to capitalize on the local tradition of the king as a divine incarnation first met with resistance on the part of the indigenous priests.[37] The belief was widespread that the kings ruled by the pleasure of the gods; the latter were ingratiated by the sacrifices offered to them. The order the rulers maintained and the victories they achieved over their enemies were regarded as replicating the primordial triumphs of the gods over their opponents. In the Hellenistic period, the maintenance of order became

34. Diodorus Siculus *Library* 1.27.2.
35. Also documented in the Kyme Inscription (1.11) and the Ios Inscription (1.8).
36. Diodorus Siculus *Library* 1.27.4.
37. Françoise Dunand, *Le Culte d'Isis dans le Bassin Orientale de la Méditerranée,* vol. 1, *Le Culte d'Isis et les Ptolemées* (Leiden: Brill, 1973), pp. 27–33.

of profound concern, not only for the sake of social and political stability, but also for dealing with the personal anxieties that had arisen as a consequence of the usurpation of rule in Egypt by foreigners (Macedonians) and the steady erosion of Egyptian traditions by aggressive Hellenization policies. Since Isis, Osiris, and Horus were the mythical guarantors of divine order, it was inevitable that the Ptolemies would capitalize on this tradition to secure their political power and to build a popular base of support. Since the gods were regarded as *theioi sōteres*, as filled with divine energy that was dispensed to their devotees and was renewed through sacrifice and ritual, the royal household's encouragement of the Osiris-Isis cult served simultaneously to raise popular esteem for the monarch and to make for social stability through widespread participation. By the second century, however, the power of the hierarchy was waxing and that of the monarchy waning.

The efforts of the Ptolemies to deal with this adverse shift in popular esteem took two forms. First, huge sums of money were expended to expand the temples, especially under Ptolemy Philadelphus (285–246 B.C.), who built a great temple of Isis in the delta and one at Philae. Under his successor, Euergetes (246–221 B.C.), the links between the patterns of relationship in the divine household and those in the royal family were underscored. Philadelphus set the pattern for this by marrying his sister, in imitation of Osiris. Euergetes' consort, Berenice II, took the next step by having herself identified with Isis, while Philopator (221–203 B.C.) had his son acclaimed as Horus. A major effect of this explicit correlation was to elevate the queens to positions of power and esteem above that of their male co-rulers, as was the case with Cleopatra II and Cleopatra III. The latter had herself represented as *dikaiosune* incarnate and as the living symbol of political and cosmic victory. When she bore a son to Mark Antony, Caesarion, she wanted to be perceived as Isis bearing the royal child. A *hieros gamos* occurred in Asia at the time of the conjunction of the sun and the moon. The offspring from this union were modestly named Helios and Selene.[38] Al-

38. Ibid., pp. 37–43.

though this elaborate and immensely shrewd public relations attempt ended in tragic failure on the part of the main characters, it rightly assessed the enduring power of the notion, popular in Egypt and in cities around the eastern Mediterranean, of the correspondence between the royal family and the divine triad, Osiris-Isis-Horus. As the one who brought back the vanished Osiris and who bore the new king, it was preeminently Isis who guaranteed stability and continuity in human life. In this capacity, she was not primarily the agent of the miraculous but the ground of cosmic and personal assurance.

Another manifestation of the cosmic power of Isis—one that is more economic and social in its implications than political—was her role as Mistress of the Sea. This was an easy transfer from her function in the boat which recovered the body of Osiris from the Nile, according to the myth. In this case, however, the *sōtēria* with which she was credited extended to her deliverance of the faithful from all dangers on land or sea. Just as she controlled the cyclic rise and fall of the Nile, so she was in charge of the changing meteorological conditions on the Mediterranean Sea which made navigation possible and relatively safe, once the winter storms had passed. A festival, which came to be known in Roman times as Navigium Isidis, was established as early as the fourth century B.C.[39] to mark the opening of navigation. In addition to her function as benefactress on behalf of mothers and newborn children, she became the deliverer of prisoners and storm-tossed sailors.[40] At Alexandria she became known as Isis Pelagia, serving as patroness of seafarers. Earlier, that role had been assigned to Ammon, but the increase in commerce through the new city was accompanied by a transferral of that beneficent assignment to Isis.[41]

From the late second century B.C. comes an inscription, found at the Sarapeum in Thessalonika, which indicates that the nau-

---

39. An inscription from Canopus, dated to 304 B.C., is the oldest surviving attestation of this perception of Isis's powers. Cf. R. Merkelbach, "Zwei Texte aus dem Sarapeum zu Thessalonike," in *ZPE* 10:46–47.

40. Dunand, *Isis*, 1:103.

41. Ibid., p. 94.

tical festival of Isis was celebrated there at least as early as that date. The details of the inscription match nicely with evidence from inscriptions, as well as from lamps and frescoes from the subsequent centuries—down to the middle of the first century A.D.—which make it possible to reconstruct the typical features of the festival.[42] These show clearly how the boat which served Isis in finding Osiris had been transformed into a symbol of her as Mistress of the Sea. That role did not fade with the Augustan Age, moreover, since Isis continued to be represented on coins as Isis Pelagia down into the Roman period.[43] Merkelbach links this role of Isis with the sacred spouted vessel that was carried in the procession at Cenchreae in preparation for the transformation of Apuleius back from ass to man, from wretched beast to devoted follower of the goddess.[44] But by the time of Lucius Apuleius, the Isis cult had passed into a stage of development significantly different from the piety that turned to her primarily as Guardian of Voyagers, as we shall see.

ISIS AND SARAPIS

In Hellenistic and Roman times, the role and fortunes of Isis were closely linked with those of Sarapis. Tacitus and Plutarch recount the story (or stories) of the importation of this divinity into Egypt under royal auspices, allegedly in the reign of Ptol-

42. Details and iconographic evidence about the *ploiaphesia* are in Merkelbach, "Zwei Texte" (see n. 39 above), pp. 48–49. Also Tran Tam Tinh, *Le Culte d'Isis à Pompéi* (Paris: E. de Boccard, 1964).

43. Dunand, *Isis*, mentions other references in inscriptions (dating from the first and second century A.D.) linked with the Navigium Isidis found in Pontus and Bithynia; see 3:105–15. Isis appears as protectress of sea-voyagers on inscriptions ranging in location from Rome and Ostia (see Vidman [chap. 3, n. 29], *Sylloge* nos. 403, 503) to Syria (ibid., nos. 355a, 358), and ranging in time down to the third century A.D.

44. Merkelbach, "Zwei Texte," p. 48. Lucius Apuleius *Metamorphoses* 11.11. Merkelbach also notes (p. 54) that the first-century A.D. inscriptional account of the dream and confirming letter of Xenainetos of Opus concerning Isis is actually a conversion experience. Mystical initiation is also mentioned among Isis's benefactions in inscriptions from Kyme (1.22) and Ios (1.9).

emy I Soter (305–285 B.C.).[45] The familiar details of the sighting
in a dream of a colossal statue in Pontus and of its subsequent
discovery and transport to Alexandria have been treated with
skepticism from Origen ("the story is lengthy and discrepant")
to modern times.[46] Suggestions have been offered that Sarapis
was neither Pluto nor the son of Heracles, as Plutarch reported,
but was of Semitic origin—perhaps Baal or Ea.[47] On arrival in
Egypt, however, he became a synthesis of Osiris and Apis, the
funerary and bull gods, respectively. Identified as Osar-Hapi, or
Osirapis, the god was designed to appeal to both Greeks and
Hellenized Egyptians, rather than to the populace as a whole.
His great appeal was his offer of a universal divine protector.[48]
Isis had a far more personal benefit to offer, and that may ac-
count for her growing appeal in spite of the competition of the
foreigner from Sinope.

In the inscriptions and the iconography, Sarapis and Isis were
closely linked. Not only in Alexandria, but wherever the cult
spread, especially in mercantile centers around the eastern
Mediterranean, the names of these two divinities were linked:
at Halicarnassus in the first half of the third century B.C.; on
Delos in the first half of the second century; on Rhodes, Cos,
Cnidus, Magnesia on the Maeander, also in the second century.[49] Of the more than 1,000 items listed by G. J. F. Kater-Sibbes

45. Tacitus *History* 4.83–84; Plutarch *De Iside et Osiride* 28. The writer acknowledges that there are other accounts of the origins of Sarapis, but after
dismissing them ("not worth while to pay attention to"), he proceeds to summa-
rize them anyway (p. 29).

46. Origen *Contra Celsum* 5.38; Franz Cumont, *Oriental Religions in Roman
Paganism* (English trans., 1911; repr. New York: Dover, 1956), on the Sarapis
cult: "We know very little of its first form and of its nature before the imperial
period" (p. 74).

47. Dunand, *Isis*, 1:49.

48. Ibid., p. 55. According to Plutarch (*De Is. et Os.* 362), Timotheus offered
to Ptolemy expert counsel on the identity of the god. The consultants were Timotheus, a professional interpreter of difficult texts, and Manetho, who was apparently an expert in matters mythological and theological. By identifying him
with both Pluto and Osiris, they provided Sarapis with divine standing, chthonic
authority, and a potential following.

49. Vidman, *Sylloge*, no. 270; P. Roussel, *Les Cultes égyptiènnes a Delos du IIIe
au I^e siècle avant J.C.* (Paris: Nancy, 1916). Relevant items listed in Vidman, *Sylloge*,

in his *Preliminary Catalogue of Sarapis Monuments*, at least 120 link
Isis with Sarapis, though both are also associated with other deities (Sarapis with 65 others), and Isis with both goddesses (Demeter, Aphrodite) and divinized personifications (Hygeia, Tyche,
Fortuna).[50] Equally important as evidence of the absorption of
indigenous Egyptian features into the Sarapis cult is the iconography, as well as its accommodation to broader Hellenistic syncretism. For example, in Kater-Sibbes's catalogue, no. 456 pictures Sarapis on a throne with Isis suckling Horus; above and
behind the throne is a serpent (Asklepios?). A medallion presents Jupiter-Ammon-Sarapis-Neptune-Asklepios, with trident
and serpent.[51]

Although the cult of Sarapis flourished during the reign of
Ptolemy II Philadelphus (285–246 B.C.), it was not until the reign
of Ptolemy III Euergetes (246–221 B.C.) that the great Sarapeum in Alexandria was erected. It was there that the colossal
statue of the god, possibly brought from Antioch or copied from
an original there, was on display. There is no evidence of a mystery cult of Sarapis; rather, his benefactions were bestowed
through dreams or by direct healing actions, as was the case with
Asklepios during this same period. We noted earlier the incident described in an inscription from the second century B.C.
found in the Sarapeum at Thessalonika in which a dream communication to establish the worship of Sarapis and Isis at Opus
is miraculously confirmed in a sealed letter.[52] In the same place—
that is, in a shrine of Sarapis—was found evidence of the celebration of the Navigium Isidis by the end of the second century
B.C.[53] From other sites, paralleling this evidence, there is a relatively small number of inscriptions that recount the miracles
(*aretai*) wrought by Sarapis.[54] Far more common are the testimo-

as nos. CE 18, CE 49, CE 60; nos. 208, 247, 268, 294.

50. G. J. F. Kater-Sibbes, *Preliminary Catalogue of Sarapis Monuments* (Leiden:
Brill, 1973); ibid., nos. 62, 283, 644; ibid., nos. 820, 875, 356, 630, 843.

51. Ibid., no. 1019.

52. Merkelbach, "Zwei Texte," pp. 45–54.

53. Ibid., p. 49.

54. The term *aretalogos* (the recounter of the *aretai* of the divinity) is attested
from the Sarapeum, at Delos (2d century B.C.) where, surrounding the imprint

nies to the miraculous powers of Isis. In a statistical study of the relative frequency of the names of Isis and Sarapis in inscriptions of Italian origin, Michel Malaise has shown that the preference for Sarapis was largely limited to those persons with Graeco-oriental names, while those with Latin names preferred Isis. He suggests the correlation that Sarapis was more widely honored in Greek resident circles, especially among members of the Greek official class. This would be consonant with the fact that Sarapis, though he is represented as a benefactor, is usually portrayed in a sovereign capacity, often in association with Zeus or Helios. By contrast, Isis, for all her majesty and power—Augusta, Domina, Victrix, Triumphalis—is primarily consoler, protectress, dispenser of personal salvation. As goddess of love, she is the symbol of maternal compassion and the patron saint of pregnant women. Added to this appeal was her great antiquity, in contrast to the parvenu Sarapis.[55]

THE PRAISES OF ISIS

The term *aretalogia* was used in antiquity to designate an account of or testimony to the virtues (*aretai*) of Isis as demonstrated to her devotees.[56] J. Bergmann's fundamental study of the Egyptian background of the Isis aretalogies has shown that they all derive from an original, very likely produced in Memphis in the third century B.C.[57] The basic content and structure

---

of the divine feet, are the words: Pyrgias aretalogos kata prostag [ma Sarapid] os to bema . . . Isi (*IG* 11.4.1263). Other inscriptions employing *aretē* as a designation of the beneficent acts of the deity date back at least to the fourth century (from Athens, *SIG*³ 3.1151) and refer to Asklepios (from Epidauros, *IG* 4².1, 128) as well as to Sarapis (from Delos, Sarapeum A, *IG* 11.4, 1299).

55. Michel Malaise, *Les Conditions de pénétration et de la diffusion des cultes égyptiènnes en Italie* (Leiden: Brill, 1972), pp. 155–70.

56. For details, see notes 57 and 60 below.

57. J. Bergmann, *Ich bin Isis: Studien zum memphitischen Hintergrund der griechischen Isisaretalogien* (Acta Universitatis Upsaliensis, Historia Religionum 3, 1968). Bergmann's thesis has confirmed the proposal made earlier along similar lines by Dieter Müller, in "Ägypten und die griechischen Isis-Aretalogien," (Abhandlungen der sächsischen Akademie 53, 1961), pp. 11–88.

of the aretalogy have long been known from the famous passage
in Diodorus Siculus (1.27.3–4):

I am Isis, the queen of every land;
She who was instructed by Hermes,
And whatsoever laws I have established,
These no one is able to destroy.
I am the eldest daughter of the youngest god, Cronos.
I am the wife and sister of Osiris, the king;
I am she who first discovered fruits for mankind;
I am the mother of Horus the king;
I am she who riseth in the star that is in the Dog Constellation;
By me was Bubastis built.
Farewell, farewell, O Egypt that nurtured me.[58]

Diodorus reports that this was the epitaph on Isis's tomb which,
together with that of Osiris, was located in Nysa in Arabia. Our
confidence in this information is not heightened by Diodorus's
having already told us (1.22) that there is disagreement about
whether Isis and Osiris were buried in Memphis or on the island
of Philae in Upper Egypt. Similarly unreliable is Diodorus's claim
that the original of this text was inscribed in hieroglyphics (1.27.3).
The close verbal correspondences among the Isis aretalogies that
have been preserved from Egypt proper, from the Greek mainland, and from the Greek islands, as well as Diodorus's own version, require us to posit a single archetype—in Greek. As D.
Müller has observed, that does not preclude that the archetype
was translated from an Egyptian original in hieroglyphics,[59] but
that source is lost. By contrast, all our evidence converges on a
Greek prototype which was modified over the years but which
preserved its essence in form and content. As we noted in our
discussion of Isis's relation to Egyptian wisdom tradition, the form
of first-person address was already present in Egyptian literature. It needed only translation into Greek and adaptation to
the new role of Isis as benefactress-healer, a transformation which

---

58. Text from Diodorus Siculus (Loeb Classical Library); translation modified from that of C. H. Oldfather (London: Heinemann, 1933).
59. Dieter Müller, "Ägypten," p. 14.

almost certainly began in Hellenistic times and in the Greek language.

Fortunately we are not left with conjecture about the antecedents of Diodorus's aretalogy. A more complete version has been found from perhaps as early as the middle of the second century B.C.[60] Discovered at the site of ancient Maroneia, the first preserved lines of the text extol Isis for her fidelity and beneficence in answering the devotee's petitions concerning his failing eyesight. At first he could see only the sun; now he can see the whole world, which belongs to Isis (lines 6–8). Her response to his petition for health (sōtēria) has persuaded him that she will help in every way. How, then, could he fail to honor her appropriately? As for what follows, his encomium comes from the mind of the god even though it is being written by human hands (lines 9–11). There follows a recital of Isis's role in the generation of the human race. Mother Earth is her daughter; she chose Sarapis as her consort, and their marriage is associated with the relationship between Helios and Selene. Though they are but two, they are known by many names; since ordinary human beings cannot comprehend the complexities of divine beings,[61] composing a hymn in their honor is a very difficult undertaking.

From this point on, Sarapis is completely forgotten in the outpouring of praise for Isis. The details recall the aretalogy of Diodorus: with the aid of Hermes, she discovered writing, including the sacred mystical writings (lines 22–23). She established justice (to dikaion), so that by nature (ek tēs physeōs—a clear Stoic affirmation) all human beings are equal in life and death. She provided human beings as a whole with a barbarous dialect, but to some (hois) she gave the Greek language, in order that the race might be harmonious, not only men and women, but also the whole of humanity. (Once more the Stoic influence is evident in the affirmation of the unity of the race.) She provided laws,

---

60. Yves Grandjean, in *Une Nouvelle Arétalogie d'Isis à Maronée* (Leiden: Brill, 1975), proposes a date somewhere between 150 and 50 B.C., on the basis of comparison with well-dated inscriptions from Thasos, Abdera, and Thessalonika (p. 20).

61. The text here (1.20) translates literally as, "For life (*bios*) knows you as gods only." The implication seems to be, "How can a mere mortal understand the divine nature and the intricacies of relationships among the gods?"

which were at first called *thesmoi* (line 29); these made possible the founding of cities and the establishment of law and order within them (lines 30–31). Parents are accordingly not merely honored but venerated as gods. Thus the grace is the greater when a goddess has written as law what is a necessity deriving from nature (lines 33–34).

After acknowledging that Isis had chosen Egypt as her dwelling-place, the aretalogy offers a compact set of tantalizing enigmas: Athens was especially honored by Isis, since there she "first revealed the fruits."[62] What is involved in this display of fertility is not specified but seems to be clearly indicated by the details that follow: Triptolemus and the sacred serpents; the sperm distributed to the Greeks; the special zeal for Athens in all of Greece, and for Eleusis in all of Athens; the designation of Athens as the crowning glory of Europe, and of the (Eleusinian) sanctuary as the crowning glory of the Athens area. The final, fragmentary lines appear to be concerned with Isis's ordination of the processes of human fertility. But the superlative evaluation of Eleusis shows that by the second century B.C. Isis was being accommodated to Demeter, and that the aspiration for new life was finding expression in the mystical dimensions of the Isis cult. These will become dominant in the imperial period, as we shall see later in this chapter, but the framework for mystical participation through Isis was established back in the Hellenistic period.

ISIS AS BENEFACTRESS

In his description of Isis, before offering the report of the aretalogy, Diodorus portrays Isis as primarily a healer:

> The Egyptians say that she was the discoverer of many health-giving drugs and was greatly versed in the science of healing; consequently, now that she has attained immortality, she finds her greatest delight in the healing of mankind and gives aid in their sleep to those who call upon her, plainly manifesting both her very

62. Grandjean translates line 36 as, "tu as révélé les fruits *de la terre*." But the final three words have no counterpart in the original, and what follows in lines 36–43 suggests far more than strictly agricultural fecundity.

presence (ἐπιφανεῖα) and her beneficence (εὐεργετικόν) toward those who ask for her help.[63]

Anticipating a skeptical response from his readers, Diodorus then asserts that her powers are manifest, not by Greek-style mythology, but by "manifest acts" (*praxeis enargeis*). As a consequence, the whole inhabited world (*oikoumenē*) bears testimony to her and offers her honors because of her self-disclosures through healings (*dia tēn en tais therapeiais epiphaneian*). He continues to depict her healing role:

> For standing above the sick in their sleep she gives aid for their diseases and works remarkable cures upon such as submit themselves to her; and many who have been despaired of by their physicians because of the difficult nature of their malady are restored to health by her, while numbers who have altogether lost the use of their eyes or of some other part of the body, whenever they turn for help to this goddess are restored to their previous condition.[64]

In the catalog of donations from the Sarapeum at Delos from the second century B.C. and later, the dominant items are various types of containers (cups, bowls, unguentaria, censers), but nearly as common are eyes (of gold or silver) and fingers; less common are ears and feet. These presentations attest to the healing actions of the god or goddess on that part of the body represented by the ex voto object.

Diodorus goes on, however, to describe another kind of medicine which Isis provides: *to tēs āthanasias pharmakon*. "By means [of this] she not only raised from the dead her son Horus," who had been the victim of plots by the Titans, but she "also made him immortal." Rounding out the naturalization of Isis into the Greek pantheon, Diodorus concludes: "They say that the name Horus, when translated, is Apollo, and that, having been instructed by his mother Isis in both medicine and divination, he is now a benefactor of the human race through his oracular responses and his healings."[65] Significantly, the role of Isis as agent of immortality is mentioned, but in rounding off his account of

63. Diodorus Siculus *Library* 1.25.3.
64. Ibid., 1.25.5.
65. Ibid., 1.25.6–7.

her beneficent roles, Diodorus returns to the theme with which he began: the gods as healers and guides of the faithful.

The other aretalogies which have survived date from the first century A.D. or later, with the exception of the Hymns of Isidorus, which seem to have been written in the first century B.C. In spite of the stylistically more elaborate framework in which Isis's theophoric-named admirer has placed his material, the substance of the hymns and much of their wording correspond closely to that of the archetypical aretalogy.[66] The same features are evident in the somewhat later hymn from Andros: Isis's instruction in letters by Hermes and the preparation of the secret words for the faithful; the kinship with Kronos; the giving of laws to humankind and the maintenance thereof; control of the heavenly bodies; the founding of Bubastis; her role as mistress of the sea; compassion toward the suffering and support of the righteous; mastery over the chthonic powers; an invitation to share in a sacred marriage.[67] Isis's cosmic sovereignty is celebrated, therefore, not as admirable in the abstract but as it bears directly on the needs of her devout followers, through her acts of compassion and healing and her ability to protect those in peril at sea. The frequent linking of Isis with Tyche and Hygeia in the inscriptions from this period reinforces that estimate of her role. *Sōtēria* at Delos and in the aretalogies concern benefactions among men and women in this world.[68]

The shrines of Isis seem to have been private, located in port cities or places of commerce, and predominantly Egyptian.[69] The festivals of Isis, on the other hand, were public and involved the

66. Text of the four hymns in *SEG* III 2, 97 ff., nos. 548–51. The role of Isis in establishing laws, in fostering both technical skills and life according to nature, as well as her ability to calm fears concerning death or dangers at sea, all are praised in these texts.

67. Text in Peek, *Isishymnus* (n. 33 above). Peek initially assigned an Augustan date to this hymn, but later revised the date to the Flavian period (A.D. 100–01).

68. Dunand, *Isis*, 2:114.

69. Ibid., vol. 2, notes that, although the evidence is too scarce to warrant broad generalization, the cult seems to have been established in Greece in the fourth century by men of commerce. It was private, lacking almost wholly in political significance or influence. From Italy there is no clear evidence of a full-time, professional clergy in the service of Isis.

masses. The procession included the carrying of a statue and a
boat in apparent reenactment of the journey of Isis to recover
the defunct Osiris. The implication is that, as Isis helped Osiris
to overcome the attack of his enemies, so Isis will aid her followers. Perhaps for many the primary focus was on the agricultural
cycle of annual renewal. But the predominant image of Isis in
the Hellenistic-early Roman period seems to have been that of
guarantor of life and benefactress to those in need. During this
period, the cult was sustained by a high priest, whose responsibility it was to maintain daily contact with the goddess, and by
auxiliary priests, whose responsibilities ranged from carrying the
sacred objects (statues, boat) to janitorial duties (*hierodouloi*). The
prophets, however, had a crucial role in interpreting the goddess's will, a function apparently viewed as continuous with Isis's
ancient role as Wisdom.[70] Others were responsible for interpreting dreams or incubation experiences. Like a modern medical clinic, the staff of an Isis shrine was expected to deal with
the day-to-day needs of those who came to the goddess to work
out their personal problems.[71] The image is confirmed in the
frescoes of Pompeii and elsewhere,[72] in which Isis's serving the
needs of the faithful is portrayed. Significantly, it is these features of the Isis frescoes that are noted by Tibullus and Juvenal.[73]

MIRACLE IN THE SERVICE OF
THE STRUGGLE FOR IMPERIAL POWER

Although the Isis cult had no inherent political implications, it
took on political connotations in connection with the power
struggle that took place during the establishment of the Julian-
Augustan principate. Antony's exploitation of the Isis-Osiris myth
to lend popular support to his union with Cleopatra we noted

70. Ibid., 2:71, 100; 3:189.
71. Ibid., 1:211; 2:113–14.
72. Tran Tam Tinh, *Isis à Pompéi* (n. 42 above). From Pergamum (in Dunand,
Isis, 3:93–96); a sarcophagus from Hierpynta in Crete, in which is represented
the fidelity of the devotees of Isis to death (Dunand, 3:207–11).
73. Tibullus 1.3, 27–28; Juvenal 12.26–28.

earlier. But Malaise makes a strong case for the theory that the Egyptian cults were perceived by the early emperors of Rome as symptomatic of political subversion on two counts. As collegia, the cult adherents could be regarded as secret conspiratorial groups. As proponents of a religion which regarded rulers as hereditary representatives of the deity, their theory of kingship was in basic conflict with the conviction that the stability of the Roman state depended on perpetuation of the cult of the Roman gods. Vergil portrayed the Battle of Actium (in *Aeneid* 8) as a cosmic victory of the Roman gods over those of Alexandria. But so great was the appeal of beneficent Isis to the Roman populace that the attempt to suppress her cult on political grounds was a failure. Her devotees would accept martyrdom rather than abandon her worship.

In spite of persecution under Tiberius, the cult began to penetrate even into the upper classes, especially among women, as the Dionysus cult had done centuries earlier. Germanicus sought to promote himself as a rival to Tiberius by visiting shrines in Egypt. Caligula took the bold step toward presenting himself as a theocratic absolute monarch on the Egyptian model by erecting a shrine of Isis on the Campus Martius, which was later rebuilt by Domitian. Although Nero had been attracted by the Isis cult, it was the Flavians who effected a fundamental change in the status of the Egyptian cults. As successors to the aristocratic Julio-Claudian line, they were perhaps compensating for their own humble origins by linking their destinies with the divinely endowed monarchs of the Osiris-Isis-Horus tradition.[74]

The clearest evidence in support of this theory comes from first-century accounts of Vespasian's ascent to power. In general, the historians of the period fill their pages with accounts of prodigies, most of which relate to the transfer of power, in connection with the birth or choice of a ruler, or his impending dismissal or death. The portents include flights of birds, movements of heavenly bodies, visions, and voices. Dio Cassius is especially fond of self-opening doors as a divine sign.[75] Unique

74. Malaise, *Cultes égyptiènnes*, pp. 384–407.
75. Dio Cassius 61.35; 63.185, 235.

among all these reports of prodigies, however, is the series of incidents reported by Tacitus and Suetonius to have happened to Vespasian while he was tarrying in Egypt prior to his return to assume power in Rome. Earlier experiences of Vespasian were similar to the omens reported as taking place in the lives of other emperors: an old oak on the Flavian estate sprouted branches when Vespasian arrived: the first was slender and withered (his daughter died in infancy); the second was very strong, portending success; the third became a tree. A cypress tree, uprooted on the family farm, became greener and stronger than ever. But at the Temple of Sarapis in Egypt, where Vespasian was awaiting signs, he was acclaimed and offered sacred boughs and garlands by one Basilides, a freedman, whose ailments (he was blind and lame) had kept him out of the shrine of Sarapis.[76] Tacitus has a variant of this, according to which Vespasian had a vision of Basilides, whom he knew to be eighty miles away, and inferred from the ailing man's name that the gods had destined him for royal power.[77]

In what may be yet another version of the same story, Tacitus describes how a blind man and a cripple devotee of Sarapis were healed by Vespasian, who moistened the eyes and cheeks of the blind man with spittle and walked on the hand of the cripple, curing both in the process.[78] These are mentioned by Suetonius, though without details.[79] Combined with the oracle from the god on Mount Carmel in Palestine, which promised divine support for his aspirations, these reports of signs from heaven were conveniently spread abroad in Italy by Vespasian's supporters, which enormously helped his cause, as both Tacitus and Suetonius note.[80] Although the divinity involved was Sarapis rather than Isis, it is obvious that the miracle-working power of the Egyptian gods was adapted to multiple purposes by the Flavians. First, the stories from the Sarapeum offer particularly vivid and appealing instances of divine approbation of a pretender to royal power. Second, there is an implied link between the monarch

76. Suetonius, *Lives*, Vespasian 5–6.
77. Tacitus *Histories* 4.lxxxii.
78. Ibid., 4.lxxxi.
79. Suetonius, *Lives*, Vespasian 7.
80. Tacitus *Histories* 2.lxxviii; Suetonius, *Lives*, Vespasian 8.

and the divine succession in the Osiris-Horus-Isis tradition. And finally, there is imperial support for the popular cult that had earlier been suppressed through imperial opposition. The centrality of the healing function of these cults is reflected in the specific nature of the miraculous attestation that Vespasian received. The convergence of these factors marks a transition in the fortunes of the Isis cult, however. From the Flavian period on into the Antonine, Isis continued to hold her following among the masses, but she also appealed to the social and intellectual elite. To them she was to become preeminently the dispenser, not of health, but, in Diodorus's phrase, of "the medicine of immortality."[81]

ISIS AND MYSTICAL ILLUMINATION: LUCIUS APULEIUS

Dio Chrysostom, writing in the reign of Trajan (98–117) and probably reflecting the beneficence of that ruler, expressed an ideal of kingship[82] which, M. Rostovtseff proposed, was adopted by the Antonines as a goal to be fulfilled.[83] Those royal duties were seen as privilege, not power; as labor, not pleasure; as beneficence, not despotism; as eliciting love from people and troops; as combining military strength with peace-making; as ruling in consort with friends (the senate) over a free people. On religion, Trajan's policy was one of encouragement for all, though some regarded him as being unduly supportive of the Jews. In a famous incident recorded in the *Acts of the Pagan Martyrs*,[84] Trajan's favoritism toward the Jews caused the bust of Sarapis to weep.

With the accession of Hadrian, however, the support for the Egyptian gods became a matter of imperial policy and example. Mystically inclined and reportedly initiated into both stages of the Eleusinian mysteries (mystic and epopt), he was also fascinated by the gods of Egypt. When his favorite, Antinous, drowned in the Nile, he was immediately identified with Osiris and ap-

81. Diodorus Siculus *Library* 1.25.5.

82. In Oration 6, *peri tyrannidos*, and Oration 62, *peri basileias kai tyrannidos*.

83. M. Rostovtseff, *Social and Economic History of the Roman Empire* (Oxford: Oxford University Press, 1957²), pp. 120–21.

84. H. Musurillo, ed., *Acta Alexandrinorum* (Oxford: Oxford University Press, 1954), lines 40 ff. Also preserved in *P. Oxy.* 1242, 40–55, the Acta Hermaisci.

propriate monuments erected for him in Egypt and Rome. The Isis cult now had the loftiest possible patronage and encouragement. The response that followed, or blossomed after decades of suppression, was of two types: popular and intellectual.

Early in the imperial period the writing in which Hermes had instructed Isis was explained as mystical in nature, as the Hymn from Andros attests.[85] Even earlier, in Diodorus Siculus, Isis is described as bringing not merely health but immortality.[86] Her role as mistress of the mysteries is implied in the vast increase in representations of her as *Isis lactans* in the first, and especially the second century of our era, as is evident on reliefs, molded lamps, and coins of the reigns of Trajan and Hadrian.[87] As V. Tran Tam Tinh has shown, the fact that this representation of mother and child is depicted in reliefs as part of a shrine with three zones (*pronaos, naos, adytum*)[88] strengthens the case for this mode of portraying Isis as part of a mystery cult. That perception of Isis is already apparent in frescoes from the second half of the first century at Pompeii and Herculaneum, in which a mystical ceremony of sacred water, sacrificial offering, music, and procession in honor of Isis is represented.[89] Fortunately, it is precisely from the Antonine period in which most of the iconographic evidence originated that we have full, detailed documentation of the Isis cult and the mode of mystic participation in it.

The classic witness is that of Lucius Apuleius in his *Metamorphoses*.[90] Although our study has been based chiefly on Egyptian elements which go back to the second millennium B.C., the over-

85. Summarized above, p. 127.

86. Diodorus Siculus *Library* 1.25.5.

87. Documentation in V. Tran Tam Tinh, *Isis Lactans. Corpus des Monuments Greco-Roman d'Isis*. (Leiden: Brill, 1973).

88. Ibid., p. 16 and fig. 13.

89. Wilhelmina F. Jashemski, *The Gardens of Pompeii, Herculaneum and the Villas Destroyed by Vesuvius* (New Rochelle, N.Y.: Caratzas Paros, 1979), pp. 137–39, figs. 216–19. These murals and the relation between structure and function in the shrines are also discussed by F. Le Corsu, in *Mythe et mystère* (Paris: Les Belles Lettres, 1977), pp. 118–35; plates 16 and 21.

90. Popularly known as *The Golden Ass*, the work appears to be a combination of autobiographical elements and a revised version of the older Greek or Helle-

all style and genre of Apuleius's work is that of the Graeco-Roman novel or romance. The location of the final events of the tale in Cenchreae suggests strongly that the material has been adapted along autobiographical lines, culminating in Lucius's recounting of his own religious experience. Before examining details of the story, and especially of the account of Lucius's conversion in Book 11, it may be useful to note some of the characteristics of the Hellenistic novel, as well as some of the distinctive features of Apuleius's employment of that genre.

Studies of the ancient romance have ranged, in conclusions about the aim of the genre, from treating it as an allegory of the destiny of the soul (so Merkelbach, following Kerenyi)[91] to the insistence of Ben E. Perry that its sole aim was to produce an artistic and creative work of fiction.[92] Perry does point out, how-

---

nistic stories, such as Cupid and Psyche, or Lucius, or the Ass. For a full and judicious discussion of the possible antecedents of Apuleius's *Metamorphoses*, see J. Gwyn Griffiths, *The Isis Book of Apuleius of Madauros (Metamorphoses Book XI)* (Leiden: Brill, 1975), pp. 7–47.

91. Reinhold Merkelbach, *Roman und Mysterium in der Antike* (Munich and Berlin: C. H. Beck, 1962), pp. 1–46; K. Kerenyi, *Die griechisch-orientalische Romanliteratur in religionsgeschichtlicher Beleuchtung* (Tübingen: Mohr, 1927).

92. Ben Edwin Perry, *The Ancient Romances: A Literary Historical Account of Their Origins* (Berkeley: University of California Press, 1967). Perry offers a salutary warning against treating a literary genre in a prescriptive sense, as though it were controlled by fixed genetic process: "To infer genre from content (externally considered) or content from genre, is to argue in a circle" (p. 18). Used descriptively to refer to categories of literary phenomena which may vary greatly, the notion of genre may be employed legitimately and fruitfully, but only ex post facto (p. 20). The changes that occur in literature are geared to artistic creativity and to basic shifts in "the way men think and react to life, both as group and as individuals." When the outlook changes in response to historical experiences, the writer and the genre change as well (p. 25). Sophie Trenkner, in *The Greek Novella in the Classical Period* (Cambridge: Cambridge University Press, 1958), has traced the origins of the romance back to Athenian folklore in the preclassical period. The "*mimēsis biou*" is provided to round out and make more vivid popular stories (novelle) through the addition of descriptive material, dialogues, and dramatic settings (p. 11). At the high point of Greek drama, Euripides draws on these motifs in his depiction of persons who are ostensibly the traditional heroes, but who are actually ordinary people of the fifth century. The themes include adventure, recognition, enslavement, ambush, exile, intrigue, self-sacrifice, wanderings over land and sea (pp. 32–33). These features are found likewise in the

ever, that (1) the adaptation of a genre is powerfully affected by the changes which occur in the society as a whole "with the passage of time and historical experience"; and (2) that in Hellenistic times there was a shift from didactic historiography to the romance, even though formal prose was expected to be historical in form, whether its content actually was or not. He sees this development as inspired by a new middle-class idealism that resulted in the transfer to the prose romance or novel of "the principal artistic aims and sanctions of serious drama." [93]

While Apuleius's novel has many features in common with the romance,[94] it is unusual in the seriousness and depth of piety with which the work comes to a close (Book 11). The attempt to account for this seeming incongruity as a pious gesture to lend a show of respectability to an otherwise breezy—even pornographic—string of tales is not only unconvincing[95] but is also insensitive to the major aims of the work, which require the integration of seemingly disparate elements. Apuleius has accented the incongruities by referring to himself in his *Apology* as a "Platonic philosopher" (10),[96] while describing his *Metamor-*

New Comedy, where chastity is threatened and preserved, where stupidity mingles with cunning, and sorcery is practiced (pp. 91–146). All these narrative clichés Trenkner traces back to Athenian storytellers. Whereas the earlier romances treated of heroes or people of the upper classes, they became increasingly democratic from the fifth century on. In Hellenistic times, however, yet another adaptation of these motifs was to occur, this time in the interest of religious propaganda.

93. Perry, *Ancient Romances*, pp. 25, 67–69; ibid., pp. 70–76. For a different assessment of Merkelbach than Perry's, see J. G. Griffiths, *The Isis Book of Apuleius*, p. 21.

94. The characteristic elements of the plot are conveniently summarized by James Tatum, in *Apuleius and the Golden Ass* (Ithaca, N.Y.: Cornell University Press, 1979). pp. 92–93.

95. Perry, *Ancient Romances*, p. 245.

96. Rudolf Helm, *Apulei opera quae supersunt*, vol. 2, pt. 1, "Apologia (De Magia)," 2d ed. (Leipzig: Teubner, 1959), sec. 10. Apuleius is probably similarly referred to in an inscription found at the site of his native North African city, Madauros: "Philosopho Platonico," in Stéphane Gsell, *Inscriptions latines de l'Algérie* (Paris: E. Champròn, 1922), 1.2115. Discussed in Tatum, *Apuleius*, pp. 106–08.

phoses in the proem of the work as "this Milesian tale."[97] What has the Platonic tradition to do with pornography? Critics of Apuleius, ancient and modern, have noted his fondness for magic and wondered how that meshes with his philosophical pretensions.

Taking up the charge of licentiousness and its inappropriateness as a theme for a philosopher, James Tatum has made a strong case that Apuleius should be regarded as a sophist and rhetor, not as a philosopher in the disciplined academic sense of the term. But further, the author's aim is that of a religious protagonist, whose strategy is to entice and engage his reader by stories which seemingly are merely entertaining and titillating. There is a dark underside to the stories, however. As Tatum perceives Apuleius's strategy, "The humor grows progressively darker and more sardonic." His intention is to show "how bad or misguided persons come to an unhappy end." If the novel begins as Milesian entertainment, "it ends with a world utterly transformed from the earlier stories of lust, revenge, or adultery." Apuleius offers only a "few cryptic signals" as to what great transformation is in the offing, "but that is not a sign that he is confused or undisciplined, only that he is a good entertainer and a subtle one."[98]

One of the few fixed points of Apuleius's life, biographically and chronologically, is his having been put on trial in the year 158–59. From this date, which is determined by the time in office of the proconsul before whom he was tried, it has been conjectured that he was born about A.D. 120 and died about 190. His *Apology* may have been delivered before or after he wrote the *Metamorphoses*; in the latter there may be some oblique allu-

97. Apuleius *Metamorphoses* 1.1.
98. Tatum, *Apuleius*, p. 103. Tatum also demonstrates persuasively the rhetorical skill of Apuleius in the carefully structured, balanced style of writing in his chapter, "The Language of the Sophist's Novel." He shows in his brilliant analysis that Apuleius intended for his work to be heard, not merely read. For evidence of this, Tatum points to puns, assonance, repetition of endings and suffixes, so that "the most salient features of his style . . . could be easily grasped at first hearing" (pp. 132–33).

sions to his having been unjustly accused on various occasions. The charges brought against him, which can only be inferred from his defense, seem to have included marrying an older woman for financial advantage, engaging in magic, and being party to the premature death of his stepson, who had urged Apuleius to marry his mother in the first place.[99] Of direct importance for our inquiry is his response to the charge of magic, and the attitude toward magic which is implicit throughout the *Metamorphoses*. Building on the etymological link between magic and *magus*, he argues in *Apology* 25 that the latter is a priestly figure schooled in ancient religious truth, which to the unlettered and ignorant may seem to be occult. It is this venerable wisdom in which he, Apuleius, has been interested and instructed. On the other hand, he rejects black magic, which is employed by the unscrupulous to harm others: "This kind of magic, so far as I know about it, is something forbidden by law from early antiquity and the time of the Twelve Tables because it causes barrenness of crops. For this reason it is occult and hidden, no less than loathesome and horrible: a thing usually guarded against by night, withdrawn into shadows, isolated from control, murmured in verses, to which not only few slaves but also few free men are attracted."[100] There is no question that Apuleius was fascinated by magic. In the *Metamorphoses* he gives a vivid picture of the tactics and capabilities of a sorceress: "By breathing out certain words and charms over boughs and stones and other frivolous things she can throw down all the light of the starry heavens into the bottom of hell, and reduce them again to the old chaos." After warning how the sorceress can ensnare and invade men whom she finds attractive, Lucius's informant also tells him that any who displease her she turns into stones, sheep, or some other beast as is her whim, while others she murders. Of such, his advisor counsels him, "I would you should earnestly beware."[101]

---

99. Details of the charges and a sketch of the family relationships are in Tatum, *Apuleius*, pp. 112–13.

100. *Apology*, p. 47, in translation from Tatum, *Apuleius*, p. 115.

101. *Metamorphoses* 2.5.

After learning through his mistress that his humiliating experience of confessing to having murdered three thieves only to find that, under enchantment, what he had stabbed was three animal bladders, his fascination with magical technique is heightened by her report of what she has seen the sorceress use: metal plates covered with strange characters; bones of birds of ill omen; limbs of corpses; nails pulled away from fingers; blood; skulls snatched from wild animals; entrails; well water; cow's milk; honey; meal; hair; perfumes.[102] Finally his sleeping companion sneaks him into the sorceress' tower as she is transforming herself into an owl. So impressed was Lucius by this metamorphosis, and so eager was he to experience it and thereby to escape from the mocking of the populace, that he persuaded his friend to procure some of the ointment used by the sorceress. On applying it to himself, he was changed—not into an owl or other kind of bird—but into *perfectus asinus*.[103] Although we know that Apuleius had a literary model on which he was dependent, he clearly has told this story, not merely as an amusing tale, but as a symbol of what befalls those whose ambition to explore the unknown ensnares them in the evil, destructive occult wisdom and malevolent techniques of magic. He achieves transformation, but the result is disastrous.

His story bears testimony to the widespread belief in magic among both upper and lower classes. The focus of magic is solely on means and results. To the extent that ends are involved, they are no more than the arbitrary, self-serving objectives of the sorcerer or of those who employ him or her for their private purposes. The *Metamorphoses* are full of such incidents: the baker's wife who hires a witch either to effect reconciliation with her husband or to destroy him by demonic possession (Bk. 9.29–31); hens that lay full-grown chickens; a well of blood that springs up from the ground; a frog leaping from a dog's mouth (Bk. 9.34); the physicians who supply fatal potions for disposing of unwanted spouses or offspring (Bk. 10.25–27). Except as portents of even greater disaster, these events have no meaning be-

102. Ibid., 3.17–18.
103. Ibid., 3.25–26.

yond themselves. They are evidences of the pervasive power of evil; they betoken the cruel fate of any who fall victim to those who employ magical techniques to destroy their opponents.

These horror stories serve to place in the sharpest contrast both the means and the ends of Lucius's ultimate transformation into a devotee of Isis. What brings meaning and fulfillment to Lucius is not metamorphosis in the magical sense but conversion in the religious sense.[104] Unlike the earlier petitioners of the aretalogies, he did not come to the goddess because of an infirmity or an ailment: he came seeking a new being. It was not restoration to human existence alone but transformation into a new mode of existence that he sought and found. The miracle of Apuleius's change from ass to human is a symbol of the more profound miracle. His petition had concluded, "Restore to me my own self as Lucius" (11.2); Isis's response promises far more: "There is now dawning for you, through my providence, the day of salvation" (11.5).

Isis is addressed and depicted by Apuleius in many of the same ways she appears in the aretalogies of the earlier period: everything is governed by her sovereign care; all bodies, heavenly and earthly, flourish and move by her power; as Ceres, she is responsible for the fertility of the crops; as Venus, she is responsible for sexual differences and for human love and procreation; as Artemis, she assists women in childbirth; as Proserpina, she is goddess of the underworld and mistress over the powers of evil. The mystical element is underscored when Isis-Ceres' role at Eleusis is mentioned (11.1–2). She is pictured as the mother of the universe and the mistress of the sea (11.5). She is the source of help to those who are in need (11.10), and all are reminded of her providential care. One of the emblems by which she is represented is justice (*aequitas*). The chief day honoring her is the public festival known as Navigium Isidis (11.5).

New, however, are several central features: Lucius's prayer is not for healing but for strength, peace, and relief from misfor-

---

104. Tatum, *Apuleius*, p. 28. On the distinction between magic and miracle, see my *Christian Origins in Sociological Perspective* (Philadelphia: Westminster, 1980), pp. 62–67.

tune, and especially for the recovery of his true selfhood (11.2);
the crown of roses which he is to devour will not only restore
him to human form but will bring about his rebirth, as the rose
as symbol is linked with the victory and resurrection of Osiris.[105]
The remainder of Lucius's life is to be dedicated to Isis; it will
be prolonged by her grace if he is obedient to her will, and he
will continue in her company in the nether world beyond death
itself (11.6). It is these promises and prospects that dawn for
Lucius on his "day of salvation." Although the details of his initiation are tantalizingly few and ambiguous, they included for
him "a voluntary death and a life obtained by grace" (11.21).
The actual ceremony involves his descent into the lower world,
where he sees the sun in the course of its nightly journey be-
neath the earth—apparently effected by artificial illumination—
following on a symbolic death.[106] Of equal importance is the appeal to Lucius to become a member of the holy army, to participate in the victory over the powers of evil, as symbolized by Seth-
Typhon—significantly depicted in Egyptian iconography as
ass-headed. It is this transformation itself which is "the wondrous miracle" (11.14); the effect of Lucius's initiation "into the
mysteries of the holy night" is for him "in some way to be born
again," to be placed "once more on the course of a new life"
(11.21).

Released from the cruel domination of a blind Fortune, under whose control he had fallen as a consequence of his "ill-
starred curiosity," Lucius is now the servant of the Fortune who
can see, "and who illumines the other gods with the radiance of
her light" (11.15). He passed through three stages of initiation,
and, after taking up residence for a period in her temple (11. 19),
he resumed his career as rhetor and lawyer. In his initial address
to Isis, Lucius had asked her to grant him heightened rhetorical

105. Griffiths, *Isis Book*, p. 161.
106. See ibid. for discussion of the possibilities of stage machinery to produce
this effect (which he considers unlikely), and the probability of unusually bright
lighting, as inferred from the extraordinarily high number of lamps found at
Isis shrines (pp. 300–01). He thinks that a narcotic may have been used to simu-
late death, though he rejects the notion that the initiate was placed in a coffin
alive, as Osiris was in one version of the myth of his death and restoration.

skills (11.3). And after the third stage of his initiation, he boasted that he "was rather nicely favored by my earnings at the bar through the generous providence of the gods" (11.30) and that he went on to win fame, favor, and fortune as a lawyer. He declared, however, that the apex of his career came when he was privileged to enter the college of *pastophoroi* (a priestly group of uncertain rank and function)[107] and was confirmed in this role by being elected to the post for a five-year term (11.30).

One aspect of the Isis cult that comes through, almost certainly unintentionally, is that it was a bourgeois movement. In spite of Lucius's claims to "high birth" and to enjoy a "position in society" (11.15), he has an increasingly difficult time scraping together the fees he is obligated to pay in order to be initiated. However gracious and beneficent Isis may have been, formal entrance into the ranks of her cult devotees was on a cash-in-advance basis only. There were no social or economic restrictions on participation in the cult, as is evident from the remark made in passing that the crowd in the procession on the occasion of Lucius's transformation consisted of "throngs of those initiated into the divine mysteries, men and women of every rank" (11.10). At the conclusion of the *Ploiaphesia* and the summoning of the conclave of the *pastophoroi*, prayers were delivered from a liturgical book "for the prosperity of our great emperor, the senate, the knights and the whole Roman people" (11.17)—scarcely what might be termed a subversive agenda. The book ends with the testimony that the man who had to sell his clothes in order to pay his initiation fee to the cult of Osiris began to enjoy life in two ways: "I was illumined with the nocturnal ecstasies of the supreme god," and he began to prosper as a result of his substantial income as an advocate (11.28). It is not at all surprising that details of Lucius's experience—including the brush with death and the passage through the elements (11.23)—should reappear in a modern middle-class movement such as Freemasonry.[108]

107. Ibid., pp. 265–66, 342–43.
108. Ibid., where the similarities are noted between this material and the libretto of Mozart's *Magic Flute* as well as the ritual in current use by the Masonic

The mystical aspects of the Isis cult as Lucius experienced it are obvious. The frequent visions and epiphanies occurred in dreams or in nocturnal incubation periods in the shrines. There is no hint of mystical union, however, nor even of a sacred marriage.[109] The abstinences enjoined upon those about to be initiated were from meat and wine, and the term involved only ten days. Thus neither sacred prostitution nor celibacy, to say nothing of emasculation, seems to have been demanded of initiates, nor were such requirements said to be binding on the priests. The shaved head for the men and the veiled face for the women, at least during the ceremonies, were all that seem to have been required (11.10, 30). The goal of mystical communion was to find fulfillment and tranquillity in life, with a hope of continued association with Isis in the life to come. What Lucius vainly sought through magic he gained through devotion to Isis.[110] The cruel, humiliating transformation he underwent through magic was overcome and itself transformed by his religious experience, which brought freedom-through-devotion, prosperity and acclaim as a public figure, and confidence about the future.

ISIS IN MYTH AND SYMBOL: PLUTARCH

F. Dunand's study of the historical evidence for the development of the Isis cult in the Mediterranean basin shows that it is in the late first and second centuries of our era that we read, from literary and inscriptional sources, of incubation in Isis shrines and interpretation of dreams along the lines documented in

order, though Griffiths dismisses the possibility of any link. At the very least, however, there is a cultural analogy between these modern phenomena and the Isis cult. And a remote dependence of the Freemasons on the Isis cult is by no means inconceivable.

109. The claim that the sacred box holding "secret things" contained the phallus of Osiris is refuted by Griffiths (*Isis Book*, pp. 222–26) after investigation of the available evidence.

110. Dunand, *Isis*, vol. 3, notes that, from Hellenistic times forward into the Roman period, the role of Isis as magician moves to the fringe of the cult and can be documented for certain only in the later Magical Papyri and in associations with sorcerers and diviners.

Apuleius's *Metamorphoses*, from the Greek Islands, from the Ionian coast, from Pontus and Bithynia.[111] But there is another rich source of our knowledge of the Isis cult in a somewhat different form than the popular, middle-class phenomenon we have been examining: this is to be found in the treatise on Isis and Osiris written by Plutarch, the eclectic philosopher-historian of the later first and early second century. It is commonly held that he wrote this essay on Isis shortly before his death, so that it probably serves to reveal to us his mature thought and also to provide additional evidence of the state of religion in the early Antonine period. Although his Isis tract performs the important function of preserving in greater detail than elsewhere the assorted myths connected with the sacred trio, Osiris, Isis, and Horus, this work makes clear from beginning to end that Plutarch's interests were not merely antiquarian and that he intended his readers to place the story of Isis and her divine companions in a very different intellectual framework from the one implicit in popular piety of the time.

From the opening lines of the work, which are addressed to his patroness, Clea, Plutarch informs his readers that the search for truth is the most sacred of human undertakings, and that in order to fulfill this obligation the gods furnish intellect and understanding so that human beings may know themselves and the nature of reality (1–2).[112] Even as he introduces the cast of characters for the myth, Plutarch tells his reader that these gods are the discoverers of wisdom, the inventors of grammar and music, and links them with justice. In short, they provide the foundation for civilization. The true devotee of Isis is not known by the linen garment or the shaved head, but by the exercise of reason and the study of philosophy in order to discern the truth within the mysteries revealed by her (3). An important reason for the intellectual to give careful consideration to the Egyptian mythological traditions is that the wisest of the Greeks all learned their truth from the Egyptians (10).

Plutarch acknowledges that, taken as literal reports, the sto-

111. Ibid., vols. 2 and 3, passim.
112. Plutarch, *De Iside*. References are to traditional chapters.

ries are incredible, since poets and prose writers indulge themselves in "loose fiction and frivolous fabrications" (20). The myths, for example, mention an impossibly large number of places where Osiris or various parts of his body have been buried. An easy way out of the difficulty is to say simply that these myths have transferred stories of deified men to the gods, since this leaves the disrepute attached ultimately to men rather than to the gods. He is reluctant to press this approach, however, since it may "dissipate the reverence and faith implanted in nearly all mankind at birth . . . degrading things divine to a human level." Plutarch escapes from the dilemma of action unbefitting to the gods yet attributed to them in the myths by following the lead of Plato and others in positing the existence of daimones, who surpass human beings in wisdom and power but do not possess "the divine quality unmixed and uncontaminated." Susceptible to pleasure and pain, their experience is subject to change, and their behavior exhibits different degrees of virtue and vice (22–24). The daimon Typhon is characterized by the wickedness of his deeds. Isis, also a daimon, commemorates her triumph over him and her restoration of order in the secret rites of her cult. Her cult, therefore, serves "both as a lesson in godliness and an encouragement for men and women who find themselves in the clutch of like calamities" (27).

Plutarch is able to carry out this interpretative scheme by using allegorical method and by relying on etymologies of names, which in turn serve his allegorical ends (32, 36, 49, 60, 61). He builds on Stoic principles of the basic elements (earth, air, fire, and especially water or moisture) and on Pythagorean numbers (41, 42, 76). His cosmology and ontology accommodate the Isis myth to Plato (53, 56). According to Plutarch, it is essential that one recognize the distinction between the natural phenomena to which the myths point and the gods who work through these natural processes and events to accomplish their divine ends. The gods are no more to be identified with the processes than one should confuse a weaver with the warp and woof he produces. The gods provide what is "everlasting and constant" in the universe (66–67). He is able to deal with the problem of evil by adopting a belief that is held by "the great majority and the

wisest of men": a form of dualism which he derives from Zo-
roastrianism (46–48). By this reworking of the myth, Osiris is
intelligence, reason, ruler and lord of all that is good. Typhon
is irrational, truculent, diseased and disorderly, and as such is
equated with Seth. Isis is the female principle of nature and is
receptive of any form of generation. She loves the good and is
the agent of creation (53), but she allowed Typhon to exist, since
"the goddess who holds sway over the Earth would not permit
the complete annihilation of the nature opposed to moisture,
but relaxed and moderated it . . . because it was not possible for
a complete world (*kosmos*) to exist if the fiery element left it and
disappeared" (40).

He struggles to offer a rational justification for the honoring
of the animals sacred to the various gods and for the offering of
animal sacrifices, and to make a clear distinction between the
gods and the natural processes—such as the flooding of the Nile
and the phases of the moon—with which the myths so closely
tie them. It is an error, he concludes, to confuse the outward
symbol with its underlying symbolic meaning (70–75). Noting
that Pythagoras, "the most noted of philosophers," saw a correlation between the sacred numbers and the myths of the gods,
Plutarch declares that "we should welcome those peculiar prop-
erties existent in nature which possess the power of perception
and have a soul and feeling and character. It is not that we should
honor these, but that through these we should honor the Divine" of which these things are mirrors (76). Isis's multicolored
robes symbolize the many facets of her sovereign power. To participate in her mystical rites is to experience the epoptic vision
of ultimate truth, to which Plato and Aristotle aspired (77). As
her devotees share in her cult, they should take as their guide
the reasoning that derives from philosophy, since everything in
human existence is to be referred to reason (*logos*) (68). Stated
more modestly, "if we revere and honor what is orderly and good
and beneficial as the work of Isis and as the image and reflection
and reason of Osiris, we shall not be wrong" (64).

Obviously not all of Plutarch's contemporaries could grasp,
much less accept for their own, his understanding of the Isis
myth and the cult in which the myth was appropriated. Equally

clear is Plutarch's disdain for those who took the myth as a literal report of divine actions in the world. The rewards of participation in the mysteries are for Plutarch purely intellectual. By contrast, for Apuleius—to the extent that the *Metamorphoses* is autobiographical—the cult provided both personal gratification and career development. In neither of these writers from the Flavian and Antonine periods do we hear of the healing benefactions of Isis. Her role is rather that of a life-orienter. Her functions are cosmic and mystical rather than practical and immediate, though in Apuleius's case there are certain practical benefits. From Hellenistic through Antonine times the myth remains as a constant. The meaning that it holds for those who take it seriously, however, varies widely with the social and cultural circumstances of the participant.

CHAPTER FIVE

Miracle and the Apocalyptic Tradition

Contemporary with the flourishing of the cults of Isis and Asklepios in their Hellenistic phases was the rise of apocalypticism in Judaism. Although the primary meaning of apocalyptic is a type of revelatory literature—of which the Revelation of John is a prime example—there lies behind the literary phenomenon a type of world-view that is distinctive and profoundly influenced the origins of Christianity.[1] The characteristic features of apocalypticism may be sketched as follows: (1) a dualistic world-view, according to which evil powers have wrested control of the universe from the creator and maintain power through the schemes of the Adversary and his demonic forces; (2) in spite of the apostasy of the religious establishment, a small band of the brave and faithful stands ready to accept opposition or even persecution in their fidelity to the divine purposes; (3) those purposes have

1. For the historical development of Judaism during the period of the rise of apocalypticism, see D. S. Russell, *The Jews from Alexander to Herod* (London: SCM, 1967). Analysis of literary and conceptual aspects of apocalyptic are set out by Russell in *The Method and Message of Jewish Apocalyptic* (Philadelphia: Westminster, 1964); by Otto Plöger in *Theocracy and Eschatology* (Oxford: Blackwell, 1968); and by Klaus Koch, *The Rediscovery Of Apocalyptic* (London and Naperville, Ill.: Allenson, 1971). P. D. Hanson, in *The Dawn of Apocalyptic*, 2d ed. (Philadelphia: Fortress, 1980), traces the links between prophecy and apocalyptic. K. O. L. Burridge, in *New Heaven, New Earth: A Study of Millenarian Activities* (Oxford: Blackwell, 1969), and Bryan Wilson, *Magic and Millennium* (New York: Harper and Row, 1973), draw on evidence from anthropological studies to analyze the social dynamics of apocalyptic movements. Gerhard von Rad's attempt, in *Wisdom in Israel* (Nashville: Abingdon, 1972), to trace the origins of apocalyptic to wisdom literature is justified in its pointing to the transmission of esoteric knowledge, which apocalyptic shares with certain aspects of the wisdom literature; but the values and themes of apocalyptic are closer to prophetic tradition, even though the apocalyptic world-view has transformed those features.

146

been disclosed to the elect remnant through visions, dreams, oracles, and marvelous acts; (4) they live in the expectation of divine judgment of the world and those who have usurped God's rule over it, but they look beyond the impending catastrophe to the triumph of God and their own vindication as his faithful people. Sociologically speaking, we might describe members of apocalyptic groups as marginal people, alienated from the authority structure and deeply conscious of their deprivation of power. Their hope looks beyond the present scene of chaos and despair. Our question is: how does miracle play a role in the apocalyptic life-world, specifically, in the early Christian tradition?

GOD'S ACTS IN BEHALF OF HIS PEOPLE

To answer that question, one must examine first the background of miracle in Jewish tradition prior to Hellenistic times. From within that perspective one can trace how the apocalyptic view of miracle took shape within Judaism in the Graeco-Roman period. In the Jewish Bible, miracle appears in two major forms: extraordinary acts said to be performed by the God of Israel, nearly always in behalf of his people or in defeat of their enemies; and acts performed by divinely endowed persons, who function as agents of God. The characteristic term for miracles of several varieties in the biblical literature is "signs and wonders." The choice of *sign* to designate these unusual acts or events is wholly appropriate, since the event does not so much carry meaning in itself as it points to some larger purpose or framework of significance.

Those who are the agents of God are regularly linked with the role of prophet. In the Exodus narrative which describes God choosing and preparing Moses for his task of leading his people out of Egypt, the doubts of the Israelites about his commission or his leadership capacities are overcome by a series of spectacular performances of Moses, including the changing of his rod into a snake, the coming and going of leprosy from his hand, and the transformation of Nile water into blood (Ex 4:1–9). When Israel's first king, Saul, is anointed for office, God's agent (Samuel) tells him of several unusual things that are about to happen to him; these include his being seized by the divine Spirit and finding himself in an ecstatic dance among the mantic prophets (1 Sm 10:1–13). Similarly, the ailing, despondent King Hezekiah learns through the prophet Isaiah that he will recover, and as a divine sign the shadow moves backward ten degrees on the sundial (2 Kgs 20:1–11; Is 38:1–8).

Although Moses' unique role as prophet was said to have been confirmed by God through the "signs and wonders" which God commissioned him to perform (Dt 34:10–12), the tradition in Deuteronomy acknowledges that there is an ambiguity in the working of miracles: they can also be performed by charlatans or evil persons (Dt 13:1–5). The significance of the extraordinary act cannot be determined from the action itself, but only from the framework of meaning in which it is placed. Stated negatively, the wonder-worker who uses his miracles to entice others into idolatry or to disobey God's commandments is to be executed. Moses, however, is said by the psalmist to have "performed God's signs" among his people. There was a fundamental congruence and a mutual support, therefore, between what Moses said about God and what he did in his behalf.[2]

Also connected with the prophetic role, but unique among the miracle-workers of the Bible are the distinctive prophets—the so-called men of God—who appear in the narratives of 1 and 2 Kings. The unnamed "man of God" who predicts the downfall of the apostate king of Israel, Jeroboam, and announces a sign to confirm his prophecy[3] (the destruction of the idolatrous altar)

2. The evidence about Samuel and Saul is from the so-called Early Source of 1 Samuel, probably from the early tenth century. The regulations about the evil miracle-workers, however, are from the Deuteronomist and date from the 6th/5th century. The basic view of miracle as sign of divine approbation remains unchanged, however.

3. A kindred theme is the prophetic sign, which is announced by Isaiah (7:10–17), that a child soon to be born will not be fully grown before the threat to Judah from Syria will have evaporated. But the birth seems to be ordinary, with no miraculous feature involved. By building on the LXX term for the young mother (*Parthenos*), the gospel tradition (Mt 1:23) finds prophetic confirmation for the story (only in Matthew and Luke) of the miraculous birth of Jesus to a virgin mother.

is himself killed by a lion for having disobeyed the Lord by accepting hospitality in the land where wickedness rules (1 Kgs 13). Better known are Elijah and Elisha (1 Kgs 17–2 Kgs 13), both of whom are known as "men of God," and both of whom perform acts which challenge the worship of Baal and the acts of the apostate kings of Israel in the name of Yahweh, Israel's God. Elijah's most spectacular actions are calling down fire from the Lord to challenge the pagan priests (1 Kgs 18:17–46) or to slay the royal messengers (2 Kgs 1:9–16). Yet his miracles include acts of mercy, such as preserving a starving widow and restoring her son to life (1 Kgs 17), as do those of his successor, Elisha (2 Kgs 4) who cures a non-Israelite of leprosy (2 Kgs 5). In each case, the remedy is placed in the context of tribute to Yahweh by whose power the enemy is overcome or the difficulty resolved. As the healed Naaman expresses it, "Behold, I know that there is no God in all the earth but in Israel" (2 Kgs 5:15).

The motif of God's acts in the life of his people undergoes a much more complex development within the biblical tradition, however, and is far more completely documented. A widely attested version of this theme recalls the "signs and wonders" which God performed *in the past* to free his people from slavery in Egypt. These texts are found in Israel's legal, prophetic, and poetic traditions, and range in time from at least as early as the later sixth century (the Deuteronomic historian) down to the late Hellenistic period (Baruch).[4] As such, the recalling of these events of direct divine action in Israel's history became the substance of Jewish confession of faith, as in Deuteronomy 26:5–9 and Nehemiah 9:6–15, where God's "signs and wonders" in deliverance of his people are celebrated.

In addition to the ongoing worship of the Jewish people, in which they find or affirm their identity by associating themselves with the God of Israel and his actions in the historic preservation of the nation, the "signs" in Hellenistic times are said to include God's maintenance of order over the creation as well as his purpose for the future (Sir 42:15–25, esp. 18). Ironically,

---

4. Jos 24:5; Jer 32:20; Ps(s) 78:43, 135:8–12; Neh 9:6–15; Sir 45:3; Bar 2:11–16.

"sign" does not connote a violation of natural law, as miracle has been widely understood by man in the post-Enlightenment period, but quite the reverse: it was the establishment of order in what we might call both nature and history that was the *sign* of God's sovereignty:

> For the Most High knows all that may be known,
>   and he looks into the sign of the age.
> He declares what has been and what is to be,
>   and he reveals the track of hidden things.

The influence of the Stoic doctrine of natural law is evident here; at the very least Sirach's understanding of divine wisdom is wholly compatible with the Stoic deterministic view of history.

From the eighth century on, the prophetic tradition looked forward to God's repeating the signs of deliverance from Egypt (Is 19:19–22). By the late sixth century and on down into Hellenistic times, the prophets and seers expected God to act on behalf of his people in ways that were analogous to the Exodus but that with the passing years shifted from the strictly historical plane to the realm of the cosmic. This significant change is evident within the prophetic oracles grouped in the second part of the book of Isaiah. In the older strand—probably written as the exile in Babylon was coming to an end by decree of Cyrus the Persian (Is 45)—the language of the prophetic promise of deliverance recalls the imagery and rhetoric of the celebrations of the Exodus:

> Fear not, for I have redeemed you;
>   I have called you by name, you are mine.
> When you pass through the waters I will be with you;
>   and through the rivers, they shall not overcome you.
> For I am the Lord your God,
>   the Holy One of Israel, your Savior.[5]

The agents through which God is here depicted as accomplishing his acts of deliverance include the pagan ruler himself (Is 45:1, where Cyrus is called "the Lord's anointed"), as well as the nation, identified under the image of Yahweh's servant (Is 42:5–

5. Is 43:2–3.

9). His actions in Israel's behalf will enable her to become "a light to the nations," and thereby bring knowledge of God to all the human race. In a curious blend of the old and the new, the story of the triumph of Israel over her enemies in the Red Sea is retold employing the ancient Near Eastern mythological imagery of God's defeat of the evil powers of the sea, depicted as dragons and submarine monsters (Is 51:9–11). Now the prophet recalls that series of acts of divine deliverance as assuring the redemption of the nation, soon to take place. This will lead to the renewal of the creation: springs in the desert, thorns and briars replaced by harmless plants, with the result that:

> You shall go out in joy, and be led forth in peace;
> the mountains and hills before you shall break forth into singing,
> and all the trees of the field shall clap their hands.
>
> [Is 55:12]

The outcome will be the transformation of human society, in that the deprived and alienated will be the objects of special divine solicitude (Is 61), and ultimately there will be renewal of the entire creation, both heavens and earth (Is 60:17). In the Hellenistic period, the prayer for the fulfillment of Jewish eschatological hopes through the defeat of the nation's enemies and the restoration of the covenant people is expressed in a prayer addressed to "the Lord, the God of the ages":

> Show signs anew, and work further wonders;
> make thy hand and thy right arm glorious . . .
> Hasten the day, and remember the appointed time,
> and let thy people recount thy mighty deeds.
>
> [Sir 36:6–8]

MIRACLE AS SIGN OF THE DEFEAT OF EVIL POWERS

Developing in Judaism concurrently with these optimistic prophetic hopes was the apocalyptic world-view. Though its antecedents go back to the sixth/fifth century, when exiled Israel was under Persian domination, the schema by which history is viewed as a succession of epochs was probably influenced by Hesiod's theory of history, the impact of which would have been felt in Hellenistic times.

The details of the apocalyptic scene of judgment are spelled out in Isaiah 24. The language recalls the initial condition of the creation in Genesis 1:2, "The earth was without form and void." Just as chaos gave way to order, then, so the creation will return to chaos before God's final redemption of it is accomplished. The cause of its disorder, however, is the failure of the inhabitants to fulfill their obligations under the "everlasting covenant"[6] (Is 24:5). The impending judgment is clearly parallel to that which earlier befell the human race and its entire earthly habitation in the flood in the days of Noah, as the prediction of the opening of the windows of heaven and the shaking of the earth's foundations reminds the reader (Is 24:18–19).[7] Although the analogy is not drawn explicitly, the implication is that participation in the elect community to whom the secret of God's judgmental/redemptive purpose has been disclosed assures deliverance, as it did for Noah and his family. In the judgment, not only rebellious human beings, but the wicked heavenly powers will be punished (24:21–22). When that work of cosmic rectification is complete, God will rule from Jerusalem, in association with the elders of his people (24:23). The renewal of the creation will be achieved, including the triumph over death and the unveiling of his sanctuary to all the nations (25:6–8). Meanwhile, however, the elect community is suffering like a woman in travail—helpless but soon to be relieved. During this interim the apocalyptist invites the faithful to withdraw until the time of judgment has passed (Is 26:20–21). Only then will the true Israel flourish and fill the earth (27:6), though the true worship

6. Probably an allusion to the covenant with Noah (Gn 9:1–17), which was believed by Jews to be binding on the whole human race and which underlies other apocalyptic writings, such as the Book of Enoch.

7. In 1 Enoch the flood imagery is used to depict the eschatological judgment (65:1; 67:3; 83), but the writer builds on Isaiah 24:19–20 rather than expanding directly on the flood story. The flood motif is also present in 1 Enoch 6–11. For a detailed assessment of the material, see David W. Suter, *Tradition and Composition in the Parables of Enoch* (SBLDS 47). (Missoula, Mont.: Scholars Press, 1979); also his "*Mashal* in the Similitudes of Enoch," *JBL* 100 (1981): 193–212.

will once again be centered in Jerusalem (27:12–13). The Adversary is depicted under the ancient Canaanite image of the dragon in the sea: Yahweh will slay him "in that day" (Is 27:1).

The fullest evidence for apocalyptic within the biblical tradition of Israel is in the Book of Daniel. The genre virtually required that the author depict his present crisis through the eyes of a worthy of the past, thereby enabling the writer to provide perspective on the present, and to look beyond it to the near future, when the divine purpose was expected to find consummation. The figure chosen from the past was Daniel, who in Ezekiel 14:14 is linked with Noah and Job, and whose wisdom is extolled in Ezekiel 28:3. The story of the Book of Daniel is set in the period of the Babylonian exile of Israel, just prior to the triumph of the Persians over the Babylonians, with the subsequent beneficences to the Jews. The actual date of writing is the reign of Antiochus Epiphanes, the Seleucid ruler who oppressed the Jews and desecrated the temple in Jerusalem.[8] His official decrees included the prohibition of prayers to alien gods and of cultic dietary restrictions and at the same time required all his subjects to offer divine honors to him. In the first six chapters of Daniel there are three stories of miraculous deliverance of those who defy the orders of the pagan king: they flourish on a starvation diet; they escape from the fiery furnace and from the hungry lions. God has intervened directly to preserve his own. Daniel's role is that of a divinely endowed seer whose visions enable him to foresee the future of the rulers and of the whole course of history, which is disclosed through the dreams and visions occupying the last half of the book (Dn 7–12). The major thrust of these visions is epitomized in the poetic words of the conclusion of the first vision (Dn 7:27):

And the kingdom and the dominion
and the greatness of the kingdoms under the whole heaven

8. On the date and circumstances of the writing of the Book of Daniel, see Louis F. Hartman and Alexander A. DiLella, *Daniel*, Anchor Bible 23 (Garden City, N.Y.: Doubleday, 1978), pp. 29–54. Also for historical background, see D. S. Russell, *The Jews from Alexander to Herod* (Oxford: Oxford University Press, 1967), pp. 1–57.

shall be given to the people who are the saints of the Most High;
their kingdom shall be an everlasting kingdom,
and all dominions shall serve and obey them.

The saints will be the vicegerents through whom God will achieve the dominion that he originally assigned to Adam ("Be fruitful and multiply, and fill the earth and subdue it, and have dominion . . . over every living thing that moves upon the earth," Gn 1:26–28). Hence the appropriateness of symbolizing those to whom the kingdom is given as "one like a son of man" (Dn 7:13)— which is to say, a human being—in contrast with the bizarre beasts who in Daniel's visions symbolize the evil, self-serving political powers. Yet it is God himself who has been at work and will accomplish the "signs and wonders" by which his enemies will be overcome (Dn 4:2–3), and it is his rule that will be established over the creation (4:34–35). At the same time, his "signs and wonders" directly benefit and preserve the life of his people: "He delivers and rescues, he works signs and wonders in heaven and on earth, he who has saved Daniel from the power of the lions" (Dn 6:27). Aiding God in the achievement of his purposes are "the watchers," who confirm his decrees (4:17) and who perform direct tasks (4:23).[9]

In the last three chapters of Daniel (10–12), there are indications of the celestial conflict between certain angels ("princes," who are partisans of the pagan nations) and those angels like Michael who champion the cause of God's people (10:13). The appearance of the heavenly messengers transforms Daniel's visage (10:8) and gives him encouragement to stand firm in the face of mounting hostility and the threat of martyrdom.

In the Dead Sea community, as we noted in chapter 2, there was total withdrawal from society on the part of a group that was persuaded that it alone was living in fidelity to the divine will, and that God had revealed to it alone the secrets of his coming judgment of the wicked and his vindication of the faith-

9. The "watchers" fulfill similar roles in other apocalyptic writings, such as 1 Enoch 12:2–3 and Jubilees 4:15. Sirach 42:17 notes, however, that even the angelic powers ("holy ones") are unable to recite all God's glorious works as he achieves his purposes in the creation.

ful. In the War Scroll found at Qumran was depicted conflict in heaven in parallel with the conflict on earth, as in Daniel. The story of Nebuchadnezzar's temporary insanity (Dn 4) is retold in the Qumranian Prayer of Nabonidus as showing that the ruler, who had been possessed by a demon, was aided and pronounced forgiven by an exorcist. Similarly, in the Genesis Apocryphon, the illness that befell Pharaoh when he took Sarah as his wife (Gn 13:17) is attributed to a demon that possessed the Egyptian ruler.

Clearly, during the first century B.C. Jewish apocalypticists were intensifying and specifying the antagonism between God and his agents, on the one hand, and Satan and the powers of evil, on the other.[10] The miracles that are being described are not always directly effected by God, but are accomplished through his agents, whose exorcisms are seen as signs of the impending defeat of the God-opposing powers. This contrasts sharply with the viewpoint toward miracle evident in the older strata of the rabbinic tradition, where miracles are depicted as occurring almost entirely as signs of divine attestation of a particular rabbi's interpretation of the law. The link with prophetic fulfillment, as in the healing of the lame and the blind (Is 35:5–6), or with the defeat of the God-opposing powers, as in the exorcisms, is missing from this rabbinic lore.[11] The miracle of healing in this apocalyptic tradition, as represented in the Dead Sea community on the other hand, is only incidentally of benefit to the one cured: its primary significance is cosmic, as a sign of a new age in which the divine will finally becomes sovereign throughout the creation.

10. In the Testaments of the XII (Test Simeon 6:6–7; Levi 5:10; 6:4; Asher 7:3; Benjamin 3:3; Test Levi [Armenian B-text] 18:12), the conflict is between God's purpose, which he is accomplishing through his own agents, and the opposition to him led by the powers of evil under Belial (or Beliar).

11. The classic study of this material by Paul Fiebig, *Jüdische Wundergeschichten im Zeitalter Jesu* (Tübingen: J. C. B. Mohr, 1911), has been sharply criticized by Morton Smith (*JBL* 90 [1971]) on the ground that the alleged parallels he adduces are actually from later strata of the rabbinic tradition. Common elements between the rabbinic stories and those in the Gospels appear to include heavenly voices, miraculous feedings, encounters with demons, and warnings of disaster.

JESUS AND HIS FOLLOWERS AS AGENTS
OF DIVINE TRIUMPH: THE Q SOURCE

Permeating the synoptic Gospels as we know them is a strand of
tradition that exhibits a remarkable degree of coherence con-
ceptually and in perspective, even though it exists only as scattered material—almost entirely sayings—incorporated and po-
sitioned independently by two of the evangelists in their respective
gospels, Matthew and Luke. Known as the Q source, it may be
defined as the material common to those two gospels but not
found in Mark.[12] One would expect such a hypothetical source
to be merely miscellaneous, but in fact the material sets forth
consistent themes of Jesus as prophet and agent of the impending Rule of God, of redefining the covenant community which
he has called into existence, of defining the roles of members of
that community.

The characteristics of the apocalyptic world-view are apparent throughout the Q material. Even before Jesus appears on
the scene, John the Baptist is portrayed as redefining "the children of Abraham" (Lk 3:7–9). Though John is represented as
having been sent by God to prepare the way for Jesus (Lk 7:27,
where the fulfillment of the prophet Malachi is attested), John's
message of impending judgment contrasts sharply with Jesus'
invitation to the deprived, the socially and religiously marginal,
to prepare for a share in the New Age. This eschatological re-
versal of roles is vividly set out in the familiar words of the Beati-

12. A brief but comprehensive history of the problem of sources of the synoptic Gospels, with bibliography, is available in W. G. Kümmel, *Introduction to the
New Testament*, trans. H. C. Kee (Nashville [and London]: Abingdon [SCM], 1975),
pp. 38–80. Efforts to account for the relationships among the synoptics on purely
literary grounds range from the mechanical (B. H. Streeter, *The Four Gospels*
[New York: Macmillan, 1925]) to the hopeless (H. Stoldt, *Die Geschichte und Kritik
der Markus-hypothese* [Göttingen: Vandenhoeck and Ruprecht, 1979], "an insol-
uble riddle"). For the evidence in support of the existence of Q as a definable
and identifiable strand of gospel tradition, see H. C. Kee, *Jesus in History*, 2d ed.
(New York: Harcourt Brace, 1977), pp. 76–83; also my essay on the present state
of synoptic studies in the forthcoming Society of Biblical Literature Centennial
Volume, ed. E. J. Epp. All quotations of Q are from Luke, since he has apparently reproduced the source more faithfully than Matthew.

tudes,[13] which promise joy to those now sorrowing, satisfaction to the hungry, vindication to those now oppressed, and participation of the "poor" in the kingdom (Lk 6:20–23).

On the specific question of miracles, Q presents both dimensions of what we have seen to characterize the apocalyptic outlook: God intervenes in world history to achieve his purpose; he enables prophetic agents to perform miracles in fulfillment of that eschatological goal for creation. The one narrative included in the Q material, the Healing of the Centurion's Slave (Lk 7:1–10), is more important as evidence of the access to divine power available to non-Jews than as merely another report of a miraculous healing. As Q makes clear, miracles can be performed on orders from the Devil (Lk 4:2–12), so that the important question from the viewpoint of this tradition is not "Can miracles be accomplished?" but "To what end do they occur?"

Central to defining the life-world in which Q understands Jesus' miracles to have taken place is the passage in which he responds to questions relayed to him from John the Baptist about the meaning of his mission (Lk 7:18–23). John's questioning of whether Jesus is "the one to come" is fully understandable: Jesus did not match up to the nationalistic hopes as they are expressed in the Psalms of Solomon, which await a triumphant king in the tradition of David (idealized); neither did he fit the Dead Sea community's expectation of a dyarchy of king and priest who would preside over a radically pure and purged eschatological Israel. The response attributed to Jesus in Q is, however, wholly in keeping with Jewish prophetic promises: "the blind receive their sight, the lame walk, lepers are cleansed, and the deaf hear, the dead are raised up, the poor have good news preached to them" (Lk 7:22). Each phrase of the response derives from the Prophets, especially Isaiah (29:18–19; 35:5–6; 61:1). What is radically new is not only the redefinition of the community benefiting from the eschatological blessings that Jesus brings, but

13. The more familiar version of the material in Matthew 5:3–12 converts the concrete social-status factors (poverty, hunger, powerlessness) into spiritual virtues ("poor in spirit," "hunger for righteousness"). That is in keeping with Matthew's aim to represent the church as the true Israel. See my discussion of this in *Jesus in History*, 2d ed., pp. 166–85.

also the claim that these prophetic promises are already in process of fulfillment among them: "Go tell John what you have already seen and heard" (Lk 7:22a).

In the somewhat fuller version of the controversy over the source of power by which Jesus performs his exorcisms found in Luke (as compared with Mark 3:19–35),[14] the specific claim of Jesus is that he casts out demons "by the finger of God." This means, he declares, that "the Kingdom of God has come upon you" (Lk 11:20). The phrase "finger of God" derives ultimately from Exodus 8:19, where it is the symbol of God's power in delivering his covenant people from their Egyptian bondage. Now the exorcisms of Jesus are signs (1) of the liberation of God's new people from the evil powers and (2) of the already begun establishment of his eschatological rule. The line of demarcation between the old age and the new has already been drawn: "The law and the prophets were until John; since then the good news of the kingdom of God is preached, and every one who enters it is involved in conflict" (Lk 16:16).

Jesus' role as miracle-worker is only one facet—important though it be—in his office as prophet. He does not perform wonders to authenticate himself. Rather, his message of the New Age and the eschatological wisdom he imparts to his people (Lk 10:21–22) are self-confirming, as were the preaching of Jonah and the wisdom of Solomon (Lk 11:29–32). Significantly, those who responded to Jonah and Solomon, as well as those who recognize Jesus as the eschatological prophet (Lk 4:24) are the outsiders. Even within the family of Jesus and those of his followers, there is sure to be disbelief and hostility (Lk 12:49–53). This prophet, lacking human credentials or the support of the established structures of society, is a radical threat to both the religious and social institutions of his culture. His followers are to carry forward both his message and his wonders (Lk 10:8–9),

---

14. Either Q has preserved an extended version of the Beelzebub controversy story, in which case Mark and Q directly overlap, or Q supplements the narrative in a substantive way. The fact that Luke's version of the tradition is scattered throughout his gospel (Lk 6:43–45; 8:19–21; 11:17–23; 12:10) suggests that only related sayings, not an alternate version of the story, stood in the Q tradition.

but they are to expect the same short-term hostility (Lk 10:16) as he experienced, as well as the same eschatological vindication. The cross is the symbol, not only of his rejection by the establishment, but of theirs as well (Lk 14:25–27). Beyond the present era of trials is the promise of a share in the Rule of God: "You are those who have continued with me in my trials; and I convenant with you, as my father has covenanted with me, that you may eat and drink at my table in my kingdom, and sit on thrones judging the twelve tribes of Israel" (Lk 22:28–30). For the Q tradition, therefore, miracle is the assuring sign of faith in eschatological vindication. Its immediate effect is personal, in meeting the specific need of the ailing or the possessed; but its frame of meaning is cosmic, in that it points to the triumph of God over the evil forces that have until now frustrated the achievement of his plan for the creation and for the human race as his agents to preside over it.

THROUGH JESUS THE NEW AGE IS DAWNING: MARK

In Mark, miracle is a pervasive element. There are not only narratives reporting miracles, but summaries of Jesus' wonder-working activity and comments on his miraculous powers made by Jesus, by the Evangelist, by Jesus' critics, and even by demons. The miracle stories range from highly compressed narrative to more extended novelistic tales.[15] Their subject matter might be loosely grouped as exorcisms, healings (including the restoration of the dead to life), and triumphs over what we could call the natural world. Framing the Markan story of Jesus are at least four indications of heavenly confirmation of his role, sketched below. At the same time, Jesus is linked throughout his career with the prophetic tradition of the Jewish scriptures, though with

15. On the classification and terminology of the gospel narratives, the classic studies are those of Martin Dibelius, *From Tradition to Gospel*, trans. B. L. Woolf (New York: Scribner, n.d.), and R. Bultmann, *History of the Synoptic Tradition*, trans. John Marsh (New York: Harper, 1963). My own proposals for generic categories—which are intended to be less technical and less value-laden than those of Bultmann and Dibelius—are offered in *Jesus in History*[2], pp. 301–06.

distinctive emphases in effect. We turn, then, to a detailed analysis of Mark's picture of Jesus, the wonder-worker.

The recounting of Jesus' public career in Mark opens with his baptism by John (1:2–11). John's link with the divine purpose is attested (1) by the appeal to prophetic tradition as finding fulfillment in his mission (Isa. 40; Mal 3), as well as in his modeling his garb and locale after Elijah (Mk 1:4; cf. 2 Kgs 1:8). It is in keeping with this role-model derived from the prototypical prophet that Jesus identified John as Elijah who has already come (Mk 9:13). But it is the heavenly voice acclaiming Jesus as God's son at the moment of his baptism which links him with both the kingly (Ps(s) 2:7) and the prophetic (Is 42:1) versions of Jewish messianic expectation. A divine acclaim similar to the one addressed to Jesus at baptism is uttered (2) in the hearing of his inner circle of followers shortly before his execution at the time of his transfiguration before them: "This is my beloved son" (Mk 9:7). (3) A third incident of divine affirmation is described as taking place at the moment of his death, when—from top to bottom—the temple veil is torn in two (Mk 15:38). (4) The final mode of heavenly confirmation of Jesus appears in the concluding verses of the Gospel (16:4–8), where we read of the stone rolled back from Jesus' tomb and the white-robed messenger who announces his resurrection. The reader is in no doubt of Mark's conviction that God stands behind the career of Jesus from beginning to the seemingly tragic end.

It is in the stories about Jesus and in various comments on him reported by the Evangelist that we receive a clear picture of what the divinely approved mission of Jesus and its significance were understood to be. The context is set for the understanding of Jesus and his miracles that Mark wants to convey by his report of three items as the story of Jesus' career begins: the testing in the desert by Satan (1:12–13), the announcement by Jesus of the incursion of God's Rule (1:14–15) into an era dominated by Satan. This is demonstrated in the first account of a miracle: an exorcism (1:21–28). The time of testing in preparation for a prophetic mission recalls both Moses and Elijah (Ex 3; 1 Kgs 19), who in fact appear at the scene of Jesus' divine confirmation (Mk 9:5). The association of Jesus with the Elijah tradition is made also by those outside the community of Jesus' followers, according to Mark. Herod Antipas's advisors (6:14–15) propose that this troublesome wonder-worker who is organizing a radical movement is, in fact, Elijah. Jesus' cry to God ("Eloi! Eloi!," 15:34) on the cross is interpreted by the onlookers as an appeal to Elijah. Even Jesus' opponents are represented as associating him with the tradition of eschatological prophets, especially Elijah. The implication of Jesus' announcement of the kingdom (1:14–15) is self-evidently in the apocalyptic tradition. That the first of Jesus' actions to be reported (following the call of the nucleus of his disciples to break with family and occupation, 1:16–20) is the defeat of the demons is paradigmatic for the Gospel as a whole.

In this incident in the synagogue at Capernaum, there is instant recognition of the authority of Jesus, not only by the worshipers gathered there (1:22), but—far more significantly—by the demons themselves (1:24). Their rhetorical question "Have you come to destroy us?" provides its own answer. The account uses a technical apocalyptic term—often weakly translated as "rebuke" (1:25)—which implies the commanding power of Jesus to control the agents of Satan.[16] Although the narrative twice refers to Jesus' action as "teaching" (1:22, 27), it is his authority that is remarkable, and that accounts for his fame among Galilean human antagonists as well as his demonic opponents.

Similarly, in the extended account of the cure of the Gerasene demoniac (5:1–20), the demons not only recognize Jesus but request from him special consideration as to how he disposes of them—namely, to be transferred to a conveniently available herd of swine (5:10, 13). In the course of the interchange, the demons themselves acknowledge Jesus' special relationship to God (5:7). In 7:24–30, recognition of Jesus' role as agent of Israel's God is expressed by the mother of a demoniac child, who is a "Greek" from the region of Tyre and Sidon, and therefore religiously and racially out of the orbit of the covenant people as defined by Jews. She acknowledges this in referring to herself

16. H. C. Kee, "The Terminology of Mark's Exorcism Stories," *NTS* 14 (1968): 232–46.

as a "dog" who might at least share some crusts fallen from the
Israelite table. The point of the story is not merely to depict an
exorcism but to show the redefinition of the potential participants in the New Age.

Perhaps most revealing of Mark's view of the significance of
Jesus' exorcisms is the Beelzebub controversy story (3:20–35).
There is no uncertainty suggested as to whether or not Jesus
can perform these extraordinary acts; the only issue is the source
of his powers. The members of his family have a simple explanation: they think he is mad (3:20–21).[17] The scribes assume
that he can control the devil's demonic aides because he is in
league with their prince.[18] There is within the story the additional acknowledgment that the scribes have their own exorcists,
so that there is by no means an implication that the ability to
command the demons is unique to Jesus. What is distinctive is
that in his exorcisms he is "plundering the strong man's house"
(3:27)—that is, is bringing to an end the epoch of Satan's control
over the creation (1:26).

Likewise in the healing stories of Mark, the point of the narrative is not merely to report Jesus' therapeutic powers. In addition, Mark has added or has preserved a dimension which treats
of an issue that must have been important for the Christian group
for or to whom Mark was writing. The healing of the paralytic
(2:1–12) involves the question of Jesus' authority to pronounce
the forgiveness of sins.[19] The cure of the man with the withered
hand involves the Jewish legal question of work on the sabbath

17. Many translations, including the Revised Standard Version, avoid the
clear meaning of the text of Mark by supplying "people" as the subject of the
verb, *elegon*. Yet the persons waiting to take him away are his family, as Mark
3:31–32 attests, and as the point of the redefinition of the family in 3:33–35
affirms.

18. The name of Satan used here—Beelzebul (= "Lord of the Divine Abode")
or its scornful equivalent, Beelzebub (= "Lord of the Flies")—derives from the
Canaanite god, Baal (2 Kings 1:2–3). It came to be used for Satan as the prince
of demons, presumably by pious Jews.

19. On the literary or editorial technique by which Mark adapts his oral or
written sources to the needs of his own situation, see my *Community of the New
Age* (Philadelphia [and London]: Westminster Press [SCM Press], 1977), pp. 54–
56.

(3:1–6). The request from the ruler of the synagogue to Jesus to heal his desperately ill daughter shifts to the issue of Jesus' victory over death (5:21–43). Other healing stories show that persistence is rewarded by a cure, as in the story of the woman with the hemorrhage, spliced into the tale of Jairus's daughter (5:24–34). Additional examples of perseverance in seeking a cure are the stories of the blind man of Bethsaida (8:22–26) and of Bartimaeus in Jericho (10:46–52). In not one of these cases is the miracle an end in itself; in each case it points to some larger framework of meaning in Jesus' mission.

In what might be conveniently grouped as the nature miracles of Mark's gospel, there are evident multiple levels of meaning within a single narrative. Although apocalyptic tradition does not hold a view of the world as divided into realms of spirit and matter, or nature and supernature, it is useful to distinguish those miracles which directly affect the health or biological life of individuals from those which change objects or forces external to human beings, such as weather, food, trees, or gravity. Yet for the apocalyptic life-world it was essential that divine sovereignty be established, not only over the human race, but also over the entire created context of human existence. This is an essential feature in the nature miracles, but does not exhaust their significance for Mark. A brief analysis of five examples of this category of miracle story will demonstrate the range of cosmic and symbolic meaning.

The story of his calming the windstorm and the raging sea (4:35–41) is to be interpreted against the ancient Semitic tradition that the sea is the source of power hostile to God, as is evident both in the biblical creation stories, where putting the waters in their places is central to God's control of the creation (Gn 1:9) and in the Canaanite mythology, where the evil god is named Yam (= sea). The interchangeability of "wind" and "spirit" in both Hebrew (Gn 1:2) and Greek makes it possible for the tradition to depict Jesus as exercising power in the realm of the spirits even as he is commanding the wind. Further, he is here described as addressing the hostile wind with the "rebuke" of power which manifests his cosmic authority, as in the exorcisms where he commands the demons.

The story of the feeding of the five thousand in the desert (6:30–44) looks simultaneously back to ancient Israel's experience and forward to the cultic practice of the Markan community. Far more is involved than merely the supernatural supply of food for the hungry crowd. Exodus 16:4–35 reports the miraculous bread that fed the covenant people in the Sinai desert in the early days of their formation.[20] The details of Jesus' provision of the bread to his people include "he took," "he blessed," "he broke," all of which appear in the eucharistic formulae of the early church, as Mark 14:22 attests in its account of the Last Supper. It might seem puzzling that Mark would have included another story so similar to this (8:1–10), in which four thousand are fed at another location. In it, not only the eucharistic terms just listed are also used, but the giving of thanks (*eucharistēsas*) is once again explicitly included (8:6). Yet another symbolic level is made evident in the comments on the two feeding stories reported by Mark (8:14–21), where the figures "seven" and "twelve" are implied to have special meaning. It is likely that these numbers represent the two phases of the early church's evangelistic mission: to Israel, whose twelve tribes were symbolized by the twelve baskets, and to the Gentiles, who were represented in Jerusalem by seven leaders, according to Acts 6:1–6. The miraculous feedings, like their Old Testament counterpart, therefore are not isolated wonders benefiting individuals but divine acts seen as constituting a covenant community.

Two other brief narratives in Mark which could be grouped with nature miracles are the previously mentioned rending of the temple veil and the cursing of the fig tree (11:12–14), with the subsequent enigmatic explanation to the disciples (11:20–25). Both incidents point to impending judgment on the old covenant people: their place of special access to God and assurance of divine presence among them will be destroyed; the image of the unfruitful plant recalls the image of God's judgment

---

20. Peder Borgen, in *Bread from Heaven* (Leiden: Brill, 1966), has traced the connections between the story of the feeding and its interpretation in Jewish Passover tradition, on the one hand, and the Christian eucharistic tradition, on the other.

on Israel in Isaiah 5 and Hosea 10, with echoes in Ezekiel 19 and Jeremiah 2:21. Both "nature miracles," therefore, are presented by Mark within a framework of apocalyptic judgment and of redefinition of the holy people and their avenue of access to God.

VISIONS OF CONFLICT AND ENCOURAGEMENT TO PERSEVERE

The most extended non-narrative part of Mark is a vision (13:4–37) in which not only the characteristics of apocalyptic are evident, but the influence of the Book of Daniel is pervasive, including direct allusions in Mark 13.[21] Indeed, it is likely that the whole of this apocalyptic discourse was developed as a free-wheeling commentary or midrash on Daniel, especially Daniel 7.[22] The predictions about what is soon to take place in the fulfillment of God's plan is, in keeping with the apocalyptic worldview, reserved for the inner circle of Jesus' followers (Mk 13:3), although no specific date is given. The disciples are to expect ever-worsening treatment at the hands of this age's rulers and established authorities (13:9–13). They are called on to persevere, even when the opposition comes from within their own families. The crucial signal for the end of the age will be directly comparable to the crisis under Antiochus Epiphanes and is described in words taken directly from the LXX of Daniel 9:27, "the desolating sacrilege" is to be set up where it has no right— namely, in the temple at Jerusalem (13:14). What Gaius Caligula had threatened to do—erect his statue there as a center for Jews to offer him divine honors—will soon take place. The consequences of this conflict will be cosmic, with stars and heavenly powers disordered as a result of this outburst of diabolical au-

21. For an analysis of Mark's use of scripture, and especially of Daniel, see my *Community of the New Age*, pp. 43–49.

22. The hypothesis is developed convincingly by Lars Hartmann, in *Prophecy Reinterpreted: The Formation of Some Jewish Apocalyptic Texts and of the Eschatological Discourse Mark 13 par.* (Coniectanea Biblica, New Testament Series, Lund, 1966). David Suter's work has shown (*Tradition and Composition in the Parables of Enoch*) that 1 Enoch 46 includes a midrash (eschatologically oriented interpretive expansion) on Daniel 7:9–14.

dacity; but the divinely chosen human, "the Son of Man," will appear, gather the elect, and reign in triumph over God's creation (13:24–27). Jesus, as Mark presents him, offers not an insight into the future of an anxious, seeking individual, but a vision of the future of God's creation.

Jesus' gift of foreseeing and foretelling the future does relate to his own destiny, however. By both explicit prediction and by implication, Jesus is depicted in Mark as foreknowing his own suffering and death, which he regards as necessary steps in the accomplishment of God's plan for regaining mastery over the creation. In justifying his disciples' failure to fast (Mk 2:18–20), Jesus compares their present joyous celebration of association with him to a wedding feast, but then notes that "the days will come when the bridegroom will be taken away from them." In response to a question about the prophetic expectation of the coming of Elijah (Mk 9:9–12), he declares that Elijah (i.e., John the Baptist) has already come, but then asks the rhetorical question "How is it written of the Son of Man, that he should suffer many things and be treated with contempt?" We do not have any text in which this specific prediction is advanced, but we have seen that the saints in Daniel must suffer before they ("one like a son of man") receive the kingdom. Thrice-repeated are the solemn pronouncements of Jesus (Mk 8:31; 9:31; 10:33–34) that he himself will suffer and die at the hands of the authorities and that God will vindicate him by raising him from the dead. Both death and resurrection, therefore, are eschatological signs.

His foreknowledge extends to the behavior and destiny of his followers, as well. He knows that one of his most trusted disciples will deny any association with him (Peter; Mk 14:30–31); that one of the twelve will betray him to the authorities (Judas, 14:17–21); that he will be put to death and his community scattered (14:26–27); and that God will vindicate him and them (14:28). Thus the pattern of suffering, martyrdom, and vindication which are common features of the apocalyptic life-world are constitutive for Mark's most extensive narrative section: the story of Jesus' death and the finding of the empty tomb.

Another feature characteristic of apocalyptic communities that affects Mark's representation of miracle is the stress on continuity between the life-style and activities of the founder and those of his followers. The very fact that apocalypses are written down is a sure indication that they are intended to serve as guides for an ongoing community, however imminent that community may expect the end of the age to be. Daniel prepared a relatively brief document to sustain his community until the consummation. The Dead Sea community, on the other hand, developed a small library of its own documents. Mark as a whole serves as a guide for the community, including regulations on such subjects as divorce, possessions, and taxes (10, 12). But most striking are the instructions to carry forward his activities of healing and exorcism. These include explicit commissionings, as in the initial appointment of the Twelve (3:13–19) and in his sending them forth to cast out demons and to heal the sick (6:7–13). But their role is also implicit in the story of their inability to cure the epileptic boy because of their failure previously to undergo the proper regimen of fasting and prayer (9:14–29). Wider public recognition of the power of those who identify with "the name of Jesus" is implied in the story of the exorcist who, though not a follower of Jesus, seeks to exploit the power of his name (9:38–41).[23]

Even if one were to take the extreme, and unwarranted, view that Mark preserved unaltered the tradition he received, the analysis of his gospel would require one all the more to take into account the summarizing and editorial passages in this document. They give explicit statement to the place of miracle in Mark's portrait of Jesus. An examination of four of these summaries will show what the evangelist's special interests were in relation to Jesus' wonder-working.

The first of the summaries comes after the description of a paradigmatic day in Jesus' public career (1:32–34), appropriately therefore "that evening, at sundown." The capsule description begins with phrases that might be used to describe nearly

23. As the Magical Papyri show, exploitation of the power of Jesus' name was—at least in the third and later centuries—a common feature of thaumaturgy. What is significant for Mark is that the use of the name by outsiders is tolerated only because this might lead the user to become an adherent to the Jesus community.

any miracle-worker of the Hellenistic-Roman epoch, "They brought to him all who were sick or possessed by demons." That the entire populace of the city would turn out to witness these extraordinary powers is, if hyperbolic, wholly understandable. What is surprising is that the demons recognize him as their conqueror and that he is able to suppress their disclosure of his identity. Secrecy about who he is makes good sense for an apocalyptic movement, to whose members, alone among their contemporaries, has been divinely revealed what God's purpose and strategy in the world are. The conceptual framework in which the exorcisms are to be understood by people of faith is implied in the link (1:39) between the control of the demons and the proclamation by Jesus of the Rule of God, as set forth in the programmatic announcement of 1:15, "The Kingdom of God has drawn near."

Another dimension of the context of Jesus miracles in the Markan view appears in the summary at 3:7–12. It opens with a list of the places from which seekers have come to hear Jesus and to benefit from the power he displays to heal and to exorcise. They orginate not only from his native Galilee and from the Jewish heartland of Jerusalem and the province of Judea, but from the regions east of the Jordan and north of Palestine— that is, from predominantly Gentile territory. Public testimony to his identity as "Son of God" by the demons is prohibited by Jesus, since the "mystery of the kingdom" is to be preserved for and among the faithful (4:11). The motif of the inclusiveness of the new community is central in Jesus' response to the accusation of the Pharisees that he enjoys the company of persons who are morally, ritually, or occupationally violators of, or traitors to, the Jewish tradition: tax collectors and sinners (2:15–16). Jesus' response is characteristically set out in a brief parable, the point of which is that those who are ailing and know it are the ones whom the physician can heal, regardless of their ethnic or ethical state (2:17).

In a section which combines features of the Markan summaries with narrative elements (6:1–6), Jesus is reported to have returned from his itinerant mission to his native town of Nazareth. In this case, however, the opposition he engendered is not demonic but thoroughly human: his fellow townspeople. Once more there is unsolicited and unexpected testimony to Jesus' wonderful powers from those who are hostile to him. His critics acknowledge two features of his activity: his wisdom and his "mighty works." Up to this point in Mark's story of Jesus—and throughout the remaining half of his gospel as well—the "wisdom" of Jesus consists almost wholly in his redefining membership in the covenant people. Sabbath observance, fasting (2:19), ethnic and social restrictions all give way before the new thing that God is doing. The rigid restraints of the old covenant must go: "No one puts new wine in old wineskins" (2:22). Yet where Jesus' words and acts elicit faith, even in his hostile hometown, healing and instruction continue (6:6).

As a lead into the story of Jesus' miraculous feeding of the five thousand, which we examined earlier in this chapter (p. 164), Mark describes Jesus as having compassion on the crowd which had gathered to see and hear him in words which employ a basic image from the prophetic tradition of Israel: the people as a flock in need of a shepherd. In contrast to the confident words of the psalmist, "The Lord is my shepherd" (Ps 23), from the time of the death of Moses onward (Nm 27:15–17) Israel had needed a human shepherd to give her guidance. In the days of the Israelite monarchy, the prophets saw the people as leaderless; as Micaiah phrased it, "I saw all Israel scattered upon the mountains, as sheep that have no shepherd" (1 Kgs 22:17). During the exile, Ezekiel lamented from Babylon that God's sheep were scattered "over all the face of the earth," while those designated as "shepherds of Israel"—the official religious leaders—neither fed nor protected the flock of God's people. God promises that he himself will seek them out, rescue them, feed them (Ez 34). The imagery of this prophetic theme and the compassion it expressed are constitutive for the wonder-working activity of Jesus as Mark portrays it.

In the final summary I shall analyze, 6:53–56, the picture of the widespread popular response to Jesus' healing is carried forward, but a dimension of early Christian healing tradition is apparent in 6:56, which is found elsewhere in Mark but becomes of major importance only in other early Christian documents representing a point of view significantly different from that of Mark (see below, chaps. 6 and 8). That factor is thaumaturgic process, which involves primarily the healing techniques. In most of the healing and exorcism stories of Mark the pattern is as follows: someone who is ailing comes to Jesus or is brought to him, or is reported to him, by a person or persons who are confident that he can effect a cure. He responds by pronouncing the cure or by expelling the demon causing the ailment. These basic features are present in stories as short as the healing of Peter's mother-in-law (1:30–31) or as long and detailed as the exorcism of the Gerasene demoniac (5:1–20). In a few of the Markan stories, however, we have mention of the thaumaturgic means, as in the spittle applied to the eyes of the blind man at Bethsaida (8:23). Also unusual about this story, but evident in miracle stories in Hellenistic texts, is the description of the stages of the cure: the man first sees others as resembling trees, and only in the second stage does he see clearly.

Akin to this interest in healing process is the detail, in two of the Markan summaries (3:10; 6:56) and in the story of the hemorrhaging widow (5:27–29), that to touch Jesus, even in passing in a crowd, was sufficient to be cured by him. Similarly, in the story of the unauthorized use of Jesus' name by an exorcist (9:38–41), the healing phenomenon is described by Mark (or his tradition) in ways that closely resemble the automatic or purely technical efficacy of magic. It is a feature that will become much more common in the later New Testament writings (see below chap. 6), and even more so in the postcanonical writings (chap. 8). Although to the modern mind, with its conviction that consistency is a virtue, Mark's inclusion of these details in a writing which clearly perceives Jesus' miracles within a framework very different from that of the Magical Papyri, for example, may seem strange, their presence warns against the imposition of absolute distinctions in the analysis of ancient world-views or of the documents that contain them.

MIRACLE AS SIGN OF THE SPIRIT: PAUL

Although Paul, like the Gospel of Mark, incorporates his understanding of miracle within an apocalyptic world-view, there are significant differences in detail between the way miracle is seen to function in Paul's letters and in the Q or Markan tradition. Although the performance of miracles is mentioned frequently in two of Paul's major letters (1 and 2 Corinthians) and at important points in Romans and Galatians as well, he is never specific about what the actual wonder was. He uses at certain crucial points the traditional biblical phrase, "signs and wonders" (Rom 15:19; 2 Cor 12:12) without designating specifically what they were. Of central importance for Paul is that through him Christ has wrought signs and wonders (Rom 15:19). Or, as he describes the working of miracles in Galatians 3:5, God effects them through the Spirit. Furthermore, they are essential signs of apostolic authority: through Paul's having performed them in all the churches, evidence is provided that he is a "true apostle" (2 Cor 12:12).

Rather than perceiving healings and exorcisms as signs of the preparation for the New Age in the sense of the defeat of the God-opposing powers, however, Paul discusses miracle-working in the context of the charismatic gifts. The aim of these special endowments is to build up the community—"body"—as a whole (1 Cor 12:4–11). In this context, not incidentally, the body is described as comprising Jews and Gentiles, slaves and free (1 Cor 12:13), which presupposes an inclusive definition of the covenant community, as it did in Mark. "Tongues" is the early Christian term to describe a phenomenon of ecstatic speech, not the miraculous mastery of a previously unknown language. Correlative with it, in Paul's view, was the gift of interpretation (12:10). Without that, the outsider attending the church gathering and observing the tongues-speaker will assume that he is mad (1 Cor 14:23). The ecstatic speech must have an interpreter, which involves yet another form of charismatic gift (14:5). Paul does not regard the gift of tongues as bad but sees it as a form of divine–human conversation that is largely a private matter for the charismatic so gifted.

The most prized of the charismatic gifts, in Paul's view, was the one that we might most expect of someone whose personal identity was in the apocalyptic tradition: prophecy. Prophetic powers for him meant to understand mysteries and to possess the knowledge of God's eschatological purposes (1 Cor 13:2).

The aim of prophecy was to build up the church (14:2) and to lead all to worship God (14:25). A specific mystery that Paul discloses is the series of events that will bring to a close the present age, culminating in the resurrection of the just and the triumph of God's rule over the creation (1 Cor 15). The climax of that series of revelations disclosed by Paul comes with the words, "Behold, I show you a mystery . . ." (15:51).

Paul acknowledges the importance of these extraordinary powers of speech and insight but deplores the fact that some who possess these charismatic gifts exploit them or display them meretriciously. Seizing upon the multiple meaning of the Greek word, *dynamis* (which in addition to its ordinary significance, "power," is also his common term for *miracle*), Paul sets out a paradox of power. The essence of divine power, he declares, is not to be seen in the manifestations of human wisdom or charismatic gifts but in the death of Jesus (1 Cor 1:18–25). The fact that he had played down his charismatic endowments, and especially his ability to work miracles, had led his ancient detractors to question his apostolic authority and to glorify their own. Paul seems to have been reluctant—nearly embarrassed—to have been forced into the position of reminding the Corinthians that he had displayed these powers (2 Cor 12:11). He would prefer to boast of his weaknesses and his sufferings, since—in the apocalyptic tradition—he regards them as the trials through which the righteous must pass as God prepares them for the final struggle against the powers of evil.

Meanwhile, however, Paul—again in keeping with the apocalyptic life-world—has been granted another kind of miraculous experience: a vision of the divine throne (2 Cor 12:1–10). Like Moses, Elijah, and Daniel before him, his privilege of seeing God was the ground of assurance for his career and the source of his courage to persevere in the face of difficulties and hostility.[24]

24. The throne mysticism of Jewish tradition, called Merkabah, is described in detail with documentation by Gershon Scholem in *Major Trends in Jewish Mysticism* (New York: Schocken Books, 1961). The mystical transport described by Paul in 2 Corinthians 12 is presented by Scholem as a prime example of this phenomenon, in *Jewish Gnosticism, Merkabah Mysticism, and Talmudic Tradition* (New York: Jewish Theological Seminary, 1960).

This is Paul's equivalent of the promise of the vindication of Jesus experienced by him at the transfiguration. Both miracle and martyrdom found meaning in the framework of an apocalyptic life-world.

CHAPTER SIX

Miracle in History and Romance
Roman and Early Christian Sources

In two widely different types of prose produced in the period from the end of the Roman republic until the end of the Antonine period miracles figure prominently. These are histories and romances. As might be expected, miracle functions in importantly different ways in each of these genres, and these differences are reflected in the comparable early Christian writings, as well. In the first section of this chapter I shall examine aspects of Roman historiography that deal with miracle, especially as related to portents. In the latter half of the chapter I shall survey the phenomenon of the Hellenistic-Roman romance and investigate its influence on the representation of miracle in early Christian writing, especially in Luke-Acts.

PORTENTS OF DIVINELY SHAPED DESTINY

For Suetonius and Tacitus, who chronicled the rise of the Julio-Claudian dynasty as well as its decline and replacement by the Flavians, miracle played an important role in their kindred views of the dynamic of history. The element of the miraculous is seen by them, not in what the actors do on the stage of history, but in how the gods reveal their purposes through the emperors by means of dreams, portents, and cosmic signs. In their histories of the earlier period, these writers link the portents with three kinds of events: (1) the birth and access to power of the emperor; (2) major shifts in the power structure of the state; (3) the death of the emperor. What happens in history is seen not so much as an overarching plan as it is a recurrent pattern according to which the gods choose a leader, prepare the way for him, either support or undermine his power, and prepare the way for his successor.

According to Suetonius, an apparently Oedipal dream of Julius Caesar, which the soothsayers interpreted as pointing to his having done violence to his mother, he understood to mean that he was destined to dominate Mother-Earth.[1] Again, when Caesar waited at the Rubicon, a being of wondrous beauty appeared, playing on a reed, the sight and sound of which attracted both soldiers and shepherds. Thereupon the apparition seized a trumpet, rushed to the river, sounded the battle-cry, and crossed over. Caesar cried out that the signs from the gods (*deorum ostenta*) summoned them to cross the river and meet their foes.[2] Likewise, his approaching murder was foreseen by signs, including (1) the discovery in a grave of a bronze tablet foretelling the death of a "son of Ilium" (= Caesar), (2) the lachrymose refusal of a horse to cross the Rubicon, (3) the warning by a soothsayer of danger in the Ides of March, (4) Julius's dream of flying above the clouds to grasp the hand of Jupiter, and (5) his wife's dream of the collapse of part of his house.[3] After his death, the appearance of a comet was understood to show that Caesar's soul had gone up to heaven. Thus the parameters of his career were perceived to be under divine guidance, the high points of which were disclosed in signs and portents.

Augustus's birth and childhood were likewise surrounded by stories of miraculous signs. His mother was visited by a serpent in the shrine of Apollo; the marks left by the reptile were interpreted by her to mean that her child was the son of Apollo. In her dreams her vitals were taken up to and spread across the heavens. In her husband's dream, the sun arose from her tomb. Others confirmed that her son was to be the ruler of the world. Perhaps the most grandiose dream— also his father's—was a kind of epiphany of the son with a thunderbolt and the sceptre and insignia of Jupiter Optimus Maximus, wearing a crown with shining rays and mounted on a laurel-wreathed chariot drawn by twelve white horses. As a child Augustus disappeared from his cradle and was found in a lofty tower with his face toward

1. Suetonius, *Lives*, Julius, 7.2
2. Ibid., 32.
3. Ibid., 81.

the rising sun. The appearance of twelve vultures at the sacrifice offered by Augustus after Julius's death was understood to foretell a glorious future for him. His success in the contest with his colleagues in the triumvirate was foreseen when an eagle attacked and struck down two ravens. Before his death, lightning struck an inscription and melted the letter C (of Caesar), by which he knew he had only a hundred days to live.[4]

Tiberius and Caligula both received solemn portents of their death, including the destruction of a lighthouse near Capri by an earthquake in Tiberius's last days, and an outburst of laughter from a statue of Zeus at Olympia on hearing that Caligula had ordered that it be moved to Rome.[5] In Caligula's own dream, he went to heaven and Jupiter threw him out.

Although sun rays shone on Nero at birth, the gloomy omens were unambiguous: his horoscope was filled with dire predictions; his father expected the worst ("Nothing that was not abominable and a public bane could be born of Agrippina and myself"); the rear end of his favorite Spanish steed was changed into an ape; the keys of the Capitol were lost; his final song, which was about Oedipus, ended with the words, "Wife, father, mother drive me to my death."[6]

In Suetonius's accounts of Otho, Vitellius, and Galba, the profound uncertainty about the future of Rome and its leadership is seen as reflected in ill omens: lightning knocked the heads from all the statues in the Temple of the Caesars and dashed from Augustus's hand the sceptre of power; the sacred chickens flew away as auspices were being prepared; an equestrian statue set up in honor of Vitellius collapsed; a cock perched on his shoulder and then on his head, which was understood to mean that he could not retain power by his own efforts.[7]

From the birth of Vespasian and his accession to power until the death of Domitian, the fate of the Flavian house was indi-

4. Ibid., Augustus, 94; 95; 96; 97.
5. Ibid., Tiberius, 74; Caligula, 42.
6. Ibid., Nero.
7. Ibid., Otho, Galba, and Vitellius.

cated by portents, Suetonius reported. The flourishing of trees thought dead, a stray dog's dropping a human hand (a symbol of power) under Vespasian's breakfast table, the defeat of two fighting eagles by a third in view of the army—all showed the divine favor attending his assumption of the imperial authority. A highly favorable judgment concerning Vespasian was rendered by an oracle of a god on Mount Carmel in Palestine, which declared that whatever he planned or wished, however great it might be, would come to pass.[8] Domitian, on the other hand, had repeated premonitions of the end of his reign and of his life, through dreams as well as through predictions of astrologers. The inscription on one of his triumphal statues was torn off in a storm. When finally he overcame the terror brought upon him by the dreams and astrological warnings, he went to his bedroom and was assassinated there.[9]

Although Tacitus in his *Histories* confirms the omens and reports additional ones, he raises doubts about the integrity of the astrologers, whom he characterizes as "a tribe of men untrustworthy for the powerful, deceitful toward the ambitious."[10] In the category of prodigies of change, Tacitus reports the portents that occurred prior to the fall of Jerusalem to the Romans: contending hosts were seen meeting in the skies; arms flashed; the temple was suddenly illuminated by fire from the clouds; the doors of the shrine opened and a superhuman voice cried, "The gods are departing," and the noise of their departure was audible. Tacitus notes that Jews interpreted these omens as indicators of Jewish supremacy, but that in reality they pointed to the victory of Vespasian and Titus.[11] Similarly, according to the late-second-century historian Dio Cassius, the changes of government were foreshadowed by lightning bolts, earthquakes, floods, strange births of or behavior by animals. Doors opened of their own accord; eclipses occurred. Laughter and chatter in

8. Ibid., Vespasian, 7.
9. Ibid., Domitian, 15, 16.
10. Tacitus *Histories* 1.xxi.
11. Ibid., 5.xiii.

a foreign tongue from the empty senate house one night presaged Rome's loss of control of Britain.[12]

Although Josephus's earlier life seems to have been devoted to exploring the various facets of his own Jewish tradition—Sadducees, Essenes, and Pharisees—and although he for a time led Jewish fighters in the nationalistic effort against the Romans, his visit to Rome and his associations with the imperial family in A.D. 64 must have persuaded him of the futility of the revolt. But further, his literary outpourings show not only his admiration for Roman culture but his ability to adopt its cultural styles and conventions. This acculturation very likely began when he was still in Palestine, but it flourished during the extended period of his stay in Rome. The obvious symbol of this outlook is his adoption of the forename Flavius as an expression of his admiration for the family whose accession to power he had foreseen.

Especially in his *Jewish Wars*, Josephus makes a sharp distinction between the prophets (whom he regards as charlatans) who promise the credulous among the Jews that God will deliver them from the Roman oppressors in process of desecrating Jerusalem and its temple, and the portents (which he regards as authentic) of the impending destruction of the city.[13] In what was apparently intended as a reenactment of Israel's conquest of Canaan in the days of Joshua, a false prophet led thirty thousand Jews through the desert and up to the Mount of Olives, proposing to force an entrance to the city from there. Instead of the "salvation" (*sōtēria*) that these prophets promised, they were slaughtered by the Roman troops.[14] The portents, which perceptive persons—including, of course, Josephus—received as divine announcements (*kerygmata*) included a star resembling a sword that hovered over the city, a comet that remained visible for a year, a cow's giving birth to a lamb in the temple courts, a brilliant light that shone around the altar and the sanctuary in the middle of the night during the Feast of Unleavened Bread,

12. Dio Cassius, bk. 42. Self-opening doors are reported in 61, 63 (in the Temple of Jupiter Victor) and 63 (Nero's bedroom and the Mausoleum of Augustus). The latter is also narrated in 66.

13. Josephus *Jewish Wars* 6.285.

14. Ibid., 6.258–60.

chariots seen in the skies, and armies hurtling through the clouds. The eastern gate of the temple, made of brass and so massive that it took twenty men to move it, opened of itself, in spite of the bolts sunk into great blocks of stone that held it fast. The learned recognized that the security of the temple had gone and saw this as an omen of desolation.[15]

Josephus did allow for authentic oracles, in spite of his scornful dismissal of the Jewish eschatological prophets. He describes in detail the appearance in the temple, four years before the outbreak of the Jewish war of A.D. 66–70, of a rude peasant named Jesus, son of Ananias. Day and night in the streets and alleys he cried out, "A voice from the east, a voice from the west, a voice from the four winds . . . against Jerusalem and the sanctuary, against the bridegroom and the bride,[16] against all the people." Though arrested, chastised, and beaten he continued his crying out for seven years. The magistrates supposed him to have been under supernatural impulse (*daimoniōteron to kinēma*), which Josephus affirms was indeed the case, but he continued until, appropriately, he was struck and killed by a stone hurled from the ballista during the Roman attack on the city.[17] In this context Josephus offers the reader his own doctrine of portents: "Reflecting on these things one will find that God has a care for human beings, and by all kinds of premonitory signs (*prosēmainonta*) shows his people the way of salvation, while they owe their destruction to folly and calamities of their own choosing."[18]

It is difficult to determine the extent to which Josephus's inclusion of the portents was a matter of personal conviction about the direct intervention of the gods, or God, in human affairs, or whether it was required of him by the historical genre which he seems to have chosen as the model for his writings.

Although the Roman historians, including Josephus, are selective in the matter of which omens and prophecies they consider to be of divine origin, their apparent common credence in

15. Ibid., 6.288–98; 292–95.
16. For this image, compare Jeremiah 7:34.
17. Josephus *Jewish Wars* 6.300–05.
18. Ibid., 6.310.

portents contrasts with the less ambiguous attitude expressed in the mid-first century B.C. by Cicero in his treatise *De Divinatione*. Although he does not rule out the possibility of divination, including direct inspiration from the Divine Mind, he is such a thorough-going rationalist that he keeps returning to the theme that what to the credulous appears to be divination is actually the outcome of inductive reasoning, based on insight and experience. Although he does not rule out frenzy and inspiration as a means of divine communication, the important thing for Cicero is that the Divine Mind has a predetermined plan for the universe, and that to attuned human minds it reveals its purposes; for the gods to fail to do so would manifest a lack of love. Faith in the institution of divination rests finally, not on reason, but on results. In his later response to Quintus on the same subject however, Cicero took a more extreme position, in which he denounced divination as superstition, "which is widespread among the nations [and] has taken advantage of human weakness to cast its spell over the mind of almost every man."[19]

Cicero's final position on the subject seems to have had no effect on the Roman historians whose views we have sketched above. For them portents were the means by which the gods (or God) conveyed approval or disapproval of leaders, by which major shifts in human history were anticipated, and by which the perceptive could discern the divine purpose at work. Conversely, for these historians, those who ignored or misread the divine signs did so at their own peril.

Beginning with the rise of the Flavians, and mounting in importance in the Antonine period, another dimension of miracle is apparent in the writings of Roman historians: by performing miracles and by personal revelations, the rulers display a personal relationship with the divine. Although Dio Cassius was writing a century later than Suetonius and Tacitus, he matches them in depicting Vespasian as the first of the emperors through whom miracles were performed, and in locating that phenomenon in Egypt on the occasion of the emperor's stay in the shrine of Sarapis. This event we have touched on in chapter 4, in connection with the Isis cult. Suetonius reports the acclaim received

19. Cicero *De Divinatione* 1.xlix; 1.xiv, xlix; 1.xxxviii, lvi, xviii; 1.ii; 1.lxxii.

by Vespasian when he visited the Sarapion in Alexandria while awaiting favorable weather for his return to Rome, where he would assume the imperial power. He was greeted by an ailing freedman with the significant name of Basilides; healings were performed by Vespasian.[20] These incidents strengthened his position enormously when he arrived in Rome, Suetonius observes.[21]

Tacitus not only expands the details of the wonders wrought through Vespasian in Alexandria but also interrupts the flow of his narrative to describe the miraculous events by which the worship of Sarapis had been introduced in Alexandria in Ptolemaic times.[22] Among the *multa miracula* linked with Vespasian's visit to the Sarapion there were, as we have noted above, the cure of a blind devotee of the god through moistening his cheeks and eyes with spittle and the restoration of a crippled hand by walking on it. Physicians confirmed the appropriateness of the emperor's thaumaturgical methods.[23] Tacitus asserts that these wonders occurred "to mark the favor of heaven and a certain partiality of the gods toward him."[24]

In addition to the report of the two healing miracles performed by Vespasian, Dio Cassius notes that the Nile flooded on the day he entered Egypt. In this way, the divine (*to theion*) was signifying its choice of him. Before his death a comet appeared, the mausoleum of Augustus opened of its own accord, Vesuvius erupted, and giants appeared on the mountains and in the cities.[25]

From the first century on, the choice and coming to power of the emperors are depicted as accompanied by divine portents. But beginning with the Flavians, the gods are portrayed as more directly involved in the lives of the emperors, including the factor of the rulers' own religious convictions.

20. Suetonius, *Lives*, Vespasian 7; Josephus *Jewish Wars* 6.616.
21. Suetonius, *Lives*, Vespasian 8.
22. Tacitus *Histories* 4.lxxxiii–lxxxiv. Tacitus mentions that delay in transferring the statue of the god from Sinope to Alexandria so annoyed Sarapis that he took off by himself in a ship, arriving two days later in Alexandria.
23. Ibid., 4.lxxxi.
24. Ibid.
25. Dio Cassius, bk. 65; bk. 66.

Although there was precedent going back to Augustus for an emperor to be initiated into the Eleusinian mysteries,[26] there is evidence that from the time of Hadrian on, the emperors took their own relationship to the gods very seriously. Hadrian was initiated into the highest grade at Eleusis.[27] On the day before he was designated as emperor, he dreamed "that a fire descended out of heaven, the sky being perfectly clear and bright, and fell first upon the left side of his throat, passing then to the right, though it neither frightened nor injured him." He then wrote to the senate asking to be confirmed as emperor.[28] When his dear friend Antinous died, Hadrian saw a new star appear in heaven.[29] Marcus Aurelius's personal involvement with Greek religious tradition was evident in that, not only was he initiated into the Eleusinian mysteries, but he also founded and endowed a school of philosophy there.[30] An oracle at Mallus in Cilicia portrayed Commodus as Hercules strangling serpents—that is, as triumphing over his rivals.[31] So important was this tradition of portents as signs of divine approbation of the ruler that Dio Cassius, after preparing and sending to Severus a book of dreams and portents which point to his [Severus's] accession to power, was commissioned by the emperor to write his history after this fashion—an undertaking which Dio believed the gods had enabled him to do and which occupied him for ten years.[32]

Another facet of the life-world of the Antonine period is evident in some of the stories included by Dio in his history of this period: the rising interest in magic among the ruling classes. Hadrian, beset by ailments ranging from dropsy to consumption, gained respite from them by certain charms and magic rites (*magganeiois tisi kai goēteias*).[33] Marcus Aurelius was aided in a battle by an Egyptian magician who brought rain by means of

26. Suetonius *Augustus* xciii.
27. Dio Cassius 69.10.3.
28. Ibid., 69.2.
29. Ibid., 69.11.
30. Ibid., 72.31.
31. Ibid., 73.7.
32. Ibid., 73.23.
33. Ibid., 72.9.

enchantments. He also had a division of Christians who objected to his use of magicians and induced him to call on their God. God heard, and loosed a thunderbolt on the enemy and welcome rain on the Roman troops, which gave rise to the division's being named the Thundering Legion.

Yet another dimension of the miraculous in the Roman historical tradition can be seen in the very fact that an Egyptian magician appeared in the midst of Roman troops fighting far from Egypt and offered his services to the emperor. The figure of itinerant miracle-worker or prophet apparently became common in the later second century.[34] Fitting into this role—and in later-third-century romanticized form, serving as its paradigm[35]—is Apollonius of Tyana. He turns up in Dio's account of the death of Domitian, inasmuch as he publicly predicted the murder of the emperor at the very moment it was taking place. Summoning a crowd in Ephesus, or somewhere else—Dio is not quite sure of the location—he commended the assassin in far-off Italy.[36] It would appear, therefore, that by the opening of the second century the professional miracle-worker/itinerant oracle was a recognizable public figure, no longer confined to shrines of Apollo, the Sibyls, Asklepios, or Isis. We shall see that this popular model affects the way in which Christian literature portrays its prophets and wonder-workers in the later second century.

PORTENT IN THE GOSPEL OF MATTHEW

From the opening genealogy to the climactic story of the risen Jesus commissioning his disciples for their world mission, Matthew's gospel exhibits the conviction that, not only is God at work in the history of Jesus from before his birth to after his death,

---

34. The evidence for the rise of itinerant wonder-workers has been assembled and judiciously assessed by David L. Tiede, in *The Charismatic Figure as Miracle Worker* (SBLDS 1), (Missoula, Mont.: Scholars Press, 1972), p. 45.

35. The trustworthiness of Philostratus's sources and the aim of his *Life of Apollonius of Tyana* are discussed in chapter 8 below, pp. 256–58.

36. Dio Cassius *History* 67.18.

but also that he has disclosed that purpose through oracles, portents, dreams, and miracles for those with the insight to discern the divine purpose. The distinctiveness of Matthew in these matters is readily apparent to the careful reader, since these features show up in material which is unique to Matthew or which we can tell he has reworked by comparing it to his major sources, Mark and Q.

Matthew's version of the genealogy of Jesus, which is significantly different from beginning to end from that found in Luke 3:23–38, shows the divine predestinarian symmetry: God has arranged the pattern of procreation among his people so that from the progenitor of the covenant people, Abraham, to David, Israel's paradigmatic king, is precisely fourteen generations. From David to the great historical tragedy of the Babylonian exile there are fourteen generations, as there are from the time of Israel's restoration in the land to the birth of her redeemer (Mt 1:1–16). Lest anyone miss the point of the divinely imposed order of human history, Matthew does the addition for the reader, and presents him in 1:17 with the arithmetic and theological results.

The portents recounted by Matthew encompass the entire career of Jesus, beginning, as we might expect, with his birth. Mary was pregnant by the Holy Spirit before she and her betrothed ever had sexual intercourse (1:18). Far off in "the East" certain magi observed the star, which they understood to portend the birth of the King of the Jews, and followed it to the land of his impending birth (2:1–2). Word of the portent of a royal birth was profoundly troubling both to the incumbent, Herod, and to the whole populace of Jerusalem (2:3). Astrological consultation between the Magi and Herod points to Bethlehem as the place of the child's birth, and the movement of the star confirms that opinion (2:7–9). The homage paid by the wider world to Jesus is foreshadowed in the gifts presented by the magi at his manger (2:11), just as the slaughter of the innocents by Herod presages the judgment on Israel which the writer understands to have occurred when the Romans harshly suppressed the Jewish revolt in A.D. 70 and destroyed the Temple in Jerusalem (2:16–18). An even more direct prediction has been introduced by Matthew into a parable from the Q tradition (cf. Lk 14:16–24), according to which the (Jewish) refusal to accept the invitation to the (eschatological) feast has these results: "The king was angry, and he sent his troops and destroyed those murderers and burned their city" (22:7).

In Mark 8:29, Peter responds to Jesus' inquiry about who his disciples think he is with the correct but ill-defined answer, "the Messiah." That term had a wide range of connotations for first-century Judaism, from High Priest to organizer of a revolution against the Romans. But in Matthew 16:16–19, not only does Peter answer in the form of a liturgical formula, "You are the Christ, the Son of the living God," but Jesus also responds with a prediction, not of an eschatological sign, but of an institutional foundation ("on this rock I will build my church"), complete with provision for ecclesiastical courts ("whatever you bind . . . whatever you loose"). It is the establishment of the church which serves as the major sign of God's authorization of Jesus, according to Matthew.

Other portents point in various ways to the divine vindication of Jesus in Matthew's account. Unlike Mark and Luke, according to which the heavenly voice addresses Jesus personally ("Thou art my beloved Son," Mk 1:11; Lk 3:22), Matthew reports a public announcement: "This is my beloved Son." (3:17). Jesus' independence of earthly authority is divinely attested in the incident of finding a coin in the mouth of a fish to pay his temple tax, and in the explicit interpretation placed on this miracle (Mt 17:24–27). This story recalls those told about the rabbis, whose teaching receives divine corroboration through miraculous events.[37] Ominous signs connected with Jesus' death—only in Matthew's account—include the suicidal death of his betrayer, Judas, by hanging (27:3–10); the earthquake, the rock-splitting, the emergence of dead saints from the tombs (27:52–53); the earthquake at the moment of Jesus' resurrection (28:2); the appearance of an angel to roll back the tombstone and to over-

37. The classic study by Paul Fiebig (chap. 5, n. 11) has been challenged on the ground that it anachronistically uses material from the second century and later, though claiming to offer a historical picture of Jewish miracle-workers in the first century.

come with terror the guard placed at the tomb (28:2–3); Jesus' appearances to the women in Jerusalem (28:9–10) and to the disciples in Galilee (28:16–20). All these incidents enhance the divine aura that surrounds the figure of Jesus and confirm his place in the divine purpose.

One story in this Gospel which not only provides a portent but also demonstrates Jesus' powers and links him with oracles (in this case, the Jewish scriptures) is that of the acclamation he received from children in the Temple on the occasion of his last visit there (21:15–16). Jesus was sought out in the temple courts by the blind and the lame. We know from the Q tradition that the early Christians saw in this capacity to heal, a fulfillment of the Prophets (see chap. 5). But when the children began to honor him as Son of David, in spite of the indignation of the priests, Jesus defended their honoring him by quoting from Psalm 8:2 the words about children offering perfect praise. The focus here is on the authority of Jesus, not—as in Mark and Q—on the signs of the New Age breaking into the present. The stories of Jesus' birth and childhood are studded with references to the divine purpose being achieved through the fulfillment of scriptural oracles: in his miraculous birth (1:22); in the priests' expectation that the child would be born in Bethlehem (2:4–6); in the return of Jesus and his family from Egypt (2:15);[38] the slaughter of the innocent male children by Herod (2:16–18); the choice of locale for Jesus' ministry (4:13–16); the decision of Joseph to take up residence in Nazareth (2:23).

Before turning to Matthew's handling of the stories of Jesus'

38. This prophecy from Hosea 11 refers to the Exodus of Israel from Egypt under Moses. In the text, "my son" is an unambiguous designation for the nation, Israel. But Matthew, like other scribes—in Christianity, among the rabbis, and at Qumran—was more concerned with what a prophecy could be made to mean in the setting of the scribal interpreter than in what the original author intended by it. Similarly, there is no mention of Nazareth or Nazarene in the Jewish Bible, but Matthew has apparently done what can be seen among the scribes at Qumran: he has taken the consonants of the Hebrew text of Isaiah 11:1, in which the Messiah is called a "shoot" (= *n-tz-r*, in Hebrew) and, by providing it with different vowels (which can be done readily in Semitic languages), he has produced a prophecy about Jesus' coming from the obscure hamlet of Nazareth.

miracles, I should mention one other medium through which the gospel writer, like his contemporary Roman and Jewish historians, understood the gods (or God) to communicate their will in history to their chosen instruments: dreams. Joseph is instructed in a dream about the meaning of Mary's pregnancy and his line of response (1:20). The Magi are warned in a dream not to report back to Herod (2:12). Joseph is told by an angel in a dream to take Mary and the Child to Egypt (2:13), just as he is instructed to return to Palestine (2:19) and to move to Galilee (2:22). Pilate's wife is warned in a dream that to harm Jesus is to invite suffering through divine punishment.

After noting that Matthew has devoted so much space to the miraculous preparations for and events within the career of Jesus, it is surprising to observe that the stories of miracles actually performed by Jesus are told in condensed form in Matthew (as compared with Mark or Q), and some are omitted entirely.[39] The other miracle stories are abbreviated, some of them drastically. Receiving the least space in the stories that Matthew has retained are the more detailed accounts of the mode or circumstances of the healing or exorcism. What Matthew is interested in instead is (1) the faith of the beneficiaries and (2) the authority by which Jesus is able to produce results. For example, his brief version of Healing the Paralytic (Mk 2:1–12) ends with the description of the fear of the crowds who "glorified God, who had given such authority to men" (9:8). A comparison of Mt 12 with the parallel accounts is instructive in this regard. In verses 5–6, which Matthew has placed in the middle of the Markan story of Jesus' condoning sabbath violation by his disciples, there appears an announcement that "something greater than the temple is here" (i.e., Jesus), and the case is rounded out by a quotation from scripture.

In Matthew's version (12:15–21) of the Markan summary of Jesus' healing activity (Mk 3:7–12), the healing is mentioned, but only as a prelude to confirmation from scripture of the divine

39. Among the stories omitted by Matthew from his Markan prototype are the exorcism in the synagogue (= Mk 1:21–28); the deaf mute (= Mk 7:31–37); the blind man of Bethsaida (= Mk 8:22–46); and the strange exorcist (= Mk 9:38–41).

mission of Jesus. In a brief depiction of Jesus as curing a blind and dumb demoniac (Q parallel in Lk 11:14), the climax is in the rhetorical question "Can this be the Son of David?" In another Q passage (Mt 12:38–42 = Lk 11:29–32) Matthew adds a unique detail: the sign of Jonah, which for Luke is the preaching of repentance by Jonah, has become Jonah's being swallowed by the whale and after three days and nights brought back: a sign of Jesus' resurrection. In Matthew's editing of the summary statements about Jesus' healing in Mk 1:32–34 and 39 (Mt 4:23–25 and 8:16–17), there is an emphasis on Jesus' ability to heal every afflicted person, and there are specific references to the fulfillment of scripture that his healing achieves (Is 53:4). Similarly, in Matthew 9:35 and 10:1, Jesus' authority and its extension to the disciples include power over "every disease and every infirmity." In his version of the Feeding of the Four Thousand (Mt 15:32–39 = Mk 8:1–10), Matthew goes so far as to say that the fish with which Jesus began the crowd-feeding process were few and small. Jesus' final miracle on the way to Jerusalem (Mk 10:46–52 = Mt 20:29–34) is to heal, not one, but two blind men. In the two miracle stories which are found only in Matthew (9:27–32; 9:32–34), the main focus is on Jesus' ability ("Do you believe I am able to do this?") and on his uniqueness ("Never was anything like this seen in Israel").

In adapting the Markan summaries of Jesus' miracles to serve his own special purposes, Matthew has sought to make an important point that once more recalls the function of miracle in the rabbinic tradition: to lend authority to Jesus' activity, and especially to his interpretation of the Law. It is no accident, therefore, that the first of the extended summaries (Mt 4:23–25) not only emphasizes Jesus' teaching and preaching activities but also leads directly into his most extended discourse section, which we know as the Sermon on the Mount (Mt 5–7). Similarly, Matthew's expanded version of Jesus' commissioning the twelve disciples to carry forward his work (10:1–40 = Mk 6:6–13) links his teaching and preaching with his healing activity. Perhaps the most dramatic instance of Matthew's modification of the tradition to exploit miracle as support for the authority and divine identity of Jesus occurs in his version of the crucifixion scene.

After introducing details of earthquake and angel visitation (which we have noted above), he depicts the centurion coming to faith, along with other onlookers. In Mk 15:39, we read that when the centurion "saw that he (Jesus) thus breathed his last, he said, 'Truly this man was a son of God.'" In Mt 27:54, on the other hand, we are told: "When the centurion and those who were with him . . . *saw the earthquake and what took place, they were filled with awe,* and said, 'Truly this was a son of God'" (italics mine). The Roman historians' argument from portent and the rabbinic argument from signs of divine approbation have been joined together in Matthew.

That these two cultural streams should flow together in the service of early Christian propaganda should not be in the least surprising. Josephus offers abundant evidence of one who absorbed and utilized Roman historiography to offer the lengthy works which are simultaneously an apology for his religious tradition and for himself, for having sided with the Romans against his coreligionists' nationalistic uprising. As careful studies of Judaism in the period of the Second Temple have shown,[40] Hellenistic language and concepts had deeply permeated the life and thought of Jews, not only in the wider Jewish dispersion, but also in Palestine itself. Matthew, wherever it was written, seems to reflect Roman literary style, although the author affirms much that is central to the Jewish heritage out of which he had come to Christian faith: the centrality of Israel's twelve tribes in God's purpose (10:6), the eternity of the Law (5:18); that the twelve tribes will share in the eschatological age (19:28). Thus, although he regards Jesus as a radical interpreter of the Law and the covenant people as including Gentiles as well as Jews (cf. Mt 5, "You have heard it said of old—but I say to you"; 28:18–20), the pervasive appeal to scripture and to precedent from Jewish history for confirmation of Jesus' role shows that Matthew is building his new Christian structure on a Jewish foundation. In

40. Saul Liebermann, *Greek in Jewish Palestine* (New York: Jewish Theological Seminary, 1942); V. Tcherikower, *Hellenistic Civilization and the Jews* (Philadelphia: Fortress, 1961); Martin Hengel, *Judaism and Hellenism* (Philadelphia and London: SCM, 1974).

developing his apologetic strategy, he utilizes miracle in the distinctive ways we have traced.

TELLING THE STORY IN GRAECO-ROMAN STYLE: LUKE AND ACTS

Although Luke shares with Matthew the concern to demonstrate the continuities between his community and that of Israel, he differs significantly from his fellow evangelist in style, strategy, and assumptions. Each of these factors influences and is influenced by the way Luke treats the element of the miraculous in his two-volume account, Luke-Acts.[41] Fundamental to all that Luke writes are his knowledge of Graeco-Roman culture and his ability to exploit that familiarity to enhance the effectiveness of his propagandistic undertaking.

Henry J. Cadbury's classic studies of the style and literary methods of Luke[42] showed—and subsequent work has not substantively modified the conclusion[43]—that Luke was familiar with the methods of Hellenistic historians and adapted them to serve his own ends. He not merely conformed his story to the dominant historiographical and literary conventions of his time, but transformed them under the influence of the tradition on which his work was based in order to achieve his own special aims. Thus, for example, the practice of depicting lives of famous men in accounts that draw recurrent parallels is apparent in Luke's implicit comparisons between Jesus and John the Baptist, between Jesus and Paul, and between the exploits of Jesus and those of the Apostles. Yet he does not allow his reader to forget the unique role that Jesus plays in the story as a whole.

41. A summary discussion of the literary origins of Luke-Acts is in W. G. Kümmel, *Introduction to the New Testament* (Nashville [and London]: Abingdon [SCM] 1975), pp. 122–51.

42. Henry Joel Cadbury, *The Style and Literary Method of Luke-Acts* (Cambridge: Harvard University Press, 1919–20); *The Making of Luke-Acts* (repr. Naperville, Ill.: Allenson, 1958).

43. An important analysis of literary details in Luke-Acts which correspond to those of Hellenistic biographies is offered by Charles H. Talbert in *Literary Patterns, Theological Themes, and the Genre of Luke-Acts* (Missoula, Mont.: Scholars Press, 1974). Taken as a complete work, however, Luke-Acts does not conform to the Hellenistic biographical genre.

Most striking among the literary conventions employed by Luke is the sophisticated, formal proem with which the work opens (Lk 1:1–4), together with its pale counterpart in Acts 1:1–3. Characteristic features include the mention of the author's aim, the work of his predecessors, and his patron's name.[44] But what is important is to discern from the work itself the aims not overtly mentioned in the prologue; with these we shall be concerned below.

Another feature of Hellenistic historiography which Luke exploits for his own ends is the composition of speeches for the leading characters in the narrative. Luke had precedent for this in the tradition he shared with the other evangelists, of course: the collection of parables and the apocalyptic discourse in Mark; the extensive sayings materials which Matthew grouped in his discourse sections.[45] But a comparison of Luke 4:16–30 with the correlative passage in Mark 6:1–6 shows how greatly Luke has expanded the passage and relocated it in Jesus' career in order to portray Jesus as presenting an inaugural address, according to which he launches his public ministry, specifies the source of his authority ("the Spirit of the Lord has anointed me"), defends his extension of salvation to non-Israelites, anticipates the hostility he will encounter, and places the entire enterprise in the context of the fulfillment of scripture: "Today this scripture has been fulfilled in your hearing." In Acts, the speeches attributed to the Apostles serve a variety of special aims for Luke: to ground the worldwide mission of the church in the divine purpose as foretold in scripture (2:16); to locate what God is doing through Jesus in the framework of the history of Israel (6:1–53); to justify the opening of membership in the covenant people to non-Jews (10:34–43); to show how an informed Christian can make effective contact with pagan intellectuals (17:22–31) and how Christians can defend themselves in civil cases when under accusation of civil disobedience (22–26). It is not merely that Luke

44. "Theophilus" (Lk 1:3) is more likely a symbolic indication that the book is addressed to "friends of God" than the name of an actual patron.

45. For a discussion of the alternating panels of narrative and discourse in Matthew, see my *Jesus in History*, 2d ed. (New York: Harcourt Brace, 1977), pp. 168–72.

knows how to imitate Hellenistic historians in writing speeches, but that he takes advantage of his literary knowledge and skill to make points that were deemed by him to be important for the Christians of his day and situation.

Another literary convention (discussed more fully below) adapted by Luke is that of establishing historical and chronological cross-references between well-known persons and events, on one hand, and the actors and events he is describing in his own narrative, on the other. In an era when there was no universal chronology this was useful for any writer, but Luke takes advantage of this historiographical convention to underscore his point that what happened through and to Jesus and his followers was acted out in full public view. As he phrases it, in a litotes characteristic of his epoch, "This thing was not done in a corner" (Acts 26:26). Accordingly, he supplements the account of Jesus' hearing before Pilate (cf. Mk 15:2–6 with Lk 23:2–16) with a report of a judicial consultation between Pilate and Herod Antipas about the fate of Jesus.[46] In the career of Paul, similar stress is laid on the public nature of his activities and, above all, on the public testimony by him as to the aim and essence of his work. This is evident in the incident of the would-be worshipers of Paul and Barnabas as Zeus and Hermes (Acts 14:8–18), in the illegal seizure of Paul at Philippi and the subsequent official apology (Acts 16:16–40), in Paul's speech at the Areopagus in Athens (Acts 17:22–33), in his defense by Gallio the governor of Corinth (Acts 18:12–17) and by the town clerk at Ephesus (Acts 19:23–41), as well as by his own *apologiae* before a succession of Roman governors and bureaucrats in Acts 22 to 25. The import is clear: there was nothing secret or subversive about this movement. Only Luke among the New Testament writers attends to this point, and he does so by employing for his own ends the literary and rhetorical conventions of his time.

Literally, the most dramatic of all the literary strategies drawn

46. On the other hand, he omits the story of Herod's irresponsible assent to the death of John the Baptist (Mk 6:17–29), probably because it reflects unfavorably on the role of a Roman-appointed civil official. Conversely, Herod Agrippa's attack on the church (Acts 12:1–23) is represented as a misguided effort to appease the Jewish leaders and, in the view of the author, an unwarranted act of hostility toward a group—the Christians—that is apolitical.

upon by Luke is that of the Hellenistic romance, which we considered briefly in connection with the Isis cult. Indeed, this genre seems to have emerged in second century B.C., perhaps even in association with the Isis cult of that era. Its antecedents were likely the oral narrators associated with her cult, who recounted her acts on behalf of her devotees, including deliverances of the faithful through trials on land and sea, works of healing performed by her in response to petitioners, and other extraordinary manifestations of her sovereignty.[47] The dominant function of the romance apparently became propaganda in connection with a cult: the earliest surviving example may be the *Ephesiaca* of Xenophon;[48] the best known is the *Metamorphoses* of Apuleius, written about three centuries later and demonstrating the genre at what was very likely the apex of its development.[49] The liter-

47. A brief sketch and bibliography of the Hellenistic romance has been offered in connection with the later Isis cult in chap. 4 above, pp. 132–34.

48. Dating from the early second century B.C., Merkelbach (in *Roman und Mysterium in der Antike* (Munich and Berlin: Beck, 1962), conjectures that similar texts appeared at least one hundred years earlier than that (p. 336). The *Ephesiaca* was reworked in the third century A.D. as propaganda for the Sol Invictus cult. Originally in ten books, the extant text interrupts the narrative and ends with a dedication to Isis for her *aretai*, and especially for her benefactions to the pair who are the central figures in the romance (p. 113), whose passionate love and marriage—with a mixture of suffering and fulfillment—are clearly symbolic of the Isis-Osiris relationship, or that of Eros and Psyche (p. 94). Fidelity in time of danger and temptation is an essential feature of this mystical piety (p. 99). Other candidates for the earliest of the romances include Chariton and the Ninos fragments. The most recently published romance, which is partially preserved in a papyrus copy (P. Colon inv. 3328), is edited by Albert Henrichs (*Die Phoinikika des Lollianos, Fragmente eines neues griechischen Romans*, Bonn: Rudolf Habelt, 1972). Henrichs shows that the author wants to claim that his work was written by Lollianos, a rhetorician in the reign of Hadrian, but that the work actually dates from the last third of the second century. Written in a "graceless" style (p. 25), the romance resembles the apocryphal gospels and Acts (p. 52), though its mythological base is in the Dionysus-Zagreus cult, said to be of Phoenician origin, and its cultic practices include child sacrifice and anthropophagy. On the analogies of the later romances with the New Testament apocrypha, see chap. 8 below, and R. Söder, *Die apokryphen Apostelgeschichten und die romanhafte Literatur der Antike* (Würzburger Studien zur Altertumswissenschaft, Heft 3. Stuttgart, 1932).

49. Merkelbach notes that, following the appearances of what he calls "Parody Romances," such as those of Petronius, Apuleius restored the original intent of the romance: as propaganda for a cult—in this instance, of Isis (pp. 337–38).

ary strategy of the romance lies in the sheer fascination of the narrative itself, but that is the means, not the end. The aim of the writing is to foster devotion to the god, and to do so by describing the experiences of the main characters in ways that mirror or even reenact the experiences of the god, as told in the mythical stories of the divine struggles and triumph. Thus, the story of the journey of Osiris across the sea from Byblos to Egypt and of the conflicts which led to his dismemberment and his being thrown into the waters of the Nile find an echo in the difficulties and deliverance-at-sea experiences of the hero and heroine of the *Ephesiaca*.

There is no reason to suppose that Luke merely invented material to serve as a basis for a Christian "romance" about Jesus and the Apostles (especially Paul). Rather, the tradition has been drawn upon and developed in such a manner as to serve this propaganda aim, thereby providing an inherently interesting story of the life, travels, and destiny of a divine figure (Jesus), and the reenactment of his experiences by his followers, culminating in death but promising ultimate vindication. The details of the stories told in Acts about confrontation with the authorities, about the perilous sea voyage and miraculous deliverance (Acts 27–28) and the sufferings experienced by the Apostles are seen as essential features of the divine plan. They serve, therefore, as assurances to a community which is threatened with or actually experiencing similar opposition. Both the basic "myth"—the story of Jesus—and the narratives of his followers serve to demonstrate in a currently popular mode of religious propaganda the basis for Christian faith and the ground of its efficacy as a way of life.

As B. E. Perry has shown in his fundamental study of the Hellenistic romance, this was not a fixed literary genre to which the author was compelled to conform. Rather, one must ask concerning each romance what the specific and distinctive aim of the author was, in the interest of which he reworked the flexible form we know as the romance. Perry observes that the reshaping of a genre like the romance is in part the consequence of the way in which "the outlook and interests of society as a whole change with the passage of time and historical experience" but that it also is affected by the specific aims of the individual writer.[50] The genre provides a literary opportunity; it is not a rigid mold demanding conformity. The dialectic between the influence of the genre of romance and the author's intent to use that form for his distinctive aims is clearly evident in Luke-Acts.

Unlike the Isis cult, which had a widely known mythological base, Luke could not merely presuppose the "myth" that was both the ground of the Jesus cult and the model for the lives of its devotees. He had to make that mythological base explicit. Its outlines and details were shaped by two central factors: the Jewish scriptural tradition and the Jesus tradition, and it was known to Luke through Mark, Q, and the other sources available to him.

For Luke, as for all the early Christians,[51] the figure of Jesus was to be understood only in continuity with the covenant people Israel, whose story and changing life-world were set forth in the Jewish scriptures. The Lukan equivalent of the Isis myth in *Ephesiaca* is the story of God's redemptive purpose for his creation as launched in the time of the patriarchs and heroes of ancient Israel, as portrayed in its later stages through the Prophets, and as culminating in the career of Jesus. Instead of a simple myth, Luke offers a mythology or theology of history. The climax of that story is set forth in volume 1 of his work, which we know as the Gospel of Luke. Drawing on contemporary styles of historiography, biography, and romance, Luke presents in Jesus the culmination of that sacred history. By contrast with Matthew's aim, Luke goes beyond the redefinition of the covenant community to show the divinely ordained role of Jesus in the universal purpose of God, as we shall note in detail below.

The universal framework of Luke's life-world is apparent in his tracing the genealogy of Jesus back to Adam (Lk 3:38), in the Nunc Dimittis of the aged Simeon ("mine eyes have seen thy salvation, which Thou hast prepared in the presence of *all people*, a light for revelation to the Gentiles, and for glory to thy people

50. B. E. Perry, as we noted (chap. 4, n. 92) warns against regarding the romance or any other genre as a fixed pattern. See his *Ancient Romances*, pp. 18–30.

51. Marcion, who rejected the Old Testament and its God, was an exception, and was in turn regarded as a heretic by the overwhelming majority of the church.

Israel," Lk 2:30–31). But this universalistic outlook is especially
evident in the words from Isaiah read by Jesus as the basis of his
sermon in the synagogue at Nazareth (4:18) and the prediction
(3:6), "All flesh shall see the salvation of God." Equally emphatic,
however, is the insistence on continuity between what God has
been working out in the past and what he is about to achieve in
the future through Jesus. The annunciation by the angel to Mary
that she is to have a child without human conception promises
the child's ascent to the throne of David and his reign forever
over the house of Jacob (1:32–33). Mary's response in the Mag-
nificat assures help to God's "servant Israel" and fulfillment of
the promise made "to Abraham and his posterity forever" (Lk
1:54–55). Similar assurances are offered in the Benedictus (Lk
1:67–69) in connection with the role of John the Baptist, which is
linked with the fulfillment of prophetic expectations (Lk 3:4–6)
and which involves the redefinition of the heirs of God's covenant
with Abraham (Lk 3:8) to include non-Israelites. In material
unique to Luke (24:27,44), he represents Jesus as making the
sweeping claim that all the Jewish scriptures speak of him and
find their fulfillment through him: "Moses, and the prophets and
the psalms."[52]

It is only in Acts that the encompassing framework of divinely
shaped history is made explicit. A microcosm of the worldwide
inclusiveness of the covenant community is to be seen, according
to Acts 2, on the day of Pentecost, when the Spirit is poured out
"upon all flesh" (Acts 2:17), as represented by the pious who
come from "every nation under heaven" (2:5). Their experience
of the Spirit is said to be in fulfillment of prophecy (Joel 2:28–
32, which is quoted in the LXX[53] version in Acts 2:17–20), and

---

52. In addition to material found in the parallel passage in Matthew (Lk 3:7–
9 = Mt 3:7–10), Luke has special tradition implying the openness of the Lukan
community, in words attributed to Jesus, toward those who by Jewish standards
would be outsiders—namely, tax-collectors and soldiers (Lk 3:10–14).

53. The author of Luke-Acts has steeped himself in the biblical style, as he
knew it through the Septuagint. Especially in the hymns and prophecies of Luke
1–2 and in some of the narrative passages in Acts (5:11–16; 7:1–53; 9:11, 32;
12:1 ff.; 14:1–18; 15:16–18) this style is evident.

in the claim that what David and the Prophets looked forward to has now begun to be fulfilled through Jesus (Acts 2:22–36).

Similarly, Peter's sermon in the temple (Acts 3) builds on the promises made by "the God of Abraham, Isaac and Jacob," but "Peter" sees now in Jesus the promise attributed to Moses (Dt 18:15–16) that in the later time God will send a prophet like Moses, to whom the covenant people will listen. His listeners are "the sons of the prophets and the covenant"; it is incumbent upon them to give heed now to the ultimate Prophet whom God has sent among them: Jesus.

The longest of the sermons in Acts, that of Stephen (Acts 7) consists mostly of a historical resumé of the dealings of God with the covenant people, from Abraham down to the time of Jesus, with special details about the call of Abraham, the migration of the sons of Jacob to Israel, their deliverance from slavery through Moses, their lapse into idolatry, their establishment in the land, and the eventual construction of God's house there. But suddenly the sermon turns to an attack on the nation as characteristically hostile to the voice of God and to his prophetic messengers, climaxing now in their rejection of Jesus, whose coming the older Prophets had foretold. The point is clear: *God is in control of history*. The promises made to the patriarchs and the predictions of the Prophets looked forward to the coming of the Final Prophet. Yet those who ought to have recognized and received him did not, with the consequence that membership in his people is now open to all humanity.

The central figure in the transition of the divine plan of history from promise to fulfillment is John the Baptist: "The law and the prophets were until John; since then the Kingdom of God is preached and everyone struggles to enter it" (Lk 16:16). Although Jesus is now visibly withdrawn from the world (Lk 24:51; Acts 1:9), the eyes of faith can perceive him already standing at God's right hand (Acts 7:56) and the faithful await his triumphant return (Acts 1:11). Meanwhile the Spirit which he has poured out on his followers (Acts 2:33) enables them to carry forward the work he inaugurated and to extend it to the ends of the earth (Acts 1:8). The narrative of Acts moves the

center of God's action from the ancestral city of the Jews, Jerusalem, to the capital of the Gentile powers, Rome. The geographical shift is symbolic of the ethnic and cultural shift in definition of who God's people are. Together Luke and Acts place
that process in a framework of cosmic history. The covenant
community is seen to be inclusive economically,[54] ethnically,[55]
sexually,[56] ritually[57] and socially.[58]

The cosmic redemption to which the author of Luke-Acts looks
forward is depicted with images drawn from the Jewish tradition, but from the wider Hellenistic-Roman culture as well.
Throughout both volumes of this work there are constant references to the promises made to David concerning the kingship.
They are first enunciated prior to his birth in the message of
Gabriel to Mary (Lk 1:27, 32). The legal links with David are
established through Joseph, Jesus' legal father, through his birth
in the royal town of David, Bethlehem (2:4,11), and through his
Davidic ancestry (Lk 3:31).[59] The connection between David as
king and Jesus is made explicit in Paul's sermon at the synagogue in Antioch of Pisidia (Acts 13:22–23), where we read
that from David's posterity God has brought to Israel the savior-
king, as promised. Elsewhere in Acts, David appears as prophet
or psalmist, whose predictions look forward to the coming of

54. Among texts which point up the inclusion of the poor and those who by
reason of station in life or occupation might be excluded from the covenant
community are Luke 2:6–7; 4:18–19; 5:1–11; 6:20–49; 14:15–30; 16:19–31;
Acts 2:44–45; 4:32–37; 6:1–6; 8:1; 13:50.

55. The inclusion of the Gentiles, especially as symbolized by the Samaritans,
is pervasive in Acts 4:23–28; 11:19–25; 2:9–11; 8:4–24; 9:15; 28:2.

56. The unusual importance attached to the place of women within the community, in contrast to the severe limitations on women in Jewish and wider Roman society, may be noted in Luke 2:36–37; 8:1–3; 10:38–42; 23:49, 53–56;
24:1–11; Acts 5:12–16; 13:50; 16:15.

57. Religious and ritual inclusiveness are set out in Luke 3:4–6; 6:17–19;
7:1–17; 7:31–35; 10:1–12; 10:29–37; 15:11–32; 17:1–2; 17:11–19; 18:15–17;
Acts 11:19–25.

58. Inclusion across Jewish social and occupational barriers is apparent in
Luke 3:10–14; 5:28–39; 7:29–30; 18:9–14; 19:1–10; Acts 9:43.

59. The enigmatic question about how "Messiah" can be both Son and Lord
of David is reproduced almost unaltered from Mark (Mk 12:35–37 = Lk 20:41–
44).

the Messiah.[60] Nevertheless, the emphasis is on continuity with David as king and spokesman for God; in both capacities, the promises to David find fulfillment in Jesus. From before his birth until after his resurrection, those who looked for Jesus' coming (Lk 2:38) and his intimate followers (Lk 24:21) expected him to accomplish "the redemption of Israel"—though presumably they thought of this along nationalistic lines, and therefore stood in need of correction.

We have already noted Luke's strategy of showing the links between the activities of Jesus and the Apostles on one hand and the authority figures of the Roman world on the other: magistrates, governors, and kings. Yet it is clear that earthly authorities were not really in control. Herod Antipas's effort to halt the gospel by imprisoning John the Baptist had failed (Lk 3:18–20). The wife of a member of Herod's administrative staff was a financial supporter of Jesus (Lk 8:1–3). A report to Jesus that Herod was trying to kill him was met by the flat declaration that the course of his career, including his death, was in God's hands, not Herod's (Lk 13:31–33).

Luke's exploitation of literary conventions of his day has also been remarked earlier. But it should also be noted that Luke uses pagan religion, philosophy, and poetry as a starting point for making his case for Christianity, especially in Acts. The address to those at Lystra who want to acclaim Paul and Silas as gods in their midst, as a consequence of the healing of a cripple by Paul, is a basic statement of a Stoic view of natural law. According to this doctrine, the order and fertility of the universe bear witness to the divine power which established it and sustains it. Paul is described as eager to move beyond that point, but thus far there is no basic conflict between his depiction of divine providence and what many devout pagans would affirm. In the address to the Areopagites in Athens, Paul's point of departure is a rejection of idol worship in favor of the god within, attested by philosophers (Epimenides)[61] and poets (Aratus). Paul

60. For example, in Acts 1:16; 2:25, 29, 34; 4:25–26, 34; 7:46; 15:16.

61. The passage is attributed to Epimenides and is surely compatible with the popular, pious, philosophical notion that the gods' providential ordering of the universe is in accord with natural law.

is reported even to go so far as to identify the God whom he proclaims with the object of their ignorant (*agnostos*) search (Acts 17:23–31). Although his turning to the theme of the resurrection of Jesus leaves behind the pagan Hellenistic sources and his Hellenistic hearers as well, there is no mistaking the strategy which seeks to build on universal religious and philosophical aspiration and to affirm, where possible, the authenticity of the human search for God.

THE DIVINE PURPOSE AT WORK THROUGH HISTORY

Yet for the author of Luke-Acts, it was not primarily in the ordering of the universe in accord with natural law that God was evident. Rather, it was in special manifestations of his power and purpose that those with true insight could discern within history the hand of God at work. The central focus of the divine purposive action within history, for both the people of God and for the creation as a whole, is what Luke refers to throughout his two volumes as "the Kingdom of God."

Although in the opening part of Luke the theme of kingdom is linked with the Davidic ancestry of Jesus (as in Lk 1:33) or with "the redemption of Jerusalem" (Lk 2:38), it becomes clear in the course of the work as a whole that to identify God's purpose with the traditional notions of Israel's achieving political or religious independence as a state or discrete community is to misconceive the divine intention. That estimate is confirmed by the misguided expressions of disappointment on the part of the disciples in the post-Resurrection scenes (Lk 24:21; Acts 1:6), according to which they speak of their forlorn hopes that Jesus would restore the kingdom to Israel. Even Joseph of Arimathea, in his generous and politically dangerous act of taking the body of Jesus for burial, attests to his "looking for the kingdom of God" (Lk 23:51), but gives no indication that he knows what sort of kingdom Jesus is to bring. From all that Luke has to say about the kingdom, and from all his careful indications that neither Jesus nor any of the Apostles was engaged in politically subversive activity, it can be inferred that for him "kingdom" connotes something very different from the traditional nationalistic aspirations.

For Luke the principal quality of the kingdom is set forth in a saying of Jesus found nowhere except in Luke's gospel: "Fear not, little flock, for it is your Father's good pleasure to give you the kingdom" (Lk 12:32).[62] The kingdom is not a human achievement but a divine gift, yet to be bestowed, although the faithful have already entered into its way of life. For the community of Luke, Jesus had already inaugurated the kingdom. Even John the Baptist, important though he was as the one who prepared for Jesus' coming (Lk 3:1–17) in fulfillment of scripture (Lk 3:4–6 = Is 40:3–5), was not a participant in the kingdom (Lk 7:28). Indeed, it is not the rich or the wise by human standards or the powerful who share in the kingdom. It is the children (18:16–17), the poor (6:20; 18:22–25), those who scorn the ordinary structures of personal identity and stability such as the family (Lk 18:29), who enter the kingdom. Sacrifice in order to attain participation in the kingdom means turning one's back on parents and means of livelihood (Lk 9:62). To share in the kingdom is not a reward for traditional or inherited piety. Instead, it is the penitent outsiders (Lk 13:28–29; 14:15–23) who enter the kingdom. The inclusiveness of the kingdom is symbolized in the instruction to invite to the "feast . . . the poor, the maimed, the blind, the lame" (Lk 14:14). It is in terms of his ministry to precisely these types of needy persons that Jesus defends his activity in response to a challenge from the imprisoned John the Baptist (Lk 7:18–23). The nature of the kingdom Jesus announces and the process by which it is coming are not humanly recognizable, even though the evidences of the kingdom are matters of public record. Rather, the truth about the kingdom is a secret that God has vouchsafed to his own (Lk 8:10),

62. Luke appends this saying to one found also in Matthew, "Seek his kingdom, and all these things [which ordinary people strive to gain] shall be yours as well" (Lk 12:31). The parallel passage in Matthew (Mt 6:33) ties in with the achievement of righteousness, which is central to Matthew's gospel as a whole. For Matthew, the church, through obedience to Jesus' new law, becomes what traditional Israel (in Matthew's view) was not: the True Israel, and a genuinely holy people.

disclosing it only enigmatically through Jesus' parables (Lk 13:18, 20; 19:11).

Nevertheless, Jesus and his followers—including the Apostles, following his death and resurrection—are sent out to announce the coming of God's kingdom (Lk 4:43; 8:1; 9:2,11,60; 10:11; 16:16; Acts 8:12; 20:25; 28:31). To preach the kingdom of God is an equivalent term for the propagation of Christianity by word and action. Yet it is at this point that miracle is so important for Luke: proclamation of the kingdom includes healing the sick as a central feature. An important corollary of the healing in this framework of meaning is the declaration that the defeat of the evil powers through the performance of exorcisms is essential to the defeat of Satan and the establishment of God's rule (Lk 11:20). Yet Jesus will not gain public approval through confirmatory signs, such as by performing miracles on demand. The only *sign* that will be given is that of Jonah: that is, the call to repentance (Lk 11:29). The signs which he does perform are not going to persuade the masses, though for those within the community the evidences of the approaching kingdom are already at work in their midst (Lk 17:20–21).

The community looks forward, therefore, to the future when God's purpose in the world will be fully achieved, and the new covenant people will be fully established. Those who have remained faithful through trials and difficulties will share in that new covenant (Lk 22:28–30). Even now they celebrate that ultimate vindication in the eucharistic bread and wine, which he will not share again with them until the kingdom is consummated (Lk 22:15–20). The symbolic penitence of the outsider and his participation in the new kingdom are dramatically represented by the appeal to the dying Jesus of the thief on the cross: "Jesus, remember me when you come into your kingdom" (Lk 23:42). That kingdom is not a human accomplishment, but an eschatological gift of grace from the God who shapes history.

We must ask, however, how miracle contributes to the overall themes and aims of Luke. First, and highlighted by its central place in Jesus' inaugural address, is the claim that what he does in his miracles is in fulfillment of prophecy. The "good news to the poor," the proclamation of "release to the captives," and the liberation of "those who are oppressed" (Lk 4:18) is not meant to be understood in a spiritual or psychological sense, nor does it carry political connotations. Rather, these actions of Jesus in fulfillment of the words of Second Isaiah are essential features of the cosmic conflict, in which God through Jesus regains control of his errant creation. These same prophetic oracles, in addition to other related passages from Isaiah,[63] are appealed to by Jesus in response to the question, relayed from John the Baptist, whether Jesus is "the one who is to come" awaited by Jews on the basis of prophetic tradition (7:18–23). Luke sees in Jesus' role as miracle-worker the fulfillment of those scriptures, but he portrays Jesus as acknowledging that many, including John, will find his interpretation of the prophetic oracles to be offensive, since they do not comprehend God's larger purpose through Him. A major factor in that offensiveness lies in the fact that Jesus healed where he encountered human need, ignoring the sabbath law against work on the seventh day—and healing was perceived to be work (Lk 6:6–11; 13:10–17). Clearly for Luke, Jesus was right in placing a higher priority on fulfilling his mission through healing than on sabbath observance, even though that practice was central to Jewish identity as the covenant people.

Luke finds precedent for healing activity that moves beyond the rules and limits of Judaism, however, in the miracles performed by the great prophets of Israel, Elijah and Elisha. Both these wonder-workers had met the basic needs of those who were outside the geographical and ritual boundaries of Israel: a widow from Sidon and a leper from Syria.[64] Indeed, the point is made in Luke that no Israelite received the miraculous benefits of the Prophets: only non-Jews were ready to be healed. The offensive implication is obvious, and led to the determination of Jesus' fellow-townspeople to destroy him. Luke leaves his reader with no ambiguity about the sources of Jesus' power, but asserts—in

63. Luke 7:22 is a mosaic of phrases deriving from Isaiah 29:18–19; 35:5–6 as well as from Isaiah 61.1.

64. The stories of the Israelite miracle-working prophets are found in 1 Kings 17:1, 8–16; 2 Kings 5:1–14. Similarly, Luke shows in 11:29–32 that only Gentiles were ready to repent on hearing Jonah's preaching, or to receive Solomon's wisdom.

phrases found only in his version of miracles reported by the other synoptic Gospels as well[65]—that the onlookers glorified God, attributing to him, rather than to Jesus' own personal resources, the extraordinary healing capacities (Lk 5:17–26; 18:43) that he displayed. Similarly, in Peter's sermon at the house of the Gentile, Cornelius the centurion (Acts 10), we read, "God anointed Jesus of Nazareth with the Holy Spirit and with power; . . . he went about doing good and healing all that were oppressed of the devil, for God was with him" (10:38). Luke wants to show that there was no question about Jesus' himself possessing miraculous powers. The only issue was the source of those capabilities, and Luke's answer was emphatic: God had commissioned and enabled Jesus for this work.[66]

From the cosmic perspective, Jesus' healings and exorcisms were regarded by Luke as essential factors in the defeat of the God-opposing powers. From the outset, Jesus' public career is set out in a context of diabolical conflict, as the so-called temptation stories show (Lk 4:1–13). In them the temptation is for him to use his powers to gain personal power rather than in the interests of the divine sovereignty. The first healing that Jesus performs, according to Luke (4:31–36) is understood by the demon itself to be a battle in the cosmic war of God and Satan. Luke modifies the Markan story of the healing of Peter's mother-in-law (Mk 1:29–31) in such a way as to stress that her fever was overcome when a commanding word (*rebuke*) was addressed to the demon that caused it (Lk 4:38–39). Similarly, Luke expands the summary of Jesus' healing activity that derives from Mark (1:32–34) in order to stress Jesus' control of the demons and that the issue at stake is his divine commissioning (Lk 4:40–41). Among his earliest followers is a woman delivered by him from demonic possession, Mary Magdalene (Lk 8:2).

It is in Luke's version of the Beelzebub controversy story, however, that the issues are most clearly set out. In both the Markan

65. Cf. with these passages Mark 2:12 (= Mt 9:1–8) and Mark 10:46–52 (= Mt 20:29–34).

66. Luke likewise underscores that God is the agent at work through Jesus in two other exorcism accounts: Luke 8:26–39 (= Mk 5:1–20) and in Luke 9:37–43a (= Mk 9:14–29).

and the Q forms of this tradition the question is raised as to the source of Jesus' authority over the demons. His opponents say that it is the consequence of his league with the prince of demons, Beelzebub. In the Q version (Mt 12:27–28 = Lk 11:19–20), Jesus responds that if all exorcists are in league with the Devil, then so also those exorcists from his Jewish opponents must have satanic ties. But he then claims as the true source of his power "the finger of God," and from this draws the consequence that to the extent that Satan's hold on the present age is being broken through Jesus' exorcisms, "then the Kingdom of God has come upon you" (Lk 11:20). Fundamental for Luke is not merely that the control of Satan over the creation will be shattered, but that it is already in process of being destroyed through Jesus' exorcisms.

Three facets of the new situation brought about by the healing activity of Jesus are pointed up in Luke's gospel: (1) the nature of the work to which he has called his disciples; (2) the privileged situation of the community of his followers; (3) the nature of the new age which is already dawning in their midst. We must examine each of these.

Luke has transformed a simple story of Jesus' calling his disciples to mission (Mk 1:16–20 = Mt 4:18–22) into a symbolic model of the scope and resources of the work to which the community is called. Instead of Mark's straightforward account of summoning his followers to leave family and job to devote themselves to preaching the Gospel, Luke describes them as fishing without results until, in response to Jesus' command, they have an astonishing catch, so great that the boats begin to sink with the load (Lk 5:1–11). There is no mistaking the symbolic import of this for the outcome of the Christian mission, if it is carried out in obedience to and reliance upon Jesus. Just as Jesus' sermon in Nazareth is programmatic for his career, so this miracle story serves as the model for all that the disciples are to do in his name.

The only miracle story deriving from the Q tradition,[67] Luke 7:1–10, serves effectively Luke's aim to show that the wonder-

---

67. See pp. 156–59.

working activity of Jesus includes reaching out beyond the bounds
of Judaism, as well as into the strata of the powerless of Jewish
society (7:11–17). The centurion in the first of these stories is
portrayed by Luke as a pious, seeking man, who loves the Jewish
people and has built a synagogue for the local congregation. But
it is his trust in the authority of Jesus that leads to the healing of
his son. The story of the widow whose only son had died (found
only in Luke, 7:11–17) recalls stories told concerning Elijah (1
Kgs 17:17–24) and Elisha (2 Kgs 4:32–37), and exemplifies how
Luke's Jesus has a primary concern for the deprived and the
oppressed. Similar significance is evident in the story of the
grateful Samaritan leper healed by Jesus (Lk 17:11–19) and the
detail added by Luke to the story of cutting off the ear of the
slave by one of the disciples in the Garden of Gethsemane (Lk
22:47–51), which tells how Jesus healed the severed ear. Here
also the case is being built that it is the outsider and the marginal
persons who are open to and who benefit from God's power at
work in Jesus. Only in Luke (10:1–20) do we learn that Jesus sent
a corps of his followers, seventy in number (corresponding to the
Jewish tradition about the number of Gentile nations), to carry
out the work of preaching and healing which he had begun. In
Matthew, by contrast, the sending of the twelve disciples (Mt
10:1–25) is explicitly limited to Israel: they are to "go nowhere
among the Gentiles, nor enter any town of the Samaritans" (Mt
10:5). The scope of the healing activity of Jesus is a model,
therefore, for Luke's portrayal of the worldwide spread of the
Apostles' work in the book of Acts.

   Luke reproduces the Markan story of the feeding of the five
thousand (Mk 6:30–44 = Lk 9:10–17). A few details are
changed: instead of a desert area, as in Mark, the miracle takes
place in the city of Bethsaida—which is consonant with Luke's
emphasis throughout both volumes of his work on the urban
setting of the mission of Jesus and the Apostles. Also, rather
than noting Jesus' compassion for the crowds, Luke notes
that he told them about the Kingdom of God (Lk 9:11). He follows
Mark, however, in using the technical language of the Eucharist
in the course of his description of the actual feeding: he took,

he blessed, he broke, he gave (9:16). That might not be re-markable in itself, but in the final meal of Jesus with his disciples in Luke's account only (Lk 24:28–35), these words are again used, this time with the point that the sharing of the bread and wine is the occasion of their recognizing him: "He was known to them in the breaking of the bread." The celebration of the Eucharist is seen as a miracle in which the risen Christ is disclosed anew to his community. We have already noted that in Luke's dis-tinctive account of the Last Supper (Lk 22:15–30) the emphasis is on the meal as a sign of the coming of God's kingdom, in which the eschatological vindication of the new covenant people will be achieved.

Closely related to the sacramental recognition of Jesus accord-ing to Luke is his emphasis on the revelatory privilege that the community enjoys. In a passage found only in Luke (10:17–20), the disciples are reported as rejoicing in their possession of the authority to command the demonic powers. They are told that this power derives from Jesus, since it is performed in his name, but there are two other privileges that they should prize more highly. One is that their names are written in heaven—that is, that they are members of the elect community of God. And the other is that knowledge of the divine purpose has been revealed to them, though God has hidden it from the wise by this world's standards. This has been conveyed to them through Jesus (10:23); by it they are enabled to perceive what prophets and kings only dimly foresaw and did not live to see fulfilled (10:23–24). The divine gift of revelation is essential, therefore, to discern what the meaning of Jesus and his works are in the divine purpose for the covenant people and for the creation.

Although, as we have seen, Luke reports Jesus as telling his disciples unequivocally that his life and actions presage the com-ing of God's Rule—especially in Luke 11:20 and 17:20–21—he represents them as unable to grasp the grand aim of God. Their hopes are still limited to his restoring the kingdom to Israel (Acts 1:6). What they have difficulty in grasping is the necessity of his suffering in order to fulfill his redemptive role (Lk 24:26). Throughout the final scenes between Jesus and his followers as

Luke represents them, there is repeated reference to the necessity of the right reading of the Prophets, if one is to understand Jesus' central role in the divine purpose.

Yet there are public signs of the turn of the ages as well, especially in the fall of Jerusalem and the destruction of its temple. Luke has moved Jesus' prediction of that event from the end to the middle of his public activity (Lk 13:34–35)[68] and has thereby heightened its symbolic significance as an indicator of a new, nongeographical locus of the worship of God. Luke also follows Mark's predictions of the destruction of the Temple (Lk 21:5–7 = Mk 13:1–4) and of the fall of Jerusalem to the Roman troops, which he describes in such specific detail as the strategy of taking the city by circumvallation (Lk 21:20–24: contra Mk 13:14–20). To this series of predictions about Jerusalem, Luke adds, "Now when these things begin to take place, look up and raise your heads, because your redemption is drawing near" (Lk 21:28). Unlike the Roman historians, for whom a portent is an indication of a change of rulers, the omen of the fall of Jerusalem and the destruction of its temple is a sign of the turn of the ages.

In addition to signs and miracles as a mode of communication of the divine purpose, Luke gives considerable space and attaches great importance to dreams, and especially to visions. Zechariah is informed about the birth of John the Baptist and his God-given role through an angel who appears to him as he is serving his priestly office in the temple (Lk 1:11–20), an experience which has a close analogy and precedent in the stories of the miraculous circumstances surrounding the birth and dedication to God of Samson (Judges 13:1–25) and of the Prophet Samuel (1 Sm 1:1–27). In both cases, angels explain what is going to occur and what its significance is in the divine plan. Similar circumstances surround the angelic appearance announcing the birth of Jesus to Mary (Lk 1:26–34). Angels advise the shepherds what is happening in David's royal city nearby, and they visit the Child lying in the manger (Lk 2:8–20). The angel's instructions are followed in the naming of Jesus (Lk 2:21). Only Luke among the synoptic evangelists tells us what the subject of

68. Cf. Matthew 23:37–39.

conversation was in the appearance to Jesus of Moses and Elijah on the occasion of the transfiguration of Jesus: his exodus, which he was to fulfill in Jerusalem (Lk 9:31). The most extended series of visions in Luke's gospel occurs in the final chapter (Lk 24). First two men appear to the women at the tomb, explaining to them the divine necessity of Jesus' death and announcing his resurrection (24:1–9). Then follows a succession of appearances of Jesus himself: to the two bound for Emmaus (24:13–31); to all the disciples gathered in Jerusalem (24:36–49); and other appearances over a period of forty days, culminating in the ascension scene (Acts 1). These visions are clearly purposive: to enable the followers to understand who Jesus is, what God has done through Him, and what He is about to begin to do through them, the Apostles.

The appearances that prepare the Apostles for their mission begin with the "tongues as of fire" that accompany the outpouring of the Spirit, which manifests itself in the miracle of simultaneous comprehension in all the world's languages (Acts 2:7–8) of Peter's sermon, presumably delivered in Aramaic though reported in Greek. An angel appears in order to release Peter and the other Apostles from the prison where they have been incarcerated by the religious authorities (Acts 5:17–21), thereby providing divine vindication for the message about Jesus that they proclaim. At the moment of his martyrdom, Stephen is granted a vision of Christ exalted at God's right hand (Acts 7:56), which affirms the validity of his message about Israel's rejection of the messenger of God.

Events of such great significance in Luke's story of salvation as the conversion of Paul and the launching of the mission to the Gentiles through Peter find divine approbation in Luke's account through visions. Not only is Paul's conversion effected through a heavenly vision, in which Jesus appears to him (Acts 9:1–9), but also Ananias, the spokesman for the Christians in Damascus, is instructed how he is to receive Paul by means of a vision. The convergence of factors which lead to the conversion of Cornelius, and hence to the opening of the Christian community to Gentiles, consists of visions: first to Cornelius, then to Peter—though his has to be repeated three times in order to

persuade him on the difficult point of allowing ritually unclean
Gentiles into the church (Acts 10). The miracle of speaking in
tongues is repeated (10:46), apparently to show continuity with
the Pentecost outpouring of the Spirit and the opening of faith
to non-Jews predicted and enacted at that decisive event (Acts
1–2). Peter is once more released from prison on the eve of his
hearing before Herod (Acts 12:6–12) through the intervention
and advice of an angel. The incident seems to indicate that the
schemes of pagan rulers cannot hinder the plans of God (12:11).

Paul's decision to shift his mission from Asia Minor to the
mainland of Europe is made on the basis of a vision of a man
from Macedonia pleading with him for help (Acts 16:9–10). His
stay in Corinth, which had such important effects on the Gentile
growth of the church, was indicated to him in a vision as well
(Acts 18:9). In his defense before his Roman interrogators, Paul
recounts his conversion, complete with details (slightly differing
in each case) of the visions he saw and the voices he heard (Acts
22:1–21; 26:9–18), just as a voice in trance had told him to leave
Jerusalem after his conversion and to launch the Gentile mission
(Acts 22:17–21).

The cumulative force of this series of accounts of visions, angelic visitations, and miracles is to show that *God demonstrates his
approbation* of each new stage in the cosmic process of redemption by a divine manifestation, for the most part publicly visible
(except for the visitations), though subject to interpretations other
than those assigned to them by the Christians: the birth of both
the forerunner of Jesus and Jesus himself; the launching of his
public ministry, the reaching out beyond the confines of Jewish
national and ritual boundaries to include Gentiles in the covenant community; the resurrection of Jesus and the commissioning of the disciples and the Apostles to carry forward the work
begun by Jesus; the outpouring of the Spirit and the resultant
confirmation of the worldwide spread of the Word; the inclusion of increasing numbers of Gentiles in the Christian community; the geographical progress of the movement across Asia
Minor to Greece and finally on to Rome itself. Each new phase
receives miraculous confirmation, as Luke depicts it in the two
volumes of his consecutive work.

Binding together all these events into a coherent whole, and meshing them into the complex of world history, are the actions and decisions of secular rulers. Often the intent of those governmental actions is to thwart or destroy the incipient movement. But the result is always furtherance of the divine plan. Imprisonments, trials, executions, even procrastination (as in the case of the succession of imperial bureaucrats who hear Paul's case and then shift responsibility to Caesar himself)—the outcome is to advance what Luke sees as God's purpose. The climax comes when the indecision of the Palestinian rulers takes Paul to Rome itself. These are by no means regarded as mere chance occurrences. The pattern of time is in God's hands, as Jesus instructs his would-be tipsters who warn him of Herod Antipas's intention to kill him. The response makes clear the view that the course of history is in the competent hands of God: "Go and tell that fox [Herod], 'Behold, I cast out demons and perform cures today and tomorrow, and the third day I finish my course.' Nevertheless I must go on my way today and tomorrow and the day following; for it cannot be that a prophet should perish away from Jerusalem" (Lk 13:32–33). The rulers think they are laying and carrying out their own independent schemes, but Luke represents Jesus as perceiving that they are merely instruments in the unfolding of the divine plan for cosmic redemption through Jesus. Once Jesus is off the earthly scene, it is the Spirit that carries forward God's work toward its predetermined end.

Two aspects of miracle appear in Acts which are not found in Luke or, to any significant degree, elsewhere in the New Testament: the punitive miracles and traces of magical technique.[69]

69. Two studies of the place of magic in the New Testament period are John M. Hull's *Hellenistic Magic and the Synoptic Tradition* (London: SCM, 1974 = SBT[2] 28), and Morton Smith, *Jesus the Magician* (New York: Harper, 1978). Both books overlook the fact that phenomena perceived as miracle or magic must be analyzed by the historian in relation to the life-world of the writer (and his community in which they appear) and to the social functions which they serve. Both writers in these studies reason backward from third- and fourth-century evidence to posit historical conditions from which they draw conclusions about the first century. For that period no adequate documentation exists. The authors assume that, because demons were dealt with by magical means in the later Roman empire, wherever demons appear in the text the appropriate way to de-

On the part of social anthropologists as well as classicists, there has been progress toward differentiating miracle from magic and in discerning how proponents of both types of phenomena ground their views in a life-world in which the manifestation of the supernatural serves an important function. Lucy Mair, in a standard work on social anthropology,[70] acknowledges that an absolute distinction between miracle and magic cannot be drawn but goes on to show that a significant differentiation between them can be made: "The efficacy of magic may be thought to depend essentially upon the correct treatment of substances used (including words spoken over them) independently of assistance from any supernatural being."[71] Both religion and magic seek to attain ends which are either not achievable by any human means, or at least not by the means humans are now using. Accordingly, they call on forces or beings outside the course of what we—in the tradition of the Stoics—call nature. If resolution of the difficulty is sought through the manipulation of forces, the activity is primarily magical. If aid is sought through communication with beings, then the activity is primarily religious.[72]

As we noted earlier (chap. 2), M. Mauss, in *A General Theory of*

---

scribe such phenomena is as magic. The consequence of this methodological confusion is that Hull, for example, simply dumps all the evidence into one undifferentiated heap and concludes "that Jesus entered without reserve into the central conflict of the magician's art" (p. 142). Smith acknowledges that the gospel evidence as it stands does not lead to such a simplistic conclusion, but he posits the existence of an older tradition behind the present picture of Jesus, which, he thinks, has been Judaized by the Christian editor and accommodated to the Old Testament. But for Smith, the real Jesus was a demoniac, who engaged in such magical acts as eating flesh, drinking blood, and participating in nocturnal lustrations in the nude with his circle of male followers (pp. 143–50). The circularity of what passes for argument and the prejudices that shape the reconstruction of the figure of Jesus will be apparent to any careful reader of these works.

70. Lucy Mair, *An Introduction to Social Anthropology* (Oxford: Clarendon, 1972[2]). See also my discussion of this question in *Christian Origins*, pp. 63–67.

71. Mair, *Social Anthropology*, p. 225.

72. Ibid., p. 229. A similar distinction is offered by John Ferguson in *The Religions of the Roman Empire* (Ithaca, N.Y.: Cornell University Press, 1970), pp. 158–59, with the valid qualification that in practice the two realms of miracle and magic may be mixed.

Magic,[73] describes as a central characteristic of magic the ritual act and the accompanying formulaic pronouncement by which actions or outcomes are coerced. The origins or initial meaning of neither act nor formula is of significance: central alone is efficacy. Failure is attributed to imprecision in rite or pronouncement. The formulae are repeated and gradually expanded by accretion, so that they end up by becoming completely unintelligible. So long as they work, that does not matter. Van der Leeuw makes the same point when he asserts that a magical formula "owes its powerfulness to precise recitation, to rhythmical sequence, to the utterance of the name together with other factors."[74]

The social function of magic is illuminatingly discussed by Peter Brown.[75] Rejecting the notion that sorcery is "an unswept corner of odd beliefs, surrounding unsavoury practices" or that it is based on confusion and decay of traditional religion,[76] Brown notes that "accusations against sorcerers occur in precisely those areas and classes which we know to have been the most effectively sheltered from brutal dislocation [i.e., in the fierce social and political struggles of the third and fourth centuries]." It was in such "stable and well-oriented groups [as the senatorial aristocracy and the professors of the great Mediterranean cities] that certain forms of misfortune" were attributed to sabotage through sorcery on the part of hostile individuals. As early as the time of Pliny the Elder we may read that "there is no one who is not afraid of becoming the subject of lethal spells."[77] Yet Pliny is almost certainly speaking primarily for the privileged class of

73. (New York and London: Norton; Routledge and Kegan Paul, 1972), pp. 55–60.

74. G. Van der Leeuw, *Religion in Essence and Manifestation* (London: Allen and Unwin, 1938), p. 423.

75. For example, in "Sorcery, Demons and the Rise of Christianity," from *Religion and Society in the Age of St. Augustine* (New York: Harper, 1972), pp. 119–46.

76. As suggested by E. R. Dodd in passing, in *Pagan and Christian in an Age of Anxiety* (New York: Norton, 1965), pp. 70–73. Dodd agrees with Brown's position, however, that magic—far from being confined to the ignorant—was found among such highly educated persons as Plotinus and Libanius.

77. Quoted by P. Brown (p. 122) from Pliny *HN* 28.4–9.

the first century, who regarded misfortune as the consequence of sorcery instigated by jealous colleagues. Down to the time of Augustine, as Brown shows, there were two major ways of accounting for miscarriage of one's hopes and plans: the machinations of Satan and the demons or the manipulation of forces from outside the system by means of sorcery. Demons were operative in both views. What distinguished the world-view was whether these hostile forces were to be controlled by God, as the Christians believed, or by magical rites and formulas, as the sorcerers and their aristocratic clients did.

The fullest documentation we have for magical practices in the Roman era dates from the fifth century A.D.[78] From it may be inferred that the efficacy of magic depended on the recitation of multiple divine names,[79] on the forcefulness of orders to the gods,[80] on elaborate recipes for magical foods and extensive ritual, on observing the proper times as derived from phases of the moon or special days, and on the use of secret magical words, many of which are nonsense.[81] The petitions are primarily negative, mostly prophylactic against demons, enemies, or disease. There are, however, repeated requests for obtaining eternal life, which include the necessity to placate the lower gods and gain access to Helios, the chief of the gods, in the hope of receiving a revelation from him.[82] Thus the aim is to coerce the powers, to force one's way into the consciousness of a distant and inaccessible god. What is required is not to know his will, but to manipulate the powers so that one can achieve one's goal.

Although commentators have sought to find traces of magic

78. *Papyri Graecae Magicae: Die griechische Zauberpapyri*, ed. Karl Preisendanz (1928), 2d ed. by Albert Henrichs (Stuttgart: Teubner, 1973).

79. *PGM* XII.136–41 represents the Great God as having 365 names (also in *PGM* XIII.100). The names derive from Egyptian, Greek, Jewish (Iao), and Christian sources.

80. The favorite term of address to the gods is *horkidzō*. In *PGM* XII.136 ff., the demon is warned that if he does not perform according to these orders, he will be reported to the Great God and hacked in pieces. Furthermore, the petitioner does not want to have to make his request a second time.

81. *PGM* XIII.890–910, includes vowels arranged in various configurations, such as groups of 3, 7, 8, and 9 each.

82. *PGM* IV.296–750; 1115–65.

in the healing stories of Jesus (such as his use of spittle) or of the Apostles (such as their invocation of the name of Jesus), the world-view of the writers of the Gospels and Acts is fundamentally religious rather than magical. None of the characteristic features of magic that we have observed in the sources is to be found in the New Testament writings, though there are traces of magic-type thinking in some of the healing stories and a kindred outlook behind the punitive miracles. All instances of these are in Acts; in six out of the eight stories, punitive and magical features are mingled.

The first story grows out of the report in Acts 4 that the Apostles and the entire Christian community in Jerusalem pooled all their resources (4:32). One couple, Ananias and Sapphira, held back part of their possessions (5:1–6). When confronted by Peter with his deceitful failure to share his wealth, Ananias fell down dead. When his wife learned of his fate and the reason for his death, she suffered a similar fate (5:7–11). There is no hint of magical technique here; rather, the fault is identified as having lied to or tried the Holy Spirit. Yet clearly the incident lies closer to the operation of unseen forces than to the fulfillment of a divine redemptive purpose. Its social function within the community of Luke-Acts seems to have been a warning against cheating rather than a positive contribution to the fulfillment of mission.

The story of the crowds flocking to the Apostles in search of healing through their "signs and wonders" (Acts 5:12–16) reads like many in the gospel tradition, but the unconscious healing effect of Peter's shadow seems more nearly automatic, and therefore magical, even than the passing of power from Jesus when the hem of his garment was touched by an ailing woman (Mk 5:25–34 = Lk 8:43–48). Similarly, in Acts 19:11 we read that healings and exorcisms were accomplished by taking to the ailing persons handkerchiefs and aprons which had been in contact with Peter. Operative here is an assumption, constitutive for magicians, that contact with a person of power, with a part of his body, or with something that has touched him, is an effective means of tapping that power. The healings as a whole, however, are set forth in Acts as essential features of the spread of the gospel in Jerusalem and the wider Mediterranean world, so that what might appear to be a magical feature—the healing effect of a passing shadow—is treated as part of the more traditional redemptive enterprise in Acts.

Similarly, the account of Paul's being bitten by a viper on Malta and his miraculous escape hints at belief in magic, or at least in some kind of automatic retributive justice: the natives think he is a criminal and wait for him to drop dead (Acts 28:1–10). When he escapes, they conclude—also wrongly—that he is a god in disguise among them. The incident seems to serve the author's aim to present Paul's life, and especially this journey to Rome, as under divine control no matter how serious the obstacles, natural or political, may seem to be. Hence, the story does conform with Luke's overarching purpose to show God's hand at work in history.

The clearest example of a punitive miracle is the story of the death of Herod Agrippa (Acts 12:20–23). After donning his royal robes and taking his seat on the throne, Herod had allowed the populace to acclaim him as a god and was forthwith smitten by an angel with a fatal disease. A similar account of his horrible death is given by Josephus (*Antiquities* xix.8.2). For both Luke and Josephus, this story is an indication of God's control over history rather than an instance of magic (no technique is hinted at) or of a miraculous action on the part of any human being.

Most significant for our assessment of the Lukan life-world are the four remaining stories, each of which combines features of a punitive miracle with clear evidence of competition between the Christian wonder-workers and contemporary magicians. Simon of Samaria was lured away from his own prosperous career as a magician by the "signs and great miracles" wrought by the Apostles (Acts 8:9–13), accepted baptism, and became a member of the Christian community in Samaria. When the Holy Spirit came among them through the apostolic laying-on of hands, he tried to buy the gift of the Spirit and was severely rebuked for having done so (8:14–24). He unwittingly attained a double fame, however: as the prototype of simony, and—as Simon Magus— as an infamous charlatan of the patristic period.[83]

83. On Simon Magus, see below, chap. 8. The Clementine Recognitions include an attack on Simon Magus as being in league with the evil powers (2.5–16).

A Jewish magician, variously known as Bar-Jesus and Elymas (Acts 13:6–12), tried to dissuade the proconsul at Paphos in Cyprus from following the preaching of Paul and was accordingly struck blind by Paul, who denounced him as a "son of the devil" and an "enemy of all righteousness, full of deceit and villainy." The bitterness of the denunciation is perhaps to be explained by heightened competition in Luke's circumstances between Christian and magical wonder-workers, or by charges that the Christians practiced magic, as we hear from Celsus in his polemic against Christianity.[84] Unwanted publicity for Paul and the God whom he proclaimed at Philippi (Acts 16:16–18) led the Apostle to expel the "spirit of divination" that provided the slave girl with her psychic powers and her owners with a fine income through fees she received. Unauthorized use of the name of Jesus by Jewish exorcists at Ephesus resulted in a struggle and their castigation by the evil spirit. When word of this spread throughout the city, magic books were burned by converted former magicians (Acts 19:13–19). The antithesis between miracles done in Jesus' name and magic, which Peter Brown describes as coming into sharp focus in the age of Augustine,[85] was already taking shape in the narrative of Acts.

Luke did not have to imagine hostility toward this dimension of the Christian tradition. We shall examine in detail below (chap. 8) the evidence that, not only was antipathy toward miracle a central thrust of Celsus's attack, but also that in the purely intra-pagan satire of Lucian of Samosata, miracle and magic are alike regarded as fraud and chicanery, as his portrait of Alexander, the False Prophet, vividly demonstrates. Similarly, in the second century Apuleius felt obligated to offer an apology against the charges that he practiced magic, especially in accomplishing his marriage to a rich widow.[86] As E. R. Dodd has noted, the ancient debate over miracle and magic was in the main not a conflict between believers and rationalists, but between two sorts of believers.[87] To analyze the evidence as though it all lay on the same

84. Quoted in Origen's *Contra Celsum*, see below, 268–70.
85. Brown, "Sorcery," pp. 132–37.
86. Apuleius, *Apology*, trans. H. E. Butler (Oxford: Clarendon, 1909).
87. E. R. Dodd, *Pagan and Christian*, p. 124, n. 1. This is discussed more fully below, 260–61.

plane is to ignore precisely the features of the relevant phenomena which are determinative for interpretation: the essential
features of the life-world which is in each case operative behind
the literature.

THE SOCIAL IMPLICATIONS OF MIRACLE
IN MATTHEW AND LUKE

Both the facts that the Gospels of Matthew and Luke were written as they were, and the existence from the outset of a reader-
ship that used and treasured these writings, show that by the
turn of the second century the church was moving out of a sectarian ghetto. Christians were able to exploit for their own special ends the means of communication available to the wider Roman world. Christian authors were not limited to reproducing
tradition in the manner of an archivist or an amanuensis. The
efforts to account for the Gospels on the basis of a simple, strict
sorting out of supposed literary sources are woefully inadequate, as recent attempts have unintentionally demonstrated.[88]
What these Gospels show us further is that there was no primitive orthodoxy or essential unity from which heretics later dis-
sented and departed. Rather, Matthew and Luke provide evidence that side-by-side in the early church were groups who were
influenced by the cultural currents of the imperial epoch, who
understood and to a considerable extent shared the assumptions
and stance toward life of their non-Christian contemporaries.
Furthermore, they read, or at least understood, the prevailing
modes of literary communication of the era. This led them,
therefore, to modify the life-world of Roman society of the time
and to exploit it as a way of setting the events of Jesus and the
Apostles in a larger framework of meaning, one that would have
appeal to non-Christians and provide a rationale for those within
the community.

Beyond these common strategies, however, and their common

88. As noted above, chap. 5, n. 12, those who deny that Mark is our oldest
Gospel and the prototype for Matthew and Luke are unable to account for the
differences among the Gospels. See my review of H. Stoldt's attempt to disprove
Markan priority in *JBL* 98 (1979); 140–41.

reliance on the traditional sources, Mark and Q, Matthew and Luke differ significantly. Matthew defines the covenant community in terms of the true Israel. Although his stance toward ancient Israel (and its first-century institutional heirs) is severely critical, there is stress on the continuities as well as the contrasts. Above all, the distinctiveness of the new Israel as the people of God is emphasized. Miracle is important to Matthew, especially as portent by which the divine control over history is manifest, but also as confirmation of Jesus as the New Moses, the preeminent and final interpreter of the will of God. The kinship with Roman historians as well as with rabbinic tradition about miracle has already been pointed out.

For Luke, however, the covenant people and the stance toward Hellenistic-Roman culture are open and inclusive. The stress falls on the universality of what God is doing through Jesus and the Apostles. In the process of this portrayal of cosmic redemption Luke comes to terms with contemporary culture: in its popular philosophical concepts, its popular literary modes (both prose and poetry), and with such widespread phenomena as magic, with which the Christians will be in competition, and against which they must defend themselves. Further, Luke-Acts displays a central feature of religion in the Antonine period, which we have seen in the changing mode of both the Isis and the Asklepios cults in this time: the importance of personal, life-transforming encounter with the divine. In the other synoptic Gospels, there is nothing that corresponds to the burning hearts of the disciples during their encounter with the risen Christ. Paul's simple, succinct references to his conversion[89] contrast sharply with the dramatic detail of antecedents, process, and results of his blinding confrontation on the Damascus road, told thrice over in Acts. Equally vivid, though not so detailed, are the conversion stories of Cornelius (Acts 9), of the Ethiopian eunuch, of the Philippian jailer (Acts 16). The mood and style of

89. Galatians 1:15–16 ("He . . . was pleased to reveal his Son in me"); 1 Corinthians 9:1 ("Have I not seen Jesus our Lord?"); 1 Corinthians 15:8 ("Last of all, as to one untimely born, he appears also to me"). See, on this, my essay on the conversion of Paul in *The Other Side of God*, ed. Peter Berger (Garden City, N.Y.: Doubleday, 1981), pp. 48–60.

these narratives of transforming religious experience are closer to such familiar conversion stories as those of Aelius Aristides and Lucius Apuleius than they are to Paul's own reports. The writer senses what his contemporaries expect and are eager to hear depicted, and he has the resources to address those interests.

For Luke miracle functions, not only to heighten the drama of the narrative, but also to show that at every significant point in the transitions of Christianity from its Jewish origins in Jerusalem to its Gentile outreaching to Rome itself, the hand of God is evident in the form of public miraculous confirmation. A corollary of this is the implicit claim that God also has shown his hand in wielding swift judgment on those who oppose the movement or who seek to exploit its extraordinary power for personal gain. And finally, miracle is always effected for human benefit, not for the accomplishment of political ends.

It is inconceivable that Christianity could have spread so rapidly and effectively as it did in the second and third centuries, that it could have penetrated the middle and upper classes of the empire so deeply, had there not been within its constituency persons able to write apologetic works of this type. Without merely abandoning their simpler, sectarian heritage, the authors of Matthew and Luke both reflected upon and facilitated the restatement of the Christian tradition in ways that synthesized it with characteristic features of the Antonine world-view.

CHAPTER SEVEN

Miracle as Universal Symbol

Thus far in our analysis of miracle we have been examining the evidence largely in descriptive terms as religious phenomena: what was experienced and what it was perceived to mean in either the public or private purview of those who reported these extraordinary events. As early as the first century of our era, however, there were those for whom miracle was an avenue to deeper or inward meaning, a symbolic vehicle by which timeless truth could be perceived behind outward event. Evidence of this significance of miracle is apparent in the account by Aelius Aristides of his inward transformation through his attendance on Asklepios, for example. But Aristides' perspective is part of a wider movement that profoundly affected the appropriation of mythological tradition in the second-century Roman world, including Jewish and Christian reappraisal of its tradition. We shall look first at the symbolic transformation of miracle tradition in the Gospel of John, and then compare this development with analogous evidence in the works of Philo of Alexandria, Plutarch, and Aristides.

THE TRANSFORMATION OF MIRACLE IN THE GOSPEL OF JOHN

In form, content, style, and strategy, the Gospel of John is a tissue of paradoxes. Its portrayal of Jesus shows clear kinship with the ahistorical models of Isis and Wisdom,[1] yet the author insists on the concrete historical existence of its central figure: "The Word became flesh, and dwelt among us" (John 1:14). Although the picture of Jesus in the Gospel of John includes such historical details as Jesus weeping, displaying his wounds, and

1. See my essay, "Myth and Miracle: Isis, Wisdom and the Logos of John," in *Myth, Symbol and Reality*, ed. Alan Olson, pp. 145–64 (Notre Dame, Ind., and London: University of Notre Dame, Ind., Press, 1980).

221

asking for food and water, the narratives are at several points simply left dangling, as in the story of the encounter between Jesus and Nicodemus (Jn 3), which trails off into a discourse devoid of a conclusion to the story line.

Perhaps the most striking feature of John is that its seeming similarity to the other three Gospels is merely apparent. All four Gospels tell the story of the career of Jesus, culminating in the conflict with the civil and religious authorities, his death, and his subsequent appearance to his followers. Yet apart from the report of the miraculous feeding of the five thousand (Jn 6) and the prediction of the destruction of the Temple (Jn 2:13–22), there is nearly no overlap between John and the synoptics, either in narrative detail or in the content of Jesus' teaching. Rather than containing discussions of ethical or legal issues, as the first three Gospels do, John's discussions are lengthy, involuted, image-laden discourses on the differences between transitory appearance and eternal reality.

Most important for our purposes is the discrepancy between the superficially analogous miracle stories in the synoptics, on the one hand, and the importantly different way that miracle functions in John, on the other. Fortunately, the author of John informs his reader explicitly that miracle is of central importance to his writing, although he paradoxically waits until the end to say so (Jn 20:30–31).[2] We shall see that in those narratives which are outwardly closest to the synoptic Gospels—the destruction of the Temple and the miraculous feeding—the differences in significance can be most clearly discerned. John's declared reason for writing his Gospel is that although "Jesus performed many other signs in the presence of his disciples which are not written in this book, these are written in order that you might believe that Jesus is the Christ, the Son of God, and that through believing, you might have life through his name" (20:30–

2. John 21 is almost certainly a later epilogue, appended to an earlier version of John which ended at 20:31. For detailed analysis and judicious theorizing about the successive stages of the redaction of John, see Raymond E. Brown's magisterial commentary, *The Gospel according to John I–XII* (Anchor Bible 29) (Garden City, N.Y.: Doubleday, 1966); and *The Gospel according to John XIII–XXI* (1970), pp. 1066–1132.

31). Nearly every word of that statement is important for assessing the special purpose of John, not only in writing his gospel in general, but in recounting the miracles in particular. The details enable us to perceive what was distinctive about the life-world within which John was operating, and especially the role miracle played in that structure.

The first implication of this concluding statement by John is that the performance of "signs" characterized the activity of Jesus in a special way, although the author has made only a selection from what must have been a far longer series of tales available to him. He does not indicate whether those "not written in this book" were preserved in oral tradition or in another writing, but all of them were done "in the presence of the disciples." This implies that they were public acts rather than secret performances, and the narratives of John uniformly bear out that inference. There is no guarantee that those who witnessed Jesus' extraordinary actions would be persuaded that his works were beneficial, much less that they were from God. Even the disciples, as official observers, were forced to come to terms with the question of what these signs implied about who Jesus was. The report of them, now being transmitted by John, has as its aim the eliciting of faith in Jesus as the Christ and the resultant bestowal of "life in his name." Several implications of this statement are important to note: (1) there is no guarantee that those who observe Jesus' signs will draw the conclusion about his divine sonship: (2) the impact of the signs performed by Jesus is by no means limited to the personal benefit deriving from his miraculous acts—whether recovery of sight, restoration from death to life, or supernatural feeding—but focuses, rather, on the acquisition of life in some special sense, as clarified and elaborated throughout the Gospel.

The ambiguity of the meaning of Jesus' miracles in John is in some limited ways similar to the response to his miracles reported in the synoptic Gospels. There, for example, the difficulty is not doubt about whether Jesus has the power to expel demons from a possessed man (Mk 3:19–30 and parallels) but concerns the source of his power: God or Satan? Another dimension of the uncertainty about the meaning of Jesus' miracles within the synoptic tradition is found in a saying that appears in two different versions: in Mark 8:11–13 and in a Q form (Mt 12:38–42; cf. Lk 11:29–32). In the first of these Jesus is asked to perform a miracle in order to confirm—or disconfirm—his claim that God is with him. His response is a flat refusal to do so. In the second form of the saying, his answer is that no sign other than "the sign of Jonah" will be given. In the Jonah story thereby alluded to (Jon 3:1–5), the reluctant prophet preached repentance, and the people—to his mingled astonishment and annoyance—believed what he had to say. In short, his message was self-authenticating; it needed no miracle to confirm it. Matthew (alone) introduces a miraculous element, the resurrection of Jesus, by way of analogy to Jonah's undersea voyage of three days' and nights' duration (Mt 12:40). But that addition basically alters the point of the other Jonah sayings: that miracles are not a mode of divine confirmation for skeptics.

Similarly, in John there are repeated requests for confirmatory signs. Thus, when Jesus cleansed the temple courts and predicted its destruction (Jn 2:13–22), he was asked to perform a sign as demonstration of his divine authorization (2:17). Instead of complying with the demand, he referred enigmatically to the raising of his "body" in three days. But did that imply his own resurrection from the dead, or the emergence of the new people, the "Body" of Christ, following the resurrection? Or both? We shall return to the matter of multiple meanings, but the popular notion of signs as indicators of God's special enabling power pervade the minds of Jesus' antagonists in the Gospel of John, even though Jesus is pictured as rejecting that understanding of miracle.

Nicodemus infers from Jesus' signs that he comes "from God" (Jn 3:2). In the subsequent dialogue between him and Jesus it becomes evident how inadequate an understanding of Jesus Nicodemus's complimentary statement about the former's miracles discloses. In 4:48 Jesus deplores the fact that his contemporaries regard "signs and wonders" as the criteria for believing that he has divine support. Similarly, the crowds follow Jesus because they want to see signs (6:2). But even more significant is his charge in 6:26 that what they are really seeking is their own physical gratification ("because you ate your fill"): not yet do they understand the meaning of his extraordinary acts (6:26–27). His unbelieving brothers urge him to go and impress others in Judea by performing miracles—presumably motivated solely by interest in notoriety for their strange brother rather than by authentic faith in him, as the evangelist sees it (7:3–5). The inability of the majority of the observers of the miracles to perceive who Jesus was, as John portrays him, is not only explicitly declared in the Gospel ("Though he had done so many signs, yet they did not believe in him," 12:37), but is even said to be in fulfillment of the Jewish prophetic scriptures (12:38–40).

The issue over the meaning of the miracles is not a matter of belief or unbelief. It is a question for John of wrong or right belief. Thus, in connection with the miraculous feeding of the five thousand reported in John 6, Jesus flees from the crowds who acclaim him as "the prophet who is to come into the world" and who undertake to seize him to make him their king (6:14–15). The opposition of Jewish officialdom to Jesus is based, not on an assumption that he is a charlatan, but that he will through his extraordinary powers rally the crowds behind him and seize political power, which will in turn trigger repressive Roman measures (11:45–48). The fickle crowd included many who were ready to affirm his messiahship on the basis of his miracles (7:31), but in his hour of trial and death, only a few women and a single faithful disciple stood by him (19:25–26). Failure to recognize Jesus for who he was, John tells us, is not for want of evidence, but for lack of *divinely granted insight*—a factor to which we shall return.

MIRACLE AS SIGN AND SYMBOL

For John, the miracles of Jesus not only have links with past and future, but they also embody the presence of eternity. Before we explore that theme of the multiple perspectives of John's miracles in detail, however, it may be useful to see how he structures his material, especially in his movement back and forth between narrative of miracle and discourse on meaning.

Scholars continue to debate over how many "signs" John included in his gospel. He notifies the reader about two of them: "the first sign" is noted in 2:11, with reference to the changing of water into wine (2:1:11); the "second sign" is the healing of the official's son (4:46–54). The other explicit accounts of miracles in John are the healing of the lame man at the pool (5:1–9); the feeding of the multitude by the sea and the stilling of the storm (6:1–21); the cure of the man born blind (9:1–12); and the raising of Lazarus from the dead (11:1–53). Johannine stories that have at times been included by scholars among the signs are the cleansing of the Temple (2:13–22), and the conversations with Nicodemus (3:1–15) and with the Samaritan woman (4:1–38). Serious but inconclusive efforts have been made to reconstruct a source of signs, which is conjectured to have been utilized by John in compiling his gospel.[3] Even if John did draw on written sources, which cannot be demonstrated but is not unlikely, he has so thoroughly integrated his material as to present a remarkably consistent point of view, particularly in relation to the miracles of Jesus.

Interwoven with the signs narratives is a series of discursive passages of various lengths and differing styles. The prologue to John (1:1–18) is the most formally rhetorical segment of the gospel. In it John asserts the eternal relationship of the divine Logos which became incarnate in Jesus with God the Creator of all. At least two of the discourses flow directly out of the signs narratives: the bread of life, from the miraculous feeding story, and the utterances about eternal life, from the report of the

3. R. Bultmann, *Gospel of John* (Philadelphia: Westminster, 1971), pp. 113, 180, 203–05, 211, 238, 289, 329, 393–95, 401, 698, 705. The source has been reconstructed by Robert T. Fortna, *The Gospel of Signs: A Reconstruction of the Narrative Source Underlying the Fourth Gospel* (Cambridge: Cambridge University Press, 1970), pp. 235–45, in which are included both the prologue and the epilogue to John, the call of the disciples, the entry into Jerusalem, the Last Supper, the arrest and trial of Jesus, the crucifixion, burial, and resurrection. In short, everything that is narrative comes from the hypothetical signs-source. By implication, all the discourse material comes from a sayings source, or sources. Serious doubts about the credibility of this sorting out of sources for John have been raised by D. Moody Smith in *The Composition and Order of the Fourth Gospel* (New Haven: Yale University Press, 1965), pp. 38–44, and W. G. Kümmel, *Introduction to the New Testament* (Nashville: Abingdon, 1975), pp. 200–17.

raising of Lazarus. Two others are in the form of dialogues: one with a Jewish ruler (Jn 3), and the other with a Samaritan woman, the subject of which, in spite of her multiple marital and extra-marital relationships, turns not to proper moral behavior but to the proper locus of worship. There are extended polemical passages, and brief ones as well: the interchange over the prediction of the Temple's destruction (2:13–22) sets forth the astonishing notion of Jesus as the replacement for the Jewish Temple; John 7 pits Jesus against Moses and the biblical tradition; John 8 contrasts Jesus with Abraham as founder of the covenant people; building on the prophetic tradition (Is 40:11; Jer 23:1–4; Ez 34:1–31), John 10 treats of true and false sheep, and the true shepherd (i.e., Jesus); John 12 (esp. 20–26) anticipates the inclusiveness of the community founded by Jesus, as the Greeks come seeking him. The discourses of John 13–17 all depict the inner life of the community, its rites, resources, and relationships to one another, to Jesus, and to God. The sayings of Jesus on the cross, according to John, announce the completion of God's redemptive scheme ("It is finished"; 19:30), and the discourses of John 20 and the epilogue (21) sketch the responsibilities of discipleship. The question may legitimately be raised: what has all this to do with miracle? The answer is: nearly everything, but in John's distinctive way.

First, we must consider the links between Jesus and the past traditions of Israel as John represents them. When John the Baptist is interrogated by the Jewish leaders concerning his identity and role, he first denies that he is the Messiah, or Elijah (whose return was expected at the end of the age; cf. Mal 4:5), or "the Prophet," whose coming was promised in Deuteronomy 18:15–18[4] (Jn 1:19–21). Similar questions are raised about Jesus (7:40, 52), although the answers are complicated by the fact that Jesus' place of origin, Galilee, did not figure in prophetic expectations about messiahs or eschatological prophets. Yet there

4. That this hope was alive in first-century Judaism is attested by the importance of this passage for the scribes and exegetes of the Dead Sea community: Psalm of Joshua 5–8; Scroll of the Rule 9:10–11, where the Prophet is linked with the advent of the kingly and priestly messiahs.

are those who see *in his miracles* of the feeding of the crowd at the sea and the restoration of sight to the man born blind evidence that he is "the Prophet" (6:14; 9:16).

Jesus' attitude toward his own miracles, as John portrays him, is one that makes a sharp distinction between "signs" and "works." The demand for signs on the part of onlookers or critics is an indicator of disbelief, of lack of perception. It is with obvious annoyance that Jesus responds to the importunate request of the official that Jesus heal his son, "Unless you see signs and wonders you will not believe" (4:48). He does, however, point to his miracles as evidence that he has been sent by God and as concrete manifestations of the "works" God has given him to do (5:36). These works must be done during the present "day" of God's special favor, since the coming night of demonic opposition will make such work impossible (9:3). The Prophet Isaiah is quoted to show, not only that few will understand what Jesus is disclosing by his miracles, but also *why* unbelief is so predominant (12:36–40). The failure to respond in faith is the consequence of a divine blinding, a hardening of the heart. As it is phrased in 10:25–26, the lack of trust in Jesus on the part of the majority of his contemporaries results from the fact that "you do not belong to my sheep." Divine determinism as to who are among the elect is the decisive factor in the reaction to Jesus and his "works": only his sheep hear his voice and follow him (10:27). The human side of the division of mankind into children of light and children of darkness is expressed in 3:19, where John declares that unbelief, or the decision to reject God's agent is man's own: "And this is the judgment, that the light has come into the world, and men loved darkness rather than light, because their deeds were evil."

Jesus is represented in John as fulfilling prophetic functions, even though they do not include his miracles. Thus, for example, Jesus' having seen Philip before they had actually met (1:48) and his knowledge of all the details of the Samaritan woman's life (4:39) manifest prophetic insight. Prophetic foresight is displayed even more extensively, however: Jesus has advance knowledge of the hour of his trial (2:4), of his betrayal and death (12:21–33), of his subsequent glorification (13:31–32), of his ascent to the Father and return to claim his own (14:2–3,

12, 18, 16:5–7, 21–22), of the coming of the Spirit (14:15–17; 15:26; 16:12–13), of the persecution of his followers (15:18–23; 16:2, 32) as well as of their glorification (17:22; 21:18–19), and of his fulfillment of his own kingly role, which is to bear witness to the truth (18:33–38; 19:14–15, 19–21). Curiously, there is an evidential value in these predictions: as Jesus phrases it in 14:29, "Now I have told you before it takes place, so that when it does take place, you may believe." The acts of Jesus, and even many of his declarations, are, as John represents them, public, yet it is only to the inner circle of his followers that the meaning of his words and actions is disclosed, and only by his own are they perceived. What is operative in John, therefore, is a special understanding of *truth*, different from both ancient and modern positivist or rationalist notions with regard both to what *is*, and how it may be known. And that brings us to a second facet of John's presentation of the Signs: the presence of eternity.

Our first clues to these ontological and epistemological dimensions of John appear in the prologue. Capitalizing on the traditional Greek philosophical distinction between being and becoming, John writes that, "the Logos *was (ēn)* the true light" (1:9). He who enlightens every human being was coming into the world, which *came into being (egeneto)* through him (1:10). After describing how, when those who might have been expected to be his people did not receive Jesus, family membership in God's true people was opened to all who would accept him, John announces: "And the Word became flesh and dwelt among us, full of grace and truth" (1:11–14). The introductory section concludes with the solemn observation, "No one has ever seen God; the only Son, who *is* in the bosom of the Father, he has made him known" (1:18). The final verb used here often means simply "report, explain, describe," but it is also a technical term for the interpretation of oracles and the disclosure of divine secrets.[5] Knowledge, therefore, is not a matter of correct information or historically demonstrable facts, but of divinely given insight, vouchsafed to the chosen community.

In quoting John 1:14 above, we stopped short of the crucial

5. See, on the term, Bauer-Arndt-Gingrich-Danker, *A Greek-English Lexicon of the New Testament*, 2d ed. (Chicago: University of Chicago Press, 1979 ad loc.)

declaration, "We have beheld his glory, glory as of the only Son from the Father." If we ask how Jesus manifested the divine glory, the answer is provided by John in his editorial comment on the first of Jesus' signs. Following the enigmatic account of the miracle at the wedding feast in Cana (2:1–10), John observes, "This, the first of his signs, Jesus did at Cana in Galilee and manifested his glory and his disciples believed in him" (2:11). It is essential to note that only the disciples believed in him. That is, of course, in keeping with what we have observed about the impossibility of faith for those who "do not belong to my sheep" (10:26). What the disciples discern in this "sign" is the divine glory, which we have learned from 1:14 is "glory as of the only Son from the Father."

A second clue concerning the privileged status of knowledge about the meaning of Jesus' acts comes in his curious, brusque reply to his mother, "My hour has not yet come." The narrative itself (2:1–10) implies that no one except the family and intimate friends knew of the potentially embarrassing lack of wine for the feast. Jesus' instructions to the servants seem to have been unobserved, even by the toastmaster or leader of the feast (2:9–10). The latter's remark about keeping the good wine until last is more than a variant on a truism about jaded palates at a feast: Unwittingly, he offers a thinly veiled prophetic pronouncement about "the best is yet to be." It is entirely legitimate to see in this scene, as well as in the comment about the best being kept until last, a symbolic eschatological picture. The abundance of wine in the days of fulfillment of prophetic hopes is a common feature of the canonical prophets (Am 9:13–14; Hos 14:7; Jer 31:12) as well of the extracanonical writings (1 Enoch 10:19; 2 Baruch 29:5). Both this story and that of the feeding of the five thousand resemble those told of the Prophets of Israel who come to the aid of hosts in times of emergency (1 Kgs 17:1–16, the breadless hostess of Elijah; 2 Kgs 4:1–7, Elisha's miraculous supplying of oil to the impecunious widow; 2 Kgs 4:42–44, the multiplication of bread given to Elisha supplies his hundred followers). Of course, the most obvious analogue to Jesus' miraculous feeding in the gospel tradition is that of the manna provided to Israel in the desert (Ex 16; Nm 11), as celebrated in the psalms

(Psa 78:21–25; Psa 105:40). That link is made explicit in John 6:31, where Psalm 78 is directly referred to.

Within Judaism of the early second century there was an expectation of the reenactment of the manna miracle in the new age, as 2 Baruch attests.[6] Similarly, the image of Israel as the adulterous wife of Yahweh is altered in the later prophetic tradition to depict the nation as the restored and radiant bride (Is 54:4–10; 62:1–5). In spite of its lack of religious content, the erotic and sensuous Song of Songs was acknowledged as part of scripture by the Council of Jamnia in the late first century A.D. largely because the poem was interpreted figuratively as describing the love of Yahweh for his people. In a passage which figures importantly in early Christian literature, Isaiah 61 (reported by Luke to have been the text used by Jesus to describe and justify his mission; Lk 4:16–20), the covenant relationship between God and his people in the day of eschatological fulfillment is explicitly compared with a bride: "He has clothed me [the eschatological covenant people] with the garments of salvation, he has covered me with the robe of righteousness, as a bridegroom decks himself with his garland, as a bride adorns herself with jewels" (Is 61:10).

To read these "signs" of John as mere wonder stories, therefore, told to enhance Jesus' reputation as a miracle-worker or attest his beneficence toward those in difficulty would be to omit the very dimensions of the narratives which are clearly of primary importance for John. These are not *signs*, in the sense that Jesus' exorcisms are signs of the defeat of Satan or of the inbreaking of the kingdom (Lk 11:20); for John they are symbols of a new reality.

6. 2 Baruch 29:8 reads, "The treasury of manna shall again descend from on high, and they shall eat of it in those years." This document was probably written between the first and second Jewish revolts (after 70 and before 135), according to A. M. Denis, *Introduction aux pseudepigraphes grecs d'Ancien Testament* (Leiden: Brill, 1970), p. 74, who assigns the date by inference from what are apparently allusions to the fall of Jerusalem. References in rabbinic materials confirm this expectation, as summarized by R. E. Brown, *Gospel of John, I–XII*, pp. 265–66, but they are of such uncertain date—probably later than the second revolt—as to be unreliable witnesses for what Jews were expecting at the time John wrote his gospel.

Suzanne Langer has made a useful distinction between sign and symbol. Signs are indicators; symbols are representations.[7] Animals respond to signs: dogs will return to their masters at the sound of a whistle; cats will come to be fed when their food container is rattled or struck. The basic process of the human brain, which distinguishes human beings categorically from animals, is what Langer calls "the symbolic transformation of experiences." That process culminates primarily in speech, in which words do not merely refer to objects but represent by symbols certain concepts, propositions, situations. Similar symbolic representation occurs also in ritual acts, which are neither practical nor communicative in the ordinary sense.[8] She rejects both the Freudian notion which equates a theory of mind with epistemology, thereby omitting the crucial role of symbolization,[9] and the logicians' assumption that "nothing which cannot be 'projected' in discursive form is accessible to the human mind, and any attempt to understand anything but demonstrable fact is bootless ambition."[10] Langer asserts instead that in this space-time world there are "things which do not fit the grammatical scheme of expression . . . matters which require to be conceived through some symbolistic schema other than discursive language," which "defy linguistic projection."[11] To adopt this approach to symbolization is not to abandon reason, however: "The recognition of the presentational symbolism as a normal and prevalent vehicle of meaning widens our concept of rationality far beyond the traditional boundaries, yet never breaks with logic in the strictest sense. . . . No symbol is exempt from the office of logical formulation, of conceptualizing what it conveys; however simple its import or however great, this impact is a *meaning*, and therefore an element of an understanding."[12]

Symbolization is not merely a private intellectual enterprise,

7. Suzanne Langer, *Philosophy in a New Key: A Study in the Symbolism of Rite and Act* (Cambridge: Harvard University Press, 1942, 1957³, 1976), p. 30.

8. Ibid., p. 45.

9. Ibid., p. 57.

10. Ibid., p. 86.

11. Ibid., p. 93.

12. Ibid., p. 97.

however, nor are the symbols assembled in the mind by a cafeteria-like style of random choice. Rather, the symbolization process is profoundly social in nature and aim. As Grace de Laguna wrote, "Some more or less organized system of beliefs and sentiments is an absolute necessity for the carrying on of social life," although the group solidarity which such a system secures may lead to "behavior ill-adapted to the objective order of nature" (i.e., ritual).[13] Robert Jay Lifton has written along similar lines, but in relation specifically to the universal problem of death and immortality: "We can understand much of human history as the struggle to achieve, maintain, and reaffirm a collective system of immortality under constantly changing psychic and material conditions. For modes of immortality to be symbolically viable . . . they must connect with direct, proximate experience as well as provide patterns of continuity."[14] He goes on to quote with approval Suzanne Langer's observation that every major advance in thinking and every epoch-making new insight springs from a new type of symbolic transformation,[15] and to describe man's ceaseless effort in every historical and cultural setting to shape images into a cosmology "which both absorbs and gives dignity to his ever-present death anxiety. . . . In the face of his potentially endless flow of images, man seeks lasting symbolic structure . . . he is ever in quest of the mental form that can contain those fragments [of shattered dreams] and balance his death terror with a life-giving vision connecting him with past and future."[16] The world-construction that is the aim of symbolization has as its development process the transformation of symbols, including not only discursive language but myth and ritual, which provide present meaning through links with the past. These writers, and others in the social sciences, emphasize that symbolization is not primarily an individual enterprise, but is instead an essential mode of socialization. Through a shared

13. Grace Andrus de Laguna, *Speech: Its Function and Development* (New Haven: Yale University Press, 1927), pp. 345–46.

14. Robert J. Lifton, *The Broken Connection* (New York: Simon and Schuster, 1979), p. 283.

15. Langer, *Philosophy in a New Key*, p. 172.

16. Lifton, *Broken Connection*, pp. 284, 292.

view of the cosmos, of man's place within it, of evil and redemption, the individual finds his or her identity, whether in the larger
society that shares those perspectives, or in a group or sect that
differentiates itself from society.[17] Mary Douglas thinks that the
process of symbolization is so fundamental to human history that,
"The whole history of ideas should be reviewed in the light of
the power of social structures to generate symbols of their own."[18]

After this excursus on symbol, but very much in light of it, let
us return to the Gospel of John. Both the miracles which we
have examined in some detail—the changing of water into wine
and the feeding of the five thousand—exhibit the transformation of symbols. Both build on Jewish scriptural tradition, but
they not merely borrow it: they adapt it to a distinctive point of
view. Further, as the discourse following the feeding story makes
clear repeatedly, the main point of the story is not "food which
perishes" but "food which endures to eternal life" (Jn 6:27; cf.
33, 40, 47, 51, 53–54, 57, 58). John 6:63 makes the point explicit: "It is the spirit that gives life; the flesh is of no avail." What
we have in these stories are not miracles of food and drink but
enacted metaphors of eternal life. The use of the technical term
eucharistēsas in 6:11, as well as the details of the participants' eating their fill and the gathering of the fragments, match precisely
the ancient eucharistic liturgy (*Didache* 9) symbolizing the rite of
participation in the "bread from heaven" which "gives life to the
world" (6:33). Although there is no explicit tie, the new, better
wine of the wedding scene in 2:10 is probably intended as an
allusion to the wine of the Eucharist.

More is symbolized in these stories than gaining a share in
eternal life, however. As we have noted, what John declares Jesus to have manifested at the wedding feast at Cana was not his
redemptive benefactions but *his glory*. In John 6:35, Jesus is not
merely the dispenser of the bread of life: he *is* that bread from
heaven. The paradox of the Incarnation is involved, since Jesus'
claim to be the bread which came down from heaven is in con-

17. See my *Christian Origins*, pp. 30–53.
18. Mary Douglas, *Natural Symbols: Explorations in Cosmology* (New York: Random House, 1970), p. 185.

flict with his known natural origin as the son of Mary and Joseph.[19] Throughout John 6 there is stress on the claim that Jesus enjoys a special relationship to God, his Father, and that he has come down from heaven. This brings us back to the theme of Jesus as the manifestation of the divine glory, mentioned in 1:14, 18, and linked with his first "sign" in 2:11.

The motif of glory is more frequently sounded in the closing chapters of this gospel. Ironically, this occurs in conjunction with Jesus' suffering and death. In John 12 the prospect of his death is linked with his glorification (12:23), as is his rejection by the mass of humanity, who did not believe in him in spite of his signs (12:37–41). Paradoxically, as the hour of his arrest, trial, and death approaches, Jesus is portrayed as referring to this as the event in which both he and God will be glorified (13:31–32). The coming Spirit will further the glorification of the Son (16:14–15), which is described in detail in 17:1–26. The work of Christ is to reveal God to the elect ("to those whom thou gavest me"; 17:6), who will one day see fully the glory which God has given him.

Another set of images through which John depicts Jesus as the embodiment of divine revelation represents him as coming down from heaven. Through a variety of symbols, John describes how God disclosed himself to his people through Jesus. There is the universal potential for enlightenment through the "true light" (1:9). The agent of creation does not find acceptance in the world, however, except among the members of the community of faith (1:10–11) who constitute God's true people, with familial ties that are not genetic or ethnic but are of God's own forming (1:12–13) among those who receive in faith his incarnate Word. The vivid image of "the open heavens and the angels of God ascending and descending on the Son of man" (1:51) is a transformation of the scene in Genesis 28:10–22, according to which Jacob has a direct encounter with God, accom-

19. While Matthew and Luke understood the incarnation as occurring through the virginal conception of Jesus (Mt 1:18–19; Lk 1:26–34), John suggests that the birth of Jesus was ordinary and directly identifies Joseph as his father (1:45; 6:42).

panied by the presence of angels, the outcome of which is that Jacob claims Yahweh as his God and Jacob is established as the progenitor of the covenant people.

A direct corollary of this "ascending and descending" link with God is the claim that Jesus came from above, since he *is*—in the sense of timeless being—in the "bosom of the Father" (1:18). Those who are members of God's family must, therefore, be "born from above," as Jesus informs Nicodemus (3:3–5, 12–13).[20] That new birth "of the Spirit" is expressly differentiated from natural birth (3:6); it takes place through the one who "descended from heaven" (3:13). A similar claim appears in 8:23 ("I am from above"); his authority derives directly from God (8:28), who has taught Jesus his role. This means, therefore, that Jesus has access to the divine secrets: Nicodemus is informed that he does not understand earthly things and is thus unable to grasp the heavenly things which Jesus is ready to impart (3:12). There is no other access to God's self-disclosure than Jesus, the "only Son" (1:14), whose preexistence is attested by John the Baptist ("he was before me"; 1:15). Through his resurrection, he ascends to "where he was before" (6:62). The symbolic mode of asserting this is set forth in a sharp contrast with the miracles of the Old Covenant people: "Truly, truly, I say to you, it was not Moses who gave you the bread from heaven; my Father gives you the *true* bread from heaven. For the bread of God is that which comes down from heaven and gives life to the world" (6:32–33). Jesus does not merely bring that bread: he embodies it (6:35).

SYMBOLIC INTENTION IN JOHN

The symbolic force of the other miracle stories in John will now be more readily apparent; similar symbolization is evident in other Johannine narratives, where prophetic insight and predic-

20. The term used by John, *anothen*, can mean "again," though it derives from *anō*, "above." In characteristic fashion, the author has used a term which his unbelieving hearers understand with literal simplicity, as does Nicodemus: "How can anyone enter the second time into his mother's womb?" (Jn 3:4), i.e., and be born again? But the discerning reader will know that Jesus speaks of a birth from above, "of the Spirit" (3:5–8).

tion blend. The "second sign," which is the healing of the official's son (4:46–54), is not merely a record of an early miracle performed by Jesus but also a symbolic paradigm of the proper response to the Word-made-flesh. The official does not have to wait to see Jesus perform a miracle in order to decide whether or not to believe in him. With no external way to determine the reliability of Jesus' assertion that the son will live, the official "believed the word that Jesus spoke to him and went his way." It is later confirmed that the recovery began at the moment of Jesus' pronouncement. The crucial factor, however, was the official's trust in Jesus' word.

The healing of the lame man at the pool (5:1–9) is recounted in such a way as to show that the response of faith is a prerequisite to the healing. Simultaneously with his obedience to Jesus' command to take up his pallet and walk, the healing takes place (5:8–9). As is the case with synoptic accounts of healing on the sabbath, Jesus' capacity to heal raises questions about the source of his power, as he performs these acts on the sabbath (Mk 3:1–6 and parallels). In the synoptics, however, the issue is posed by Jesus as to whether acts of mercy, including the saving of life, are not acceptable deeds to be performed on the sabbath. In John 5, on the other hand, the basic question is Jesus' relationship to God. He justifies his setting aside the sabbath law on the grounds that he is carrying out God's ongoing work ("My Father is working still, and I am working"; 5:17). This claim is understandably perceived by the Jewish leaders as tantamount to placing himself on an equal level with God (5:18). That implication is spelled out in 5:19–21, where Jesus declares that his unique filial relationship with God is the basis for the works he performs, which are in fact the works of God, a feature of John to which we shall return.

The symbolic meaning of the signs includes not only who Jesus really is but how the believer in him discovers his own identity. The crucial text, John 20:31, not only designates Jesus through his signs as Son of God, but also announces that those who trust in him have "life in his name." Here also we have a pervasive motif in the Fourth Gospel. Already in the prologue, John's readers learn that this new life, this being born of God, constitutes one as a member of God's family (1:11–12). Another collective image is used in the oracle about the destruction of the Temple and its replacement by Christ's "body," which is made possible through his resurrection from the dead (2:20–21). Following the dialogue with Nicodemus, John declares that God gave his Son in order that those who believe in Him might have life (3:14–21). The miracle stories of 4:46–54 and 5:1–9 lead on to pronouncements concerning the attainment of life (5:21). Indeed, eternal life (5:24–25) is not merely a hope for the day of resurrection (v. 25) but is already experienced by those who believe Jesus' word. Similarly, the bread which Jesus provides does not merely sustain life from day to day but guarantees it for eternity (6:33, 35, 40, 51): "I am the living bread which came down from heaven; if anyone eats of this bread, he will live forever." There is no other source of life eternal but this living bread (6:54), and it completely supplants the divine sustenance of the Old Covenant people through the manna in the desert experience of Israel (6:58). The agency by which that life is experienced is the Spirit which Jesus sends, symbolized by the "living water" (7:38–39).

Other life-images used by John include "the light of life" (8:12), a symbol which is then developed in narrative form in John 9: the man born blind who receives sight through "the light of the world" (9:5). Those who respond to the light in faith join the company of believers, in contrast to the official religious leaders, who remain in darkness (9:25–40). The image of the shepherd and the flock is elaborated in John 10, where those who heed the shepherd's voice demonstrate thereby that they are members of his fold. They thus share in the life which he makes possible for them by laying down his own (10:11). The motifs are woven together in 10:27, "My sheep hear my voice, and I know them, and they follow me; and I give them eternal life, and they shall never perish, and no one shall snatch them out of my hand."

The related themes of eternal life and vicarious death are set forth in the "sign" story of the Raising of Lazarus (11:1–44). There is an explicit contrast between the traditional Jewish belief in the resurrection at the last day and the pronouncement of Jesus that he *is* the resurrection and the life, and that whoever believes in him shall never die. The death of Jesus, which makes possible the resurrection life for believers, is ironically described by the Jewish leaders as necessary for national survival (11:51–52). Its necessity is affirmed by Jesus in the image of the grain seed which must "fall into the earth and die" if it is to bring forth the fruit, which is the new people of God (12:24). Again the interconnected themes of faith, light, and life are set forth in 12:44–50, culminating in the declaration that the Father's "commandment is eternal life."

Similarly, in the extended discourses of John 14–17, participation in the corporate life of the new people is symbolically portrayed. The architectural image of the house of God (14:1–6) leads to the qualification that admission to God's household is only through the One who is the "way, the truth, and the life." The horticultural image of the vine is immediately interpreted as the transmission of life and fructification through the one who is "the true vine," a picture taken over from ancient Israel (Is 5:1–7; Ez 19:10–14) but now transformed and personalized in the figure of Jesus. John 15:18–16:33 furnishes advice to the community concerning the persecution it will undergo after Jesus has gone back to the Father and the Paraclete (the Spirit) has come among them, and how during that time of duress they are to be bold in prayer and forthright in teaching. At 16:25 Jesus reportedly acknowledges that he has been talking in veiled figurative language[21] but will now speak openly. The explanation which follows contains no surprises, however. It is a somewhat more prosaic statement of what has been set out in discursive and metaphorical language throughout the Gospel: Jesus' special relationship with the Father, past, present and future; and the comfort the disciples are to experience through their link with the Father by means of him. Many of the Johannine themes are interwoven in one of the concluding lines of the prayer

21. The term used here, *paroimia*, can mean merely proverb or maxim, but according to the late testimony of the Byzantine period lexicon, Suidas, it meant "hidden pronouncements," which suits well this context (Jn 16:25). The word also appears in Sirach 47:17 in connection with *hermeneia* but the terms there are in parallel, rather than implying that the *paroimiai* are in need of explanation.

of Jesus (17:24), "Father, I desire that they also, whom thou hast given me, may be with me where I am, to behold my glory which thou hast given me before the foundation of the world."

In her study of symbolization, Suzanne Langer shows that symbolic transformation in its nonverbal form gives rise to ritual, the primary aim of which is to strengthen a sense of group identity. Ritual arises around an important individual, whose utterances are preserved in stylized liturgical form, repetition of which reinforces the meaning and purpose of the group. She describes the ritual acts as "part of man's ceaseless quest for conception and orientation. They embody his dawning notions of power and will, of death and victory; they give active and impressive form to his demoniac fears and ideals." Although ritual gives expression to these deep, cosmic concerns, it is "usually a homely, familiar action, such as washing, eating, drinking . . . an act that is essentially realistic and vital."[22]

It is precisely in these modes that ritual appears in John's gospel. The most obvious narrative of ritual depicts Jesus washing the feet of his disciples (13:1–11), which symbolizes his humility, the need of all for continued cleansing from the defilement of the world, the concrete expression of mutual love. That this was not understood as a unique occurrence is evident from the specific instruction (13:14): "If I then, your Lord and Teacher, have washed your feet, you also ought to wash one another's feet." We have already noted that the bridal feast and the miraculous feeding symbolize the sacred feast of the Eucharist, including traces of the liturgical usage of the later church. This meal is reenacted in the final miracle story of John (21), where we read of the miraculous catch of fish (symbolizing the success of the mission of Jesus' followers) followed by the meal of bread and fish, through which Jesus is once more revealed to his disciples (21:14). The import of these ritual acts is spelled out in the subsequent instructions to the disciples to display their love concretely by feeding and tending to the needs of Christ's flock (21:15–19).

Miracle for John is far more than a benefaction attesting to

22. Langer, *Philosophy in a New Key*, pp. 131, 157, 159.

divine favor or compassion. It is more than a sign of the impending New Age, in which God's will triumphs over the powers of evil, as we saw to be the case in the apocalyptic strand of the New Testament writings. It is an avenue or medium by which men and women of insight and faith can experience the transcendent in the midst of earthly life. That goal was by no means unique to John, though John is the only evangelist who makes explicit his convictions about the centrality of signs/symbols in his story of Jesus.

SYMBOL AND MYTH IN PHILO AND PLUTARCH

An attitude toward miracle which, like John's, regards the outward event as the symbolic representation of an inner change or disclosure is to be found in non-Christian writers of the first and second centuries as well. In a wide range of miracles, portents, and visions, Philo of Alexandria takes his reader behind the external narrative to an interior meaning. What is important for our purposes is to note Philo's epistemological and ontological assumptions, not merely his allegorical method, which he shares with biblical writers.[23]

In Philo's *On Flight and Finding*, the miracle of Israel's divine food in the desert (based on Ex 16:4–21)—which, of course, is directly linked in John with Jesus' miracle of feeding (Jn 6)—is not reported by Philo as a divine provision for human sustenance in the absence of earthly food. Although initially the Israelites "knew not what it was" (Ex 16:15; in Hebrew, *manna*), Philo tells us that "they became learners and found it to be a

23. The allegory of Israel as the unproductive vine in need of pruning appears in Isaiah 5:1–2 and is developed in the earlier gospel tradition (Mk 12:1; Mt 21:33–44) to justify (1) the founding of the church, which considers itself to be the New Covenant people, and (2) the catastrophe of the fall of Jerusalem in A.D. 70, which Christians regarded as a divine judgment on Israel, the unfruitful vine. In Galatians 4, Paul offers an allegorical interpretation of the story of Sarah, Hagar, and Abraham in order to provide a biblical precedent for his doctrine of justification by faith as the ground for admission to the New Covenant community. In all these cases, however, the thrust of the allegory is to explain historical change, and particularly to account for social redefinition—a very different aim than that of Philo, whose allegorical method serves to internalize truth.

saying of God, that is the Divine Word,[24] from which all kinds
of instruction and wisdom flow in perpetual stream." This heavenly nourishment which "God drops from above" is the ethereal
wisdom which falls on "minds which are by nature apt and take
delight in contemplation," even though they do not fully recognize it for what it is. But on inquiry they learn that "this divine
ordinance fills the soul that has vision alike with light and sweetness, flashing forth the radiancy of truth, and with the honeyed
grace of persuasion [imparts] sweetness to those who hunger
and thirst after nobility of character."[25]

The biblical account of the divine intervention through which
God seeks to thwart human conspiracy against his purposes in
the world by confusion of human language (Gn 11:7) provides
Philo the occasion for a cosmological statement about the unity
of God and the multiplicity of the divine potencies.[26] Though
"there is only one sovereign and ruler and king," there are
"around him numberless potencies which all assist and protect
created being." Through them "the incorporeal and intelligible
world was framed, the archetype of this phenomenal world, the
former being a system of invisible ideal forms as the latter is of
visible material bodies." The base on which this philosophical
disquisition rests is the simple biblical statement of God, "Come
and let us go down and confuse their tongues." A similar philosophical elaboration is offered by Philo in his report of Jacob's
dream of the stairway to heaven on which the angels of God
ascend and descend (Gn 28:12), with the Lord God standing
above it (28:13). Philo seizes the occasion to offer a detailed geo-
physical and astronomical description of the air, which in turn
leads to a depiction of the exalted souls which mount up to or
float down from the heavenly presence. God is represented as
walking among his people (Lev 26:12) and as mounted on a
chariot.[27] The last detail recalls the throne mysticism found in
Judaism in the period of the Second Temple and subsequently,

24. Surprisingly, Philo uses *hrēma*, not *logos*, though the concepts are akin.
25. Philo, *On Flight and Finding*, pp. 137–39.
26. Philo, *On Confusion of Tongues*, pp. 168–79.
27. Philo, *On Dreams* 1:133–35; 148; 157.

according to which the seat of God's power is a celestial chariot by which the faithful ascend in mystical transport.[28]

Abraham likewise is represented in his dealings with God as the model of ecstatic mysticism. His call by God, reported in Genesis 12:1–3, leads to his release from his body.[29] The curious turn of phrase in the LXX of Genesis 15:5, according to which God "led him out outside" is explained by Philo as a vivid way of contrasting "life in the body which is a sojourning in a foreign land,"[30] with God's leading the faithful person "outside of the prison-houses of the body, of the lairs where the senses lurk, of the sophistries of deceitful word and thought," and out of confidence in human wisdom, out of allegiance to oneself.[31] Obviously the focus of interest in Philo's version of the patriarchal narrative has shifted from a physical descendant for the childless Abraham and Sarah to the attainment of divine knowledge, and of the divinization of the self: "For when the mind is ministering to God in purity, it is not human, but divine."[32] The trance into which Abraham fell at the climax of his conversation with God (Gn 15:12) is seen by Philo as an "inspired and God-possessed experience," For Philo, the occurrence of this ecstasy at the setting of the sun is richly symbolic of his divine possession: "While the radiance of the mind is still all around us, when it pours as it were a noonday beam into the whole soul, we are self-contained, not possessed. But when it comes to its setting, naturally ecstasy and divine possession and madness fall upon us. For when the light of God shines, the human light sets; when the divine light sets, the human dawns and rises. . . . And therefore the setting of reason and the darkness which surrounds it produce ecstasy and inspired frenzy."[33]

28. See chap. 5, n. 24. Also Gershon Scholem, *Jewish Gnosticism, Merkabah Mysticism and Talmudic Tradition* (New York: Jewish Theological Seminary, 1960). Traces of this mystical tradition are also evident in the Dead Sea Scrolls: in the Angelic Liturgy (4QSL), where the cherubim "bless the likeness of the Throne of the Chariot," a phrase also used in 3 Enoch 46:7 and Sirach 49:8.

29. Philo, *On the Migration of Abraham*, pp. 2–3.

30. Philo, *Who is Heir?* p. 82.

31. Ibid., p. 85.

32. Ibid., p. 84.

33. Ibid., pp. 264–65.

Thus Philo evinces no interest in the historical experiences of Israel and her patriarchs as such, nor in the questions of genealogical descent and political survival. Rather, his attention is turned inward, looking through the traditional accounts of God's miraculous interventions, portents, and epiphanies granted to the leaders of Israel, concentrating instead on the mystical participation of the faithful in the divine wisdom, sharing in the divine life itself, transported—not from Egypt to the land of Canaan, in any literal sense—but upward into the presence of the One who sits on the throne-chariot. The miracles are not signs of divine favor but symbols of divine participation.

This consciously symbolic interpretation of miracles was not limited to Jewish and Christian writers of this period, however. We have already examined in some detail (chap. 4) how Plutarch undertook to interpret the Isis myth "more philosophically"— that is, to treat the myth as a medium of rational perception of reality. It may be useful to observe more specifically how he described his own hermeneutical method, since it is clearly akin to the symbolic approach we have been observing in John and Philo. He is scornful of those who take the myth literally, especially of those who glory in the gory details of some versions of the myth. He describes those who report such "infamous tales . . . as that about the dismemberment of Horus and the decapitation of Isis," remarking that "if they hold such opinions and relate such tales about the nature of the blessed and imperishable (in accordance with which our concept of the divine must be framed) as if such deeds actually took place, then "Much need there is to spit and cleanse the mouth, as Aeschylus has it."[34] He expresses assurance that his patroness "detests those persons who hold such abnormal and outlandish opinions about the gods."[35]

Plutarch likewise rejects purely rational explanations of the myths of the gods. He discusses sympathetically the theory that these narratives concern demigods or daimones. He suggests that

34. A fragment from Aeschylus, now published by Nauck in *Trag. Graec. Frag.*, Aeschylus, no. 354.

35. Plutarch, *De Iside*, p. 20. All subsequent references in parentheses are to the section numbers of this treatise.

his readers "follow the lead of early writers on sacred subjects" and consider that the subjects of the myths were "stronger than human beings, yet not possessing the divine quality unmixed and uncontaminated, but . . . share also in the nature of the soul and in the perceptive faculties of the body, and with a susceptibility to pleasure and pain and to whatsoever other experience is incident to these mutations . . ." (25).

On the other hand, Plutarch rejects the notion, proposed by "numerous and tiresome people," of confusing theological insights with seasonal changes and agricultural patterns of sowing and growing (65). Similarly, he has no patience with naturalistic explanations of the myth offered by those who "unwittingly erase and dissipate things divine into winds and streams and sowings and ploughings, developments of the earth and changes of the seasons," since they thereby confer "the names of gods upon objects which are senseless and inanimate" (66). He characterizes as "a play of fancy surpassing all the wealth of monstrous fable" those interpretations of myth which assume that the gods changed themselves into animal forms, or which see in the narratives totemic meaning (72). He also reports without comment the idea that the myths were conjured up by "later kings"—presumably Hellenistic rulers, who imposed themselves on Egypt—to confuse the "light-minded" populace, so that by planting among them "an everlasting superstition" they were divided among themselves by "unceasing quarrelling" (72).

For those who accept the myth literally, to the point of assuming that Osiris actually dwells in the earth among the bodies of the dead, Plutarch has only pity. Yet he is confident that "when these souls are set free and migrate into the realm of the invisible and the unseen, the dispassionate and the pure, then this god becomes their leader and king, since it is on him that they are bound to be dependent in their insatiate contemplation and yearning for that beauty which is for human beings unutterable and indescribable" (78). Plutarch insists, rather, on interpreting the myths "more philosophically" (32), not only the narratives themselves, but the rituals and the sacred objects linked with the Isis myth as well. He sees the entire range of his world-view—including physical and astronomical features of the cosmos—as

mirrored in the myth (41–43). Mingling several Greek myths
with those of Isis and Osiris, Plutarch asserts that the birth of
Apollo from Osiris and Isis means "allegorically" that before this
world was made visible and its rough material was completely
formed by Reason (*logos*), it was put to the test by Nature (*physis*)
and brought forth of itself the first creation imperfect. That god,
"born in darkness" and "a cripple," was the elder Horus, "for
there was then no world, but only an image and outline of a
world to be" (54). The mythic accounts of the struggles of Horus
and Hermes with Typhon instruct us that "Reason adjusts the
universe (*to pan*) and creates concord out of discordant elements
. . ." (55). Combining mathematical features, especially the Pythagorean theorem of the right triangle, Plutarch discerns complete harmony between the mythic triad—Isis, Osiris, Horus—
and Plato's doctrine of creation as set forth in the *Republic* and
the *Timaeus* (56).[36]

The symbolic treatment of the Isis-Osiris myth leads Plutarch
to observe that Osiris symbolizes the combined relationship of
things in the heavens and things in the lower world (61). The
gods are one, in spite of the different ways they are named among
different peoples of the earth, "For that one rationality which
keeps all things in order and the one Providence which watches
over them and the ancillary powers that are set over all" is known
among different peoples in various ways and honored by different rituals and customs. "Thus men make use of consecrated
symbols, some employing symbols that are obscure, but others
those that are clearer, in guiding the intelligence toward things
divine," even though some fall into superstition on the one hand
or atheism on the other (67). The identification of animals as
sacred need not be merely superstitious, however: for example,
"the crocodile, certainly, has acquired honor which is not devoid
of a plausible reason, but he is declared to be a living representation of God, since he is the only creature without a tongue; for
the Divine Word has no need of a voice . . ." (75).

Against the background of this rich and varied array of sym-
bolizations, Isis is for Plutarch the symbolic medium through

---

36. Plato *Republic* 546; *Timaeus* 50.

which men and women may participate in the ineffable beauty of ultimate reality. "With this beauty Isis, as the ancient story declares, is forever enamoured and pursues it and consorts with it and fills our earth here with all things fair and good that partake of generation" (78). In her wisdom she "discloses the divine mysteries to those who truly and justly have the name of 'bearers of the sacred vessels' and 'wearers of sacred robes.' These are they who within their own soul, as though within a casket, bear the sacred writings about gods clear of all superstition and pedantry. . . . For this reason, too, the fact that the deceased votaries of Isis are decked with these garments is a sign that these sacred writings accompany them, and that they pass to the other world possessed of these and naught else" (3).

In all this setting forth of promise and participation in the divine Isianic mysteries, there is not a trace of Isis, the beneficent healer. She and her consort, Osiris, symbolize the maintenance of natural order in the Stoic sense; they do not voluntarily effect the change of seasons and the cycles of crops. The details of the myths that tell of Isis are treated as symbolizing ontological and cosmological issues, which have been set forth more prosaically by the philosophers Plato, Pythagoras, and Zeno. Only the foolish and misguided read the myths literally. The wise regard the myths as mirrors of reality (76). The attuned ear can hear through the outwardly incredible myth the Divine Word of eternal truth, by which the universe was brought into being and is maintained in tension, but also in accord, with divine order. One turns to Isis for truth and meaning, not for healing or solutions to transitory problems. In expressing this world-view, Plutarch is the spokesman for a significant segment of the Roman populace in the early second century.

SYMBOLIC INTERPRETATION OF ASKLEPIOS: AELIUS ARISTIDES

The symbolic function of the Isis myth in the exposition of Plutarch recalls the symbolic transformations of the Asklepios myth in Aelius Aristides (see chap. 3 above), although there are important differences to be noted as well. Aristides did continue to have problems with his health throughout his life, so that healing, or at least alleviation of his ailments, was important for him to carry on his work. We have observed earlier[37] that he was impatient with those who wanted to discuss only their physical disabilities, passing by in silence "those things which at the same time raised my body, strengthened my soul, and increased the glory of my rhetorical career." We have seen how abundant is testimony to the god's enabling him to reach the summit of rhetorical achievement, on a par with the military prowess of Alexander the Great.[38] But the communion with the god effected not only his superlative rhetorical attainments; it also led to his own union with the divine, which in his fifth Sacred Discourse he envisioned in a form nearly identical to that of Jacob, as pictured by Philo,[39] and of Jesus as quoted by John: "Truly, truly, I say to you, you shall see the heavens opened, and the angels of God ascending and descending upon the Son of Man" (Jn 1:51). Direct access to the divine presence is claimed in each of these mystic accounts.

Though Aristides claims that the god granted him unique rhetorical skill, and though he is annoyed with his fellow dwellers in the Asklepion who speak only of their diseases and cures, he speaks for an important segment of Roman society in his yearning for and depiction of union with the divine. Although Lucius, in the *Metamorphoses*, is interested in his own transformation by Isis and his devotion to her, he makes it clear that he is a participant in a cult. When he achieves his spiritual change and emerges resplendent in his sacred robes from the sanctuary, he is acclaimed by the crowd of devotees of the goddess.[40] In the cases of both Apuleius and Aristides, there is a shared life-world and a common experience of renewal through the divine, however personal and direct are the benefits. Yet for Plutarch and John, the divine transformation is of cosmic dimensions. There is no calling upon the gods for direct, divine intervention in order to achieve political or ethnic goals, as was the case with

37. Chap. 3, p. 95, with reference to *Sacr. Disc.* 5.36.
38. Chap. 3, p. 97, with reference to *Sacr. Disc.* 4.22–29, 48–54.
39. Philo, *On Dreams*, pp. 133–59, based on Genesis 28:12.
40. Apuleius *Metamorphoses* 11.24.

the prophets denounced by Josephus when the climax came in the Jewish struggle for military overthrow of Roman domination of Palestine.[41] Neither are signs awaited for eschatological vindication of the faithful, as in the Dead Sea community, or in the Q tradition and in Mark.[42] The quest in Plutarch, Aelius Aristides, and John is for the meaning of human existence in a cosmic setting, for an understanding of ultimate reality, for a sense of participation in a divine order and purpose which transcends the powers of evil and triumphs over the human sense of anxiety and helplessness in a vast universe.

In spite of the features he shares with Jewish and pagan contemporaries, John is distinctive in important ways. Philo plays down the historical base of the scriptures which he is interpreting allegorically. That practice did not in the least diminish his sense of belonging to and his devotion to his Jewish heritage, as is attested in his having led the delegation to the emperor Gaius Caligula to protest the maltreatment of Jews in Alexandria.[43] Yet the symbolic and allegorical meaning of the scriptural material, whether narrative or legal, was the overwhelming preoccupation of Philo, who sought to correlate his reading of these texts with the eclectic philosophy in which he had been reared in Alexandria. Plutarch begins with the Isis-Osiris myth but moves quickly and pervasively to universalize that material by linking these Egyptian divinities with other Greek and oriental gods. His goal is a universally inclusive system of symbols for the divine renewal of the human mind.

John, by contrast, insists on the historicity, the corporeality, the true humanity of his revelatory figure, "Jesus of Nazareth, the son of Joseph" (Jn 1:45). No miracle surrounds his birth; no glory surrounds his birthplace, as the link with Bethlehem does in Matthew and Luke by associating Jesus with the royal line of David. John's consistent paradox identifies this hill-country carpenter's son with the divine Logos, through which both the evangelist and the philosophers of the period understood God

---

41. Josephus *Wars*.
42. See above, chap. 5, pp. 155–70.
43. Fully documented in Philo, *Legatio ad Gaium*.

to have created the universe. The Fourth Gospel focuses on the universal hopes and human needs, and does so in precisely those omnipresent symbolic forms to which Robert Lifton has drawn attention: death and the transformation of life.[44] Yet for John, this is not merely an individual search for immortality. The symbols of life that he employs are uniformly corporate, attesting to the commonality of the divine benefaction that brings renewal: the flock, the vine, the Israel of God. His life-world is reinforced through ritual and extended through the mission to which his community is seen to have been called, all of which is symbolically portrayed in his narratives and discourses.[45] John binds together the whole of his life-world, even while demonstrating his links with other contemporary symbolic schemes and his sympathies for those human aspirations thus symbolically represented, by transforming the structure that he received from the tradition. Miracle is no longer a sign of divine intervention; it is a symbol of divine transformation.

As we observed above, in reference to the insights of Suzanne Langer, the "symbolic transformation of experiences" is a characteristically human enterprise. That it is to be seen taking place in the writings of John, Philo, Aristides, and Plutarch in relation to miracle is in no sense unique. What is distinctive, however, is that all these writers make explicit what it is they are doing, in that they differentiate between a literal reading of texts or interpretation of events on the one hand, and the symbolic meaning of words and acts on the other. In comparing and contrasting this phenomenon as it appears in sophisticated writings, such as those of Plutarch and Aristides, and in such a stylistically simple

44. Lifton, *Broken Connection*, p. 283.

45. The communal focus of John's symbolic transformation of the tradition recalls Emile Durkheim's classic formulation: religious representations are collective representations which express collective realities; the rites are a manner of acting which take rise in the midst of the assembled groups and which are destined to excite, maintain, or recreate certain mental states in these groups. So, if the categories are religious facts, they too should be social affairs and the product of collective thought. From Emile Durkheim, *The Elementary Forms of the Religious Life*, trans. from the French by J. W. Swain (New York: Free Press, [1915], 1965), p. 22.

Christian writing as the Gospel of John, one can perceive typical features of a life-world that took shape in the late first and early second centuries, just as one can discern how a certain wing of the rising Christian movement was also adopting this life-world even while adapting it to the peculiarities of the Christian tradition.

CHAPTER EIGHT

Miracle as Propaganda in Pagan and Christian Romances

By the end of the second century of our era both pagan and Christian writers, both believers and skeptics, were exploiting the possibilities of a popular Hellenistic genre,[1] the romance, to propagandize for their particular values and aims. Whether the message was that of the scornful satire of Lucian of Samosata concerning Alexander the False Prophet or the credulousness of the apocryphal Acts of Paul, whether it was an extended narrative in praise of Apollonius of Tyana as philosopher or the vivid account of the bewitching and conversion of Apuleius, devotee of Isis, the medium was that of the romance.

As we noted earlier (chap. 4, n. 92) with regard to Apuleius's *Metamorphoses*, the ancient romance was far more than mere entertainment (see chap. 6, pp. 193–95): it served as a vehicle for conveying religious truth or as an apology for a philosophical view. Or, in the case of Lucian, the romantic style was the instrument to expose the fraudulence of the claims made by a kind of propaganda agent or public relations officer for the oracle of Asklepios. Similarly, the refutation by Eusebius of Caesarea of Philostratus's claims in behalf of Apollonius of Tyana derives its evidence from the latter's romantic tale of the peripatetic, wonder-working philosopher. Evident in all these romantic accounts is the conviction, not far below the surface, that the journeys undertaken by the heroes and heroines are not random wanderings reported as diverting exotica, but rather life pilgrim-

1. The very different estimates of the intention of the romance, as represented respectively by R. Merkelbach (Munich and Berlin: Beck, 1962) and B. E. Perry (Berkeley, 1967), are sketched and assessed above, p. 133. The scholars share the opinion, however, that the genre emerged in the late Hellenistic period (probably early second century B.C.) and that interest in it greatly revived in the second and third centuries of our era.

ages, searches for truth, whereby the pious seeker, through trials and a questing journey, gains insight into ultimate reality and is thereby transformed. The humor, the earthy features, the seemingly extraneous elements are included by way of contrast, in order to heighten the seriousness of purpose of the earnest seeker who finds the meaning of life. Thus the story of Psyche and Eros, with its variations on the Isis/Osiris myth, is told to depict the journey of the soul, including a sacred marriage and a ceremonial death: what Merkelbach has rightly called a *hieros logos* of the Isis mystery.

The closest affinity of the romance is with New Comedy,[2] with its common elements of love story, human intrigue, and the feature of recognition or reunion of the leading characters after separation and severe difficulties. Also influential in the style and substance of the romance is rhetoric, particularly the practice of having the plot unfold through contrived situations, with formal descriptions of works of art, exotic animals, strange royal courts, and public gatherings,[3] and above all, the lengthy speeches and disquisitions of the characters in the romances.

The romance functions primarily as propaganda, either for a cult or for a philosophical point of view, or both. The phenomenon of miracle is a frequent feature of the romances. External forces are depicted as initiating and sustaining the action of the narrative. The reader discerns that the gods are liable for what happens to the characters and are appealed to when the heroes and heroines are in difficulty.[4] In the case of the philosophically oriented romances, such as Dio Chrysostom's *Hunters of Euboea*, the hero's fidelity to his philosophical outlook—implicitly, the

2. Moses Hadas, *Three Greek Romances* (Indianapolis: Bobbs-Merrill, 1953), p. vii. Also Johannes Helms, *Character Portrayal in the Romance of Chariton* (The Hague: Mouton, 1966), pp. 14–15. Pierre Grimal, *Romans grecs et latins* (Paris: Librairie Gallimard, 1958), p. viii, sees the roots of the romance as ranging widely across Greek literature: Homer's *Odyssey* has the travel and adventure; Menander and Terence, as well as Euripides, have the human conflict and aspirations, the exotic features and brutal passions, set out in myth as well as in historical narrative.

3. Hadas, *Romances*, p. viii.

4. Helms, *Chariton*, p. 118.

Cynic-Stoic commitment to freedom attained by a life according to nature—enables him to overcome the schemes of outrageous fortune, and thus he is vindicated. The tractarian intent is as clearly evident whether the perspective is that of a cult or of a philosophy. The distinctive features of the romance include the decision or the necessity to leave one's native place and an emphasis on the marvelous as an indication of the direct involvement of the gods in human affairs, so that human destiny is seen to be under divine control.[5]

Efforts to classify the romances, such as that of Hadas (propagandistic, pastoral, and utopian) are suggestive but not ultimately useful, since the paradigm of the "pastoral" romances—Longus's *Daphnis and Chloe*—also serves as a tract for the wisdom and power of Eros Protogonos.[6] The characterization of Eros by the sage Philetas in *Daphnis and Chloe* makes it clear that Eros is not to be viewed as the god of erotic love alone: "The Lord of the elements, the Lord of the stars, the Lord of all his fellow-gods. . . . All flowers are the works of Eros, trees and plants his shaped creations. He makes the rivers flow and the winds to breathe."[7] The cosmic role of Eros is implicit in Longus's having geared the plot of the story into the cycle of solstices and equinoxes, and is explicit in the way the plot unfolds as a consequence of the movement of wind, waves, and storms.

The working out of the divine purpose in the lives of the heroes and heroines of the romances is characteristically marked by miracle. It is not so much that the gods directly intervene—though they not infrequently do that—as that they reveal their special care for the leading characters in these ancient novels by public disclosure of their supernatural powers. In those cases where the apologetic aim of the romance is to display the superiority of a philosophy, the miracles occur as manifestations of wisdom. Where the aim of the romance is propaganda for a cult, the miracles occur as divine confirmations of the claims made in

5. Grimal, *Romans*, pp. viii–ix.
6. Christopher Collins, *Daphnis and Chloe by Longus* (Barre, Mass.: Imprint Society, 1972), p. 9.
7. Ibid.

behalf of a particular god or goddess. Hadas sees a sociological factor at work, in that the apologetic intent of the romance is offered in service of a "cultural minority who are . . . devotees" of a cult. He proposes that the propaganda is used an an instrument "on behalf of rejected minorities or unpopular cults," as in the case of Heliodorus's *Ethiopica* and of Apuleius's *Metamorphoses*, which we have already considered in connection with the Isis cult (chap. 4, pp. 132–42). Judging by the quantity of literary evidence, the romance became a more common instrument of religious and philosophical propaganda as the empire moved from the second down into the third century.

The links between the romance and the cult become even more evident in this period, as can be observed in the second century A.D. redaction of the *Ephesiaca* of Xenophon.[8] Although this tale describes the Temple of Artemis as the launching site for the complex adventures of Habrokomes and Antheia, the details of the imagery of the experience and the glorious climax of their deliverance through supernatural intervention focus on Isis. There are recurrent entombments and restorations; when Habrokomes is delivered from crucifixion at the hands of brigands by an earthslide, he floats down the Nile, reenacting the struggle with death and the ultimate redemption from it that Osiris underwent in the myth of Isis. Antheia's prayer for deliverance and for reunion with her beloved are uttered in the temple of Isis. On being rejoined, the lovers enter the shrine of Isis to express to her their gratitude for their preservation and deliverance from all their adversities. As befits narratives concerning divinities whose roles include those of love and fertility, such as Isis and Eros, the romances written in praise of these deities are highly erotic, yet the stress falls on the chastity and fidelity of the heroes and heroines. The modern reader may be fascinated by the tales of attempted rape or alienation of affections, but the motivation behind the romance is by no means primarily that of

8. Hadas dates the surviving form of the *Ephesiaca* in the late second or early third century (*Romances*, p. iv), rather than in the early second century, as does Merkelbach. Yet it is most probable that antecedents, and perhaps the prototype, of the romance go back to the second century B.C. (Merkelbach, *Roman*, p. 336; Helms, *Chariton*, p. 17).

entertainment.[9] The blend of fully human characters and of divine providential care serves the objective of fostering the cult and encouraging devotion to its patron divinity.

APOLLONIUS AS DIVINELY ATTESTED
MAN OF WISDOM: PHILOSTRATUS

The stock-in-trade features of the romance are well represented in Philostratus's *Life of Apollonius of Tyana*: journeys to distant lands, with accounts of exotic animals and the customs of foreign courts; astonishing coincidences as evidence of the actions of the gods; the fidelity of the leading characters to principle, with the consequent triumph of virtue.

The author claims to be utilizing as his chief source the diary of Apollonius's traveling companion, Damis.[10] Many scholars think that Philostratus is appealing to a literary convention and that he has invented Damis and his travel narrative.[11] The material allegedly drawn from Damis is so full of historical anachronisms and gross geographical errors that one could not have confidence in Damis as a reporter if there actually were a diary. For example, "Damis" reports visits to Nineveh and Babylon, both of which had lain in ruins since the fourth and third centuries B.C., respectively. The border of the empire was almost certainly not at Ctesiphon in the reign of Tiberius, as Philostratus assumes. Seleucia, which had replaced Babylon in 275 B.C., was

9. B. E. Perry's insistence that the intention of the romance is solely entertainment requires him to omit from the genre the Alexander Romances of Pseudo-Callisthenes, Philostratus's *Life of Apollonius of Tyana*, and the Apocryphal Acts. Yet the chief characteristic feature of the romance, as we have already noted—namely, propaganda—is clearly evident in all these works excluded by Perry.

10. Philostratus *Life of Apollonius* 1.19. Damis is said to have reported every word of Apollonius, on the analogy of collecting crumbs of ambrosia from the table of the gods.

11. Fritz Täger, *Charisma: Studien zur Geschichte des antiken Herrscherkultes* (Stuttgart: W. Kohlhammer, 1960), 2:603–05; John Ferguson, *The Religions of the Roman Empire* (Ithaca: Cornell University Press, 1965), pp. 180 ff. Martin Hengel, *Nachfolge und Charisma* (BZNW 34, Berlin: W. de Gruyter, 1968), p. 30; E. R. Dodds, *Pagan and Christian in an Age of Anxiety* (Cambridge: Cambridge University Press, 1965), p. 59.

destroyed in A.D. 164, and in turn replaced by Ctesiphon. In part the account offered is apparently dependent on older sources, going back to Herodotus, and cannot be considered eyewitness testimony. The Damis diary reportedly includes description of the Caucasus as (1) providing the divide between Babylon and India,[12] and (2) as the location of the sources of the Indus.[13] There is an account of the "formidable manner" in which the Hyphasis discharges into the sea, although in fact it is a tributary of the Indus and joins it far inland.[14] There are straightforward accounts of encounters with dragons whose eyes bear mystic gems,[15] and of a successful trick whereby a lascivious satyr is intoxicated.[16] A plausible explanation for the mix of the fantastic and misinformation is that Philostratus invented most of it or borrowed it in eclectic fashion. In any case, what Philostratus reports tells us a great deal about the author and his time—that is, at the turn of the third century—but provides no unassailable evidence about Apollonius and his epoch.

The dominant role of Apollonius in Philostratus's portrait of him is not miracle-worker but philosopher. The hero adopted the ascetic way of life in the Pythagorean tradition, whose follower both he and others observing him considered him to be.[17] According to one of the letters attributed to Apollonius, his detractor, Euphrates, linked him with Pythagoras as well.[18] The bare subsistence mode of life he led saw him clothed in linen, unshaven and with long hair, wearing no shoes, and taking neither meat nor wine.[19] His renunciation of possessions and worldly position was demonstrated by his gift of most of his patrimony to the Temple of Asklepios in order to convert it into a Lyceum and Academy, in the philosophical tradition.[20] There were ele-

12. Philostratus *Apollonius* 2.5.
13. Ibid., *Apollonius*, 2.17.
14. Ibid., *Apollonius*, 2.52.
15. Ibid., *Apollonius*, 3.7.
16. Ibid., *Apollonius*, 3.6–8.
17. Ibid., *Apollonius*, 6.27; 1.13; 8.7.
18. Apollonius *Epistles* 16.
19. Philostratus *Life* 1.7; 6.11. Apollonius is said to have gone beyond Pythagoras in asceticism, in that he abstained totally from sexual relations (1.3).
20. Ibid., 1.13.

ments of Stoicism in his philosophical position, as well. Apollonius is reported, however, as identifying his own way of life, especially in its asceticism, with the tradition of Pythagoras.[21] With Pythagoreanism he shared the belief in the transmigration of souls.[22] Traces of Stoicism are evident in the major features of Philostratus's picture of him: self-control and the life according to nature, *kata phusin*.[23] The trials and persecutions he underwent during the reign of Domitian are compared with those experienced by Zeno, Diogenes, and Crates, thereby linking him in yet another way with the Cynic and Stoic traditions.

For Philostratus this is not mere rhetoric, since he portrays philosophy as the highest of human attainments and as the factor which links Apollonius with the divine. In India, the king observes that the Greeks regard philosophy as the divinest of human achievements.[24] It is in the wisdom of Apollonius that the king rejoices: he urges the Indian sages to receive Apollonius and his companions hospitably, since they are "philosophers and followers of a divine man."[25] Like the king, Iarchos, the chief of the Indian sages, greets Apollonius as divine by reason of his superior wisdom.[26] Later, in Alexandria, Vespasian sought an interview with Apollonius in order to draw on his wisdom concerning his own impending accession to power and as to whether or not he should restore the republic—a proposal rejected by Apollonius. In gratitude for the philosopher's insight and sage advice, Vespasian pronounced his utterances to be divine.[27]

Apollonius, according to Philostratus, is not lacking in extraordinary gifts. He has an innate knowledge of all languages and thus has no need to learn any.[28] Pervading the narrative is

---

21. Ibid., 4.16; 6.11; 8.7.

22. Ibid., 3.19–24; 8.7. On an underground journey, A. receives a volume of Pythagorean writings, which were presented to Hadrian (8.19).

23. Ibid., 7.14–15; 2.14; 5.36; 6.29.

24. Ibid., 2.29.

25. Ibid., 2.40.

26. Ibid., 3.28.

27. Ibid., 5.27–35; 5.36.

28. Ibid., 1.19.

the claim that he possesses foreknowledge and the ability to see what is happening at a great distance. Thus he predicts the short terms of office during the year of the four emperors, informs Vespasian that he will indeed become emperor, and notifies Titus concerning the manner of his death.[29] The gift of foresight enables Apollonius to escape a shipwreck and also a plot to ensnare him sexually.[30] He is reported as explaining to Damis that this gift is a manifestation of wisdom: "We have reached men who are unfeignedly wise, for they seem to have the gift of foreknowledge."[31] In a discussion of the gift of divination between Apollonius and Iarchos the Indian sage, the latter asserts that this capacity to foresee the future is an endowment from Apollo, by means of which the equivalent of the Delphic oracle is resident within the human breast, and the consequence of which is that the person thus blessed by the god is thereby rendered divine and contributes to the salvation of the human race.[32] The same applies to the ability to interpret dreams as signs of the future, since dreams are a medium for the perception of truth. The discussion of divination takes place in the context of considering which philosophy is fitting for a king.[33]

Furthermore, the gift of healing is associated by Philostratus with wisdom. The explanations offered for Apollonius's miracles are frequently rational, evidencing his reliance on natural therapy. For example, he cured a profligate Syrian by cutting down on his intake of food and alcohol.[34] When Apollonius restored to life the daughter of a consular family as she was being carried on a bier to her grave, he did so by whispering something secretly into her ear. But the explanation is then offered that she merely seemed to be dead and that he perhaps recognized a spark of life in her, or else it was the warmth of his touch that revived her. Philostratus alias Damis observes that to decide among these possible explanations constitutes "a serious prob-

29. Ibid., 5.11; 5.35; 6.32.
30. Ibid., 5.18; 6.3.
31. Ibid., 3.12.
32. Ibid., 3.42.
33. Ibid., 2.37.
34. Ibid., 1.19.

lem which neither I myself nor those who were present could decide."[35] Apollonius scoffs at those who see something super-natural in his ability to understand the twittering of the spar-rows, as apparently this skill is a part of his superior knowledge of language and of the natural world.[36] In *Life* 4.4, Apollonius predicts that there will be a plague in Ephesus. Later this pre-diction was the basis for the accusation that he was a wizard. His explanation for his capacity of prescience was purely physical: his light diet enabled him to be peculiarly sensitive, so that he could detect the approaching plague. God foresees the future, whereas ordinary men see only what is before them. It is the wise who are enabled to see what is approaching.[37]

Several of the miracles attributed to Apollonius border on the magical. A woman who approached him on behalf of her de-moniac child was sent off with a letter to the demon, the ghost of a man who had been offended by his wife's speedy remarriage following his death.[38] A mixture of magical technique and nat-ural therapy is apparent in another demoniac story, this one concerning a demon transferred from a mad dog to a boy, which is brought under control when the dog licks the boy's wounds and then is itself cured—of hydrophobia—by drinking water.[39] Yet Philostratus turns aside from his narrative about Apollonius, precisely at the dramatic point when the sage is facing death, to inform the reader about the difference between miracle—which Apollonius *does* perform—and magic, which he does not.[40] The distinction made between the two phenomena closely resembles that offered by modern anthropologists, in that magic is repre-sented as being concerned with the manipulation of forces, while religion involves communication among beings, although in many cases the features of both tend to merge.[41] Abandoning the pos-

35. Ibid., 4.45.
36. Ibid., 4.3.
37. Ibid., 8.7.
38. Ibid., 3.38.
39. Ibid., 6.42.
40. Ibid., 7.39.
41. A more complete statement is found in my *Christian Origins*, pp. 61–67.

ture of dependence on Damis, Philostratus portrays magic as a practice in which technique or the use of a specially endowed object produces certain results. A failure of the outcome is a misuse of the technique. Magic is a commercial enterprise, in which wizards perform certain requested feats in exchange for a fee. Philostratus objects strenuously to magic on both these counts and warns young persons against becoming involved in it.[42] As Philostratus portrays our hero, on the other hand, his relationship with the god provides him the wisdom and insight to know how to perform cures and exorcisms.

Toward the end of the work, the specific question is raised as to what precisely *is* Apollonius's relationship to the gods. This matter is directly addressed in the apologia prepared by Apollonius for presentation to Domitian, after the sage was accused of wizardry.[43] His defense begins with the assertion that he is merely a philosopher with none of the external sources of power. When Vespasian came to Egypt and sought his advice, what the emperor-to-be asked of him was not a string of portents or miracles to support his claim to the imperial authority, but counsel concerning the laws, proper worship of the gods, and just rule over the empire. The conversation took place in a temple, which is not the setting sought by wizards. Apollonius, then and always, refused remuneration for his services—once more in contrast to the greedy wizards. His unusual dress and diet—no meat, no clothing made from animal material, long hair—derive not from the wizard tradition but from the rule of the philosopher Pythagoras.

Although he has been accused of doing so, Apollonius never sought divine honors. He has been the instrument of healing and of purification, but these deeds have been performed out of concern for and in order to benefit others, rather than to set himself up as *theon*. There is, however, "a certain kinship between man and God which enabled human beings alone of the animal creation to recognize the gods, and to speculate about human nature and the manner in which it participates in the

---

42. Philostratus *Life* 7.39.
43. Ibid., 8, the whole of which is taken up with Apollonius's apologia.

divine substance."[44] Those human beings like himself who are endowed with such capacities, which come from the gods alone, are near to God, (*anchitheous*) and may be regarded as *theious*. The human race requires that someone fashioned in the divine image should administer and care for undisciplined souls, who can enable others to overcome avarice and passion. Such an agent is *theos hypo sophias hēkōn*, a god who comes under the power of wisdom, which is a synonym for "the Wise."[45] The latter are to be differentiated from both the gods (*hoi theoi*) and from ordinary human beings (*hoi anthrōpoi*). When the plague was stayed at Ephesus, Apollonius gave credit to Hercules rather than claiming the achievement for himself as a wizard would do. Similarly, in a contest at Corinth with a lamia, Hercules accomplished the victory; Apollonius was merely the instrument of it. The explanation for the sage's seeming triumphs is that the gods disclose their intentions to the wise and holy. Apollonius's reputation, therefore, rests on his god-granted wisdom.

For Apollonius as Philostratus portrays him, philosophy means "the rule of Pythagoras." That is the factor which determines his dress and manner of life, which prohibits him from any contact with blood, and which persuades him that his soul has been incarnate in other bodies and will continue its transmigratory course after his bodily death. It is on the basis of this philosophical conviction that we are to understand his applying to himself the line from the Iliad: "For thou shalt not slay me, since I tell thee I am not foredoomed to die [*morismos*]."[46]

It is this factor which accounts for Apollonius's disappearance from the court of Domitian following his acquittal of the charge of being a magician. His only explanation of the miraculous transport from Rome to Dichaearchia, where he appeared to his followers in the Cave of the Nymphs, is that he was conveyed thither by a divine escort.[47] That his presence is not merely an apparition is made certain, Philostratus tells us, by his insisting

44. Ibid., 8.7.
45. Ibid., 8.7.
46. Ibid., 8.5. *Iliad*, 22.13.
47. Ibid., 8.12.

that his followers touch him, thereby confirming that this is his bodily presence. His followers are aware that his actions and words are cared for "by some god." It is only when the imprisoned and shackled Apollonius removes his leg from the fetters and then voluntarily replaces it that Damis is persuaded that Apollonius is *thespesios*, "divine-sounding." Even this, however, is linked with the sage's role as philosopher: the act of self-liberation is an indication that he possesses true freedom: "It rested with himself to release himself." His freedom proved to Damis that all ordinary human wisdom and knowledge were transcended by Apollonius.[48] It is the role of wise men, attuned to the gods and their purposes, that makes possible the extraordinary actions of Apollonius. Philostratus is clearly not ready to place Apollonius among the gods, as his choice of synonyms for *theios* indicates: *anchitheos, thespesios*.

Apollonius's philosophy, derived from Pythagoras, is for him far more than an intellectual system and a life-style, however. The symbolic significance of it for death and survival beyond death is implied in the vivid tale toward the close of the *Life* which reports a visit by the sage to Lebadaea, a pilgrimage to the shrine of Trophonius, Apollo's son. The priests refused to allow Apollonius to enter the subterranean complex linked with the shrine even though he came with the request, "I wish to descend into the cave in the interests of philosophy." Claiming that he was a wizard, the priests offered pretexts to exclude him from consulting the oracle there. But with the aid of some of his eager disciples he was able to remove some of the physical barriers blocking entrance to the passage and did indeed descend, wearing his philosopher's mantle. He emerged one week later, having traversed the underground passages a far greater distance than all his predecessors, and having received a tangible response to his question to Trophonius asking what was the truest and most complete philosophy: a volume of the teachings of Pythagoras.[49] From the symbolic journey through death he returned with this epitome of wisdom.

48. Ibid., 8.13.
49. Ibid., 8.19.

Indicating that he is proceeding beyond the information included in Damis's memoirs of Apollonius, Philostratus offers two accounts of the sage's death: one in Lindus, the other in Crete. The latter tale includes the fawning of the fierce guard dogs at the shrine of Dictynna upon Apollonius's approach, his imprisonment and self-liberation, the opening of the temple doors spontaneously at his coming, and the song of the virgins from within the shrine calling him to "Go up from the earth."[50] Following his ascension, he continued to appear to his disciples, proclaiming wisdom and instructing them concerning the soul and immortality.[51] From the beginning of his career to its glorious end, therefore, he is portrayed by Philostratus as a philosopher whose endowments and sensitivity, and above all, whose perception and wisdom, manifest his kinship with the divine. Accordingly, the miracles are told, not to display his magical powers, but as testimony to his superior wisdom.

The literary vehicle which Philostratus chose to convey this picture of Apollonius was the Hellenistic romance. All the major features of that genre are evident, as we have noted above. The cause for which the *Life of Apollonius* serves as propaganda is not a cult in the ordinary sense of the term, but the religious and personal values of the Pythagorean tradition as it was understood in the late second and early third centuries. There are some details which might indicate that the author commissioned by a vigorous opponent of Christianity to do this work was writing consciously a pagan gospel, as Eusebius of Caesarea maintains. For example, the injunction to the followers of the sage, who has just been miraculously rescued from his would-be executioners at Rome, to touch him in order to assure themselves of his bodily presence recalls the scene of Jesus' reunion with his disciples after his crucifixion, when he invites them to convince themselves of his bodily resurrection by fingering his wounds (Jn 20:26–29). The instructions offered in the post-ascension accounts of Apollonius resemble some of the gospel reports of Jesus' post-Resurrection appearances. But the more important factor is the way in which—whatever his sources and conscious

50. Ibid., 8.30.
51. Ibid., 8.31.

aims may have been—Philostratus has employed the immensely popular medium of the romance to promote the philosophical wisdom of his miracle-working hero, "the man from Tyana," as he delights to call him.

DISCREDITING MIRACLE-WORKERS: LUCIAN, CELSUS, AND EUSEBIUS

From the second to the early fourth century there was a series of polemical writings which treat of the theme of miracle-working, both pagan and Christian. Some are satirical and some credulous. Fortunately for our purposes, in a few instances these authors took up strong positions in direct opposition to other writers with whom we are concerned, with the result that the differences among them are specific and their respective points of view sharply contrasting. Thus Origen, writing in the middle of the third century,[52] in his *Contra Celsum* defends Christianity and its claims for the miracles performed by Jesus. Fortunately, he quotes at length from Celsus, who was probably writing during the reign of Commodus (A.D. 177–80).[53] He was thus a contemporary of Lucian of Samosata, (125–90), the satirist who heaps burning ridicule on miracle-workers and on Christians—though he does not (as does Celsus)[54] explicitly attack Christian claims about miracles. Our final author in this section treating of competing attitudes about miracle in the period from the Antonines to Constantine is Eusebius of Caesarea, who counters the claims of one Hierocles that Apollonius of Tyana (as portrayed by Philostratus) was superior to Jesus as a performer of miracles. We begin our sketch with a consideration of Lucian and his portrait of Alexander, the highly successful prophet and miracle-worker.

52. A discussion of the date of the *Contra Celsum* in Henry Chadwick, introduction, translation, and notes, *Origen: Contra Celsum* (Cambridge: Cambridge University Press, 1965), p. xv.
53. For the evidence about the identity of Celsus and the date of his writing his work, *The True Doctrine*, see Chadwick, *Contra Celsum*, pp. xxiv–xxix.
54. The network of relationships under consideration would be tighter if this Celsus, answered belatedly by Origen, were identical with the Celsus mentioned by Lucian in his *Alexander the False Prophet* (1.21), who wrote a book attacking magicians. Lucian's friend was an Epicurean, however, while Origen's target is clearly a Middle Platonist, as Chadwick has noted (p. xxv).

From beginning to end, Lucian's depiction of Alexander the False Prophet is the story of an imposter, whose stock-in-trade is deceit and whose willing victims are fools. The terms in which Lucian describes Alexander are, in addition to impostor (21),[55] scoundrel (16), fraud, sham (17), one who operates by means of lying, trickery, perjury, malice and who is facile, audacious, and skilled in deceit (4). His techniques Lucian describes as a mixture of buncombe, humbug (25), quackery, and sorcery (6). Those taken in by him are characterized as fatheads and simpletons (9), superstitious (9), thick-witted. They include uneducated fellows (17) as well as the rich (9). All are driveling idiots (20).

Lucian details how Alexander tricked the unwary by opening sealed letters with a hot instrument, resealing them, and giving the answer to the writer. In his nocturnal response technique, he slept on scrolls containing questions and then gave ambiguous answers next morning (40). The most detailed description of his techniques for chicanery is that of his Asklepios oracle. Alexander placed a newly hatched snake in a blown-out eggshell and hid it in the foundation of a building, where it was "discovered" alive and wriggling and was promptly identified as Asklepios. After seemingly rapid growth, the snake-god appeared in Alexander's carefully arranged shrine. The god having been fitted out with a fake head (15), the mouth and tongue controlled by horsehairs (12), and a snake's tail extending from behind his body, everything was ready for the gullible to consult the oracle. Asklepios gave audible responses to his questioners, thanks to a crane's windpipe, which functioned as a speaking tube for a confederate concealed behind the draperies (26). By strapping some gilded leather to his thigh, Alexander was able to pass himself off as the incarnation of Pythagoras (40). In addition to the satisfaction Alexander gained from his enormously skillful and effective schemes of deceit, the prophet took in large sums of money which the credulous showered upon him in gratitude for his advice and oracular messages.

In Lucian's piece on The Passing of Peregrinus, miracle does

---

55. Numbers in parentheses refer to sections in Lucian's tract on *Alexander the False Prophet*, from *Lucian* 4, Loeb Classical Library (Cambridge: Harvard University Press, 1969).

not figure significantly. The gullible are taken in by Peregrinus's show of piety on the Cynic model, his renunciation of all but the bare necessities. He is portrayed with long hair, a dirty mantle, a wallet and staff. His temporary conversion to Christianity elicits more scorn from Lucian, because the Christians were duped into offering generous financial support to this pious exhibitionist. Lucian claims to have been an eyewitness to Peregrinus's self-immolation, carefully timed and staged at the Olympic Games in order to assure that his final act of philosophical ostentation would take place in front of the largest possible crowd of awed admirers. Lucian notes, however, that the last-minute plea to save himself that Peregrinus seems to have hoped for was not forthcoming from a mob fascinated by the gruesome sight of his leap into the fire. Lucian reports, however, that he told the gullible that at the moment of Peregrinus's death there had been an earthquake and a voice from heaven which called out, "I am through with earth; to Olympus I fare" (40). Not only, therefore, do the faithful have reports of his being taken up to join the gods in their traditional abode, but there are also accounts of his having appeared to his devotees after death. Thus the portents that we have seen to characterize the Roman historians' accounts of the death of the great are now associated with Peregrinus. The stage is set, Lucian suggests, for a cult of this Cynic saint, whom our author regards as a charlatan. The longest of Lucian's treatises, *Hermotimus*, is a satirical sketch of the various philosophical schools. It ends with the observation, "If in the future I ever meet a philosopher while I am walking on the road, even by chance, I will turn around and get out of his way as if he were a mad dog." Clearly, no one can accuse Lucian of exploiting his literary skills for propagandistic purposes on behalf of a philosophical or religious system.[56]

Celsus's attack on the Christians is of quite another order than that of Lucian's on itinerant preachers and miracle-workers. The main thrust of Celsus's *True Doctrine* is a denunciation of Christianity on the ground that it undermines devotion to the traditional gods and thereby threatens the stability of the Roman

56. Lucian, *Hermotimus*, p. 86.

state.[57] Instead of honoring the appropriate *numina*, the Christians, including their founder, are magicians who have gained the power they possess "by pronouncing the names of certain daemons and incantations."[58] It was by magic that Jesus had been able to do the miracles which he appears to have done. Because he foresaw that others, too, would get to know these formulas and do the same things, boasting that they did so by God's power, he expelled them from his society. It was during the sojourn of the family of Jesus in Egypt that he had learned his magical tricks. Returning to Palestine full of conceit, he claimed to possess divine power and took to himself the title of God.[59] Indeed, Jesus unwittingly gave himself away when he said that others who performed the same miracles as he, did so by means of sorcery, as he thereby admitted that his own acts were not signs of divine nature, but "signs of certain cheats and wicked men."[60]

Unlike Lucian, therefore, Celsus does not regard Jesus' miracles as deception or fraud but as magical actions accomplished in league with the evil powers. His reaction closely resembles that of Jesus' opponents in the Gospel narratives, who acknowledge that he can expel demons but attribute his power to his being in league with Satan, or Beelzebul (Mk 3:22–23). Nevertheless, he does compare Jesus to "sorcerers who profess to do wonderful miracles . . . who for a few obols make known their sacred lore in the middle of the marketplace and drive demons out of men and blow away diseases and invoke the souls of heroes." They perform illusions of meals and apparitions of heroes, "although they are not really so, but only appear as such in the imagination."[61] The claims of extraordinary events, such as the descent of the dove at Jesus' baptism and the resurrection of Jesus, rest respectively on "nothing more than partisan claims," and on "a hallucination of an hysterical female."[62] It is only the gullible and the uneducated who are taken in by the Christian

57. *Contra Celsum* (ed. Chadwick), 5.41.
58. Ibid., 8.55; 1.6.
59. Ibid., 1.28.
60. Ibid., 2.49.
61. Ibid., 1.68.
62. Ibid., 1.41; 2.54.

claims.[63] Their propagandists are "able to convince only the foolish, dishonorable, and stupid, and only slaves, women and little children," the most "illiterate and bucolic yokels."[64] The universalism of Christianity is an indication of its appeal to the vulgar and the ignorant.[65]

Yet Celsus does not deny that Jesus did indeed perform some of the miracles reported by his adherents, even though he regards them as evidence of sorcery.[66] The claims made in behalf of Jesus are identical with those made by followers of Cybele, Mithras, and Sabazius: the miracles they do are performed by magical techniques.[67] It is on this acknowledgment by Celsus that Jesus possessed extraordinary powers that Origen builds his case in behalf of the truth of Christianity.

Origen wrote his response to Celsus nearly seventy years after the appearance of the *True Doctrine*; that is, probably during the reign of Philip the Arab (244–49).[68] For him the bedrock on which the truth of Christianity rested was twofold: the fulfillment of prophecy and the prodigious miracles of Jesus.[69] Furthermore, he believed that the miraculous powers were still evident within the Christian community.[70] Origen freely acknowledged that miracles were done among Jews in the past—especially through Elijah and Elisha[71]—and that they might take place among Greeks as well.[72] His main concern was to refute the charge of Celsus that Jesus was a sorcerer. The argument builds on both logical and pragmatic considerations. In answer

63. Ibid., 1.9.
64. Ibid., 3.44; 3.55.
65. Ibid., 1.27.
66. Ibid., 2.14.
67. Ibid., 1.9; 6.39.
68. Chadwick, introduction to *Contra Celsum*, pp. xiv–xv. Chadwick gives credence to the report of Eusebius in his *Ecclesiastical History* (6.36.2) that this work was produced in the period during which Origen was looking back over his career as well as forward to a period of renewed persecution of the Christians (*Contra Celsum* 3.15).
69. *Contra Celsum* 1.2.
70. Ibid., 1.2, 46; 2.8.
71. Ibid., 2.58. The day of miracles is past, however (2.8).
72. Ibid., 5.57.

to Celsus's declaration that Jesus did indeed perform miracles but did so by magic powers, Origen retorts: "I do not know why a magician should have taken the trouble to teach a doctrine which persuades all human beings to do every action as before God who judges each for all his works, and to instil this conviction in his disciples whom he intended to serve as ministers of his teaching." When they, too, performed miracles in his name, is it plausible to suggest that they were magicians, when they risked their lives in great danger for a teaching that forbids magic?[73] The evidence as Origen sees it points in the opposite direction from Celsus's interpretation of it: it is the sorcerers who invoke the name of Jesus, thereby acknowledging that it is in him that real power for human renewal lies.[74] If they use the power of his name for self-serving ends, why cannot miracles be done in his name for admirable ends?[75]

Celsus had been particularly put off by the Christian claim that Jesus had raised the dead, in addition to having risen from the dead himself. Origen asserts that the Christian's claim that Jesus raised the dead is true. Spectacular as is this miracle attributed to Jesus, it is said to have occurred only a relatively few times, whereas if it were a fraud, there would have been many such alleged occurrences. Furthermore, those who are said to have been raised are named; anyone wanting to refute the claim could have presented evidence to the contrary by showing how long they had been in the tombs.[76] What Jesus did was in fulfillment of scripture and had precedent among the Jews, through Elijah and Elisha. He did the same, only better.[77] The ultimate miracle is Jesus' resurrection, but Jesus did not make a great public show of it, as Celsus would have preferred. Rather, he appeared only to those who were prepared to see him, to those who were spiritually worthy.[78] He did not escape from the cross,

73. Ibid., 1.38.
74. Ibid., 2.49.
75. Ibid., 2.51.
76. Ibid., 2.48.
77. Ibid., 2.58.
78. Ibid., 2.61–63.

as Celsus proposed he should have done, because he came as a human being, died as a human being, and was buried as a human being.[79] As he promised, (Jn 14:12) his disciples are doing even greater works than he accomplished, in that they are opening the eyes and ears of others to God's truth and enabling them to enter into new life.[80]

Had Celsus survived to read Origen's response, he would not likely have been persuaded by the arguments, but he could not have scorned the whole of the body of Christians as uneducated and ignorant. Origen reverses on Celsus the line of reasoning that seeks to show how Plato is superior to the Christian Scriptures, which are written in such crude style. Book 6 of the *Contra Celsum* opens (sec. 1–21) with an attempt to show the basic compatibility between Plato's cosmology and that of the New Testament, and of the underlying unity of truth. Origen's erudition is likewise evident in his counter to Celsus's effort to demonstrate the superiority of Mithraism and Gnostic speculation to Christianity.[81] In short, Celsus might have disagreed with Origen, but he could not have dismissed him as a fool.

During the reign of Diocletian (284–305), a provincial governor by the name of Hierocles wrote a work in which he compared Jesus and Apollonius of Tyana to the latter's decided favor, basing his case on the *Life of Apollonius* produced early in the third century by Philostratus. It is possible that the stimulus for Hierocles' tract in behalf of Apollonius was the construction by Alexander Severus (205–35) of a shrine to what one might broadly call "divine figures": Alexander the Great, Orpheus, Abraham, Jesus, and "the man from Tyana."[82] As the last great persecution of the Christians came under Diocletian, the time was auspicious for a polemical response to Hierocles. Eusebius

79. Ibid., 2.68.
80. Ibid., 2.8, 48.
81. Ibid., 6.22–23.
82. Ibid., proposed by F. C. Conybeare, in his introduction to Philostratus, *Life of Apollonius of Tyana* (LCL), original edition 1918, repr. 1960 (Cambridge: Harvard University Press), pp. xiv–xv.

rose to the challenge in a treatise against Philostratus's life of Apollonius, "occasioned by the parallel drawn by Hierocles between him and Christ."[83]

To the extent that we can reconstruct Hierocles' argument from Eusebius's rebuttal, there are some superficial similarities to the attack by Celsus on the Christian claims about Jesus. For example, he alleges that the stories about Jesus have been vamped up by Peter, Paul, and others, "who were liars and devoid of education and wizards," whereas Apollonius's *Life* was based on records kept by educated contemporaries of the sage, especially his companion Damis. Eusebius's response, however, is much more in the spirit of Celsus, with its exposure of inner contradictions in the narrative of Philostratus, an extended lesson in cosmology, and a concluding discourse on theodicy.[84] The laws of nature, according to which all creatures have limits imposed on them, preclude the practice of levitation that is reported to have been seen by Apollonius in India. The contradictions are many, according to Eusebius: if Apollonius knew all languages innately, why did he need instruction in Attic Greek or an interpreter in India?[85] If he possessed the gift of foreknowledge, why did he have to ask the Indian philosopher how he had learned Greek, and why did he prepare a long apology which he was never able to deliver?[86] Eusebius also finds incredible the reports of stone tripods, flowing with wine and hot and cold water, which move about by themselves at the establishment of the Brahmans.[87]

More serious is the challenge to Apollonius's integrity and his right to be called a philosopher. He claims to have learned philosophy directly from Pythagoras, yet he had to acquire his knowledge from humanly transmitted tradition. His deceitfulness is apparent in his false claim to have made Vespasian em-

83. Text and translation in *Philostratus* 2:484–605, referred to in this study as Eusebius.

84. Eusebius, 6, 17–19; 42.

85. Ibid., 8–9; 13–14.

86. Ibid., 15, 38.

87. Ibid., 18–19.

peror. He praised the philosopher Euphrates to Vespasian, and later denounced him when he exposed Apollonius as a wizard. He flattered Domitian when he was under his power, but later in Ephesus sought to alienate supporters of the emperor.[88] Such duplicity makes a mockery of the title Hierocles had chosen for his tract: *Lover of Truth.*

With regard to his miracle-working, Apollonius is guilty of both deception and complicity with the demons. He claimed to have innate miraculous power, yet he had to learn the techniques from the Arab and Indian shamans.[89] His boast to have foreseen the plague at Ephesus through his vision of an aged beggar is in conflict with medical theory about the noxious vapors which give rise to plagues.[90] The accusations that Apollonius was a wizard were made frequently and never refuted, except by his own counterclaims. He was denounced as such by the philosopher Euphrates in Rome and by the priests at the sacred caves in Lebadaea as well as by the Roman authorities.[91] In spite of his claims to possess divine powers, there is in the Roman annals no mention of his having performed miracles.[92] Even faithful Damis remained unpersuaded of his divine powers until just before his death.[93] The only conclusion to be drawn is that he was in league with the demons and performed his feats by deception and wizardry. Apollonius is neither a lover of wisdom nor an honest man. As in Celsus's attack on Jesus as miracle-worker, Eusebius does not deny that Apollonius performed extraordinary feats. The issue is the source of his power, and his conclusion is that his power was demonic in origin. In this epoch, both champions and critics of miracle-workers are agreed as to what the basic issues are: are miracles evidence of divine wisdom and power, of demonic power and wizardry, or of fraud and chicanery?

88. Ibid., 11; 28; 29; 39.
89. Ibid., 23.
90. Ibid.
91. Ibid., 26; 40; 33–35.
92. Ibid., 31.
93. Ibid., 35.

MIRACLE AS EXPLOITED BY CHRISTIAN PROPAGANDISTS

The Christians in the second and subsequent centuries made full use of the widespread fascination with miracle in writing the propagandistic material known in modern times as the New Testament Apocrypha.[94] The tone of this literature is set in large measure by secondary features. The genre that most directly influenced these writings is, not surprisingly, the Hellenistic romance, since both the original pagan model and the Christian exploitation of it are eager to fascinate the reader even while propagandizing for a religious conviction. Accordingly, in addition to miracle—the primary motif of this literature—there are the characteristic features of the romance: travel, often to exotic places; a mix of erotic interest and ascetic counsel; speeches, usually in the presence of public figures and before crowds, which serve to put across persuasively the point of view that is being promulgated; recognition scenes, in which by a curious chain of circumstances those long separated are reunited or the dead reappear.[95] A few examples of each from the New Testament apocryphal material will demonstrate how miracle functions in the hands of these pious writers.

In the Acts of Thomas, the Apostle is sold into slavery by Jesus disguised as a merchant and journeys to India, thereby reluctantly fulfilling the commission he had received by lot that India was to be his mission field. Peter, Paul, and the latter's companion, Thecla, travel around the Mediterranean and to Rome, often under divine protection, as in the case of Peter's voyage from Caesarea to Puteoli, for which both Peter and the ship captain were prepared by visions.[96]

More striking is the blend of the erotic and the ascetic in these

94. The edition here used is that of Edgar Hennecke, *New Testament Apocrypha*, 2 vols., ed. W. Schneemelcher; Eng. trans. by R. McL. Wilson et al. (Philadelphia: Westminster, vol. 1, 1963; vol. 2, 1965; repr. 1976).

95. The features here noted as typical correspond on the whole with those noted in the classic study by Rosa Söder, *Die apokryphen Apostelgeschichten und die romanhafte Literatur der Antike* (Wurzburger Studien zur Altertumswissenschaft, Heft 3. Stuttgart, 1932).

96. Acts of Peter 2.5.

narratives. Characteristic is the episode from the Acts of John (49–54) in which John meets a young man outside Ephesus who has just killed his father in an argument that arose from the young man's having loved a married woman. On the promise that he (John) will raise the father from the dead if the son will renounce further pursuit of the woman he loves, John does restore the father to life, and the young man guarantees that he will fulfill his pledge by castrating himself. Also in the Acts of John (62-115) we read of Drusiana, a Christian woman who had separated from her husband out of pious conviction that chastity was the moral ideal, but who was pursued by a would-be adulterer, Callimachus. She became ill on learning of this evil desire and asked to be released from this life, which she soon was. Her husband realized what her motivation had been and commended her posthumously for her purity. The lover's passion was so great, however, that he bribed her husband's steward, Fortunatus, to open her tomb so that he might copulate with her corpse—an act from which he was prevented only by the intervention of a snake, which first bit the steward and then entwined itself about the feet of the frustrated lover so that he fell down to the ground. The next day the husband and his entourage, together with John, went to the tomb to celebrate the Eucharist. They found the tomb opened and were greeted by a handsome young man who urged John to raise the late wife from the dead. On the other side of the tomb they discovered the dead steward and the lover, alive but still wrapped in the coils of the snake. Callimachus describes a vision he had seen of a young man who, by covering the nearly naked body of Drusiana, had prevented him from defiling her. He repents of his evil intent and is converted. Drusiana is restored to life and is the agent through which Fortunatus the steward is raised to life as well. Neither the conversion of Callimachus nor the reports of the appearance of the young Christ-figure can persuade Fortunatus to repent, however, and he is shortly thereafter found bitten and turned black from another bite of the snake. With the transformation of her former passion-ridden pursuer, Drusiana is now able to resume her life of chastity in peace. John's dying prayer of thanks expresses gratitude that he had been prevented from marriage and had been cured of the desire even "of looking closely at a woman" (113).

In the Acts of Peter[97] there is a story about his daughter who, even as a child, had been so beautiful that men sought to seduce her. She had become partially paralyzed and then had died. Peter was urged to restore her to life and did so, but was instructed that she should resume her crippled state so that she would not be so great a temptation. In the Acts of Paul, the Apostle's relationship with Thecla is never on a sexual basis. Indeed, Thecla had been betrothed when she first heard Paul's words about the beauties of the life of virginity. She visited Paul in prison and kissed his fetters,[98] but their relationship remained pure. The moral values involved are succinctly set forth in Paul's variant on the Beatitudes:

> Blessed are they who have kept the flesh pure,
>   for they shall become a temple of God.
> Blessed are they who have wives as if they had them not,
>   for they shall be well pleasing to God.
> Blessed are the continent,
>   for to them shall God speak.[99]

Encratism is the standard for the pious in the Acts of Andrew; and in the Acts of Thomas, God is portrayed as androgynous.[100] In the ninth and tenth of the Acts of Thomas, the wife of a close kinsman of the king is converted by Thomas and refuses to cohabit with her husband under threat of death to her and to the Apostle. When the king commands that Thomas place his bare feet on red-hot iron plates, water gushes up from the ground and dissolves the plates. For Thomas the paramount virtue is chastity, but the narratives concerning it are filled with erotic detail. In his death speech John praises God that he has been

97. From what is designated in Hennecke-Schneemelcher as "Fragments of the First Section" of the Acts of Peter; translated from Berlin Coptic Papyrus 8502, pp. 128–32 and 135–41.

98. Acts of Paul 3.18.

99. Acts of Paul 3.5.

100. Acts of Thomas (Second Act), p. 142.

kept "pure for Thyself and untouched by union with a woman."
He describes the sexual urge as "the foul madness that is in the
flesh" and "the secret disease of the soul" (Acts of John 113). By
refusing to take part in sexual acts, the pious are enabled to
overcome the pattern of male-female relationships established
by Adam and Eve, which lie at the root of human sinfulness.
The paradigm for the asexual way of life is shifted back from
the virginal conception of Jesus (Luke 1–2) to the miraculous
conception of Mary in the Protevangelium of James. The fact
that Joseph has honored her virginity is confirmed by his drinking the water of conviction, as decreed in Numbers 5:11–31. As
a new race of humanity, the Christians regard themselves as following the model of Mary and Joseph, who broke with the pattern of sexual reproduction set by the sinful progenitors of the
human race.

As is the case both in the canonical Acts of the Apostles[101] and
the romances, the authors of the Apocryphal Acts represent the
Apostles as seizing the occasion now and again to deliver themselves of a public oration calculated to convince both the crowd
and the local rulers—to say nothing of the readers—of the truths
of the Christian claims. Thus, in the Acts of John (31–36) the
Apostle promises to heal elderly women and to convert some of
the onlookers. Before performing as promised, however, he ha-
rangues the crowd for their greed, licentiousness, and worldli-
ness, threatening them with the fires of hell unless they repent
of their evil ways. Similarly, in the Acts of Paul (7)—likewise in
Ephesus—there is an address before the governor, although in
this case it is more explicitly evangelical, detailing how God has
provided salvation for the human race through Christ. Paul is
visited in prison by the "young man," who is Christ, and his fetters are removed. One of the women who had fainted before
the surging waves as she was being baptized is restored, lest Paul
be charged with having killed her and then having escaped from
prison. In Acts of Thomas (Ninth Act), there is an address on
chastity, and in the Clementine Homilies (3.58.2) there is a pub-

101. Acts 2:14–40; 3:11–26; 7:1–53; 14:14–18; 17:22–31; 22:1–21; 23:26–
30; 26:1–23.

lic disputation with the arch-villain, Simon Magus. One may infer that the speeches actually did more to strengthen the faith
of the faithful than to convince the unbelievers, but the addresses are public as a reminder that faith is open to all who
respond to the message.

Yet another feature of these narratives which shows affinity
with the life-world of the romances is the motif of recognition
of, or reunion with, the lost or departed. These familiar elements in the plot of the romances are adapted for Christian purposes by the writers of these Apocryphal Acts, as well. In the
Acts of Peter, the Apostle is met repeatedly by the risen Christ
(16, 51, 35–36). The last of these is the famous "Quo vadis?"
legend, according to which Peter was encouraged to flee from
Rome in order to escape martyrdom. The Lord met him and
spoke of his own crucifixion, about to take place once more in
Rome. Peter came to realize his own responsibility to follow in
the steps of his lord, and returned to accept crucifixion. In both
the Clementine Recognitions and the Homilies there are incidents in which chance meetings or unexpected reunions figure
importantly. Clement, for example, on hearing reports of a "man
from Judea" who announces God's rule and performs marvelous signs, journeys to Palestine and there encounters Peter, the
disciple of this man. In Clementine Homily 12 there is an account of a man's search for his lost wife and child. In Tripoli,
Peter comes upon a beggar woman, who is in fact the lost mother
of Clement (8.21–23). In addition to their inherent human interest, these recognition scenes serve to underscore the Christian conviction of God's sovereignty over individual human history. This brings us, then, to the larger, pervasive factor of miracle
in these writings.

Miracle functions in this literature preeminently as a mode of
manifestation of divine power. That factor shades over into two
corollaries, one positive and the other negative. The positive implication is that the person through whom the miracle was performed is divinely attested as an agent of God.[102] The negative

102. This is a function of miracle common in the rabbinic tales, as collected
and analyzed by Paul Fiebig, in *Die jüdische Wundergeschichten im Zeitalter Jesu,*

corollary of miracle is that the opponents and competitors of Christianity practice magic. Further, miracle serves as a medium of divine reward for the faithful and of punishment for the impious, with the result that miracle offers an encouragement to the pious to persevere. Each of these facets of miracle is abundantly evident in these apocryphal documents; from among the range we shall examine some representative samples of each.

Among the earliest surviving fragments of Jesus tradition (Papyrus Egerton 2, from before 150)[103] there is an account—unfortunately with lacunae at the crucial point—which apparently describes Jesus as sowing grain in the Jordan Valley and then harvesting it immediately. The question raised repeatedly in the papyrus fragment as a whole is whether or not Jesus has been sent by God. In the Gospel of Peter there is a heightening of the portents, such as the shaking of the earth when the body of Jesus is taken down from the cross and laid on it (6.21). There is a loud voice from heaven as the soldiers are guarding the tomb, and the stone rolls back of itself. From the tomb emerge two men leading another, with the cross bringing up the rear. The heads of the two reach to the heavens, but the head of the other reaches still higher. As the soldiers discuss reporting this to Pilate, a man descends from heaven and enters the tomb, whereupon the soldiers declare, "In truth he was the Son of God" (9.35–11.45).

The second-century anti-Gnostic document *Epistula Apostolorum* is content (in its extant portions, at least) to offer little more than a rapid summary of the miracles attributed to Jesus in the

---

(Tübingen: J. C. B. Mohr, 1911), where the miracle that occurs confirms the interpretation of the law implicit in the action of a rabbi or explicit in his legal interpretation. Recent study of the mishnaic traditions has raised fundamental questions about the age of this material, and it is therefore not a dependable resource for the attitudes in the first century. On the other hand, it seems to provide useful insights into the perspective on miracle in the period during which the Talmud began to take shape—that is, in the second and subsequent centuries.

103. First published by H. I. Bell and T. C. Skeat, *Fragments of an Unknown Gospel* (London: British Museum, 1935); also *The New Gospel Fragments* (London: British Museum, 1935). Bibliography in *New Testament Apocrypha* 1, 96. The text referred to here is from lines 70–75.

synoptic Gospels and John (5). The rest of the work (6–50) is occupied with a description of the events that accompanied and followed Jesus' resurrection, and with predictions about the mission to the Gentiles led by Paul and the final judgment. The Protevangelium of James, from the second half of the second century, reports miracles in connection with the birth of Mary that closely resemble those recounted in Luke concerning the divine power evident in the conception and birth of both John the Baptist and Jesus.

It is in the Infancy Gospel of Thomas, however, that the most elaborate effort is made to persuade the reader of the divine nature of Jesus by means of the miracles he performs as a child prodigy. In this late-second-century "Account of Thomas the Israelite Philosopher concerning the Childhood of the Lord," as it is called,[104] stories of Jesus portray him as displaying his miraculous powers with a mixture of ostentation and petulance. When he is rebuked for shaping clay to form pigeons on the sabbath, he claps his hands and they fly away (2.1–4). When a playmate spoils Jesus' pools of water, he withers the child, after denouncing him as an "insolent, godless dunderhead" (3.2). Another child who knocked against his shoulder, it would seem inadvertently, is struck down dead by Jesus' word. Joseph's attempts to dissuade Jesus from such punitive acts, on the ground that they are fostering hatred on the part of the neighbors, is dismissed as unwise by Jesus, who warns him, "Do not vex me" (5.1–3). Similarly, the attempt to teach Jesus letters results in his confusing and humiliating his teacher with a string of rhetorical declarations and utterances about the allegorical significance of the letters of the alphabet (6.1–7.4). The only conclusion that father, neighbors, and would-be teacher can draw is that his words and deeds are marvelous (5:2) and that "he is something great, a god or an angel," but no one knows quite what he is (7.4). Other marvels include his carrying water in an apron (11.1–2), making a single grain of wheat produce one hundred measures (12.1–2), and stretching to proper length a piece of wood that his carpenter-father had wrongly cut (13.1–2). In the latter part of

104. Title and text (in translation) in *New Testament Apocrypha* 1, 392–99.

the extant text (16.1–18.2) there are also stories of his restoring to life those who had died. The present ending of the document consists of an expanded exaggerated version of the story in Luke 2:41–52 of his confounding the Scribes in the Temple at age twelve. The point of this writing is to heighten the sense of the divine powers of Jesus, not only to heal, but even more significantly to punish, as well as to teach. An Arabic Infancy Gospel[105] reports the even more fantastic power of Jesus who, after tossing all of a dyer's cloths into a cauldron of indigo, tells the dyer that each cloth as it is withdrawn from the pot will be the color the dyer desires. The onlookers are reported to have praised God, but the function of this and all the other miracles of this material linked with Thomas is solely to heighten awareness of the supernatural powers of Jesus.

In the apocryphal narratives of the Acts of the Apostles, there is a powerful tendency to surround the Apostles themselves with a supernatural aura of authority. Although they perform acts of compassion, as did Jesus and the Apostles in the canonical texts, in some instances the miracles attributed to the Apostles are whimsical, as in the case of the cooperative bed-bugs which, on apostolic command, leave their accustomed place in the bed of an inn in order that John and his traveling companion can get a good night's sleep, and which then return to the bed on the Apostle's departure (Acts of John 60–61); or the tale of the lion that was to have attacked Paul but instead asked to be baptized, an act Paul thereupon performed (Acts of Paul 7).

There are serious amplifications of the miraculous dimension of the New Testament in the apocryphal writings, however, aimed at expanding the religious significance of Jesus, or heightening the force of apostolic authority, or fostering the cult of the saints, especially Mary (as in the Protevangelium of James).[106] In the Acts of Pilate we read, not only accounts of the post-Resurrection

105. *New Testament Apocrypha* 1, 400–01.
106. Examples would include: John's restoring to life a certain Cleopatra at Ephesus (Acts of John 19–26); Paul restoring to health a man sick with dropsy (Acts of Paul 4); Andrew performing exorcisms (in a Coptic Papyrus, Utrecht 1); and Paul restoring to life the daughter of a man who had ordered her put to death along with Paul, after Paul had converted her (Acts of Paul 9).

appearances of Jesus to his followers, but also descriptions of his liberating the souls of the dead in hell, thus overcoming both Satan and Hades, the personification of the power of death (Acts of Pilate 17–27). These authority-confirming events range from heavenly voices to divine portents that attend the martyrdom of the Apostles (Acts of John 18; Acts of Paul 11). The latter document also reports a post-Resurrection encounter of Paul with Nero, who forthwith halted his persecution of the Christians (10.6). Veneration of the Apostles is clearly evident in the story of the exorcistic power of the dust left from the bones of Thomas (Acts of Thomas 170).

The therapeutic function of Thomas's dust, and the elaborate story of the docile wild asses who assist Thomas in the dispatching of the demon-possessed women and the expulsion of the demon beyond the reach of human habitation (Acts of Thomas 68–78), make evident how narrow the line between miracle and magic in this literature has become. Even so, there is an explicit attack on magic, especially as it is represented by its most notorious practitioner in the early Christian tradition, Simon Magus.

Nearly the whole of the Acts of Peter is occupied with the contest between (Simon) Peter and Simon Magus. Even the story of Peter's martyrdom is set out as the consequence of his having successfully overcome Simon's magic, with the result that some of his former adherents, now converted to Christianity, refuse to have sexual relations with their husbands or owners (34), who in turn conspire to destroy Peter. It was while Peter was still in Palestine that he had visions of the work of Simon in Rome and how it was luring members away from the church there, following the departure of Paul for Spain (2). Simon's spectacular public stunts, which included flying over the city in midday, resulted in the apostasy of most of the church in Rome. After the divinely protected voyage to Italy, which we noted above (p. 274), Peter hastens to the capital city, where the church gathers to hear him. He recites the great things that happened to him in his association with Jesus, though he also confesses how Satan led him to deny Jesus. The church repents of its enchantment with Simon, and Peter vows to expose him as the instrument of Satan in their midst (3–4). Marcellus, a wealthy Christian still under Simon's spell, is also brought to repentance when Peter visits his home and pacifies the fierce watchdog there, which asks Peter for instruction and is ordered to go in and tell Simon of Peter's challenge (4). A young man who had laughed as Peter was foretelling the contest with Simon describes the argument under way between the dog-messenger and Simon, and then is freed from the demon that has taken possession of him. He thereupon kicks to pieces a statue of Caesar, which causes grave anxiety to the owner of the house, as it would be considered a subversive act. Peter, however, reassembles the shattered statue.

When the contest proper begins publicly, Peter persuades many to believe in him when he makes a smoked tuna fish swim. Simon, on the other hand, is dressed down by a seven-month-old child, who warns the magician of his peril. An appearance of Jesus to Peter assures him that Simon's actions will be exposed as mere "charms and illusions of magic" (6). The other charge brought against Simon implicitly in the narrative is that he is a thief and a deceiver, as is evident in his having smuggled out of Judea a jewel-encrusted golden satyr. Peter discovered the scheme and exposed it to a would-be buyer, Marcellus. On hearing what a scoundrel his late guest (Simon) is, Marcellus purifies his house with holy water (7).

After Peter performs a string of healings, and Marcellus has a dream in which Peter hacks to pieces the demon that controlled Simon, a public contest in the Forum ensues. Peter declares that Christ is the source of his power, while Simon's acts are mere sorcery. Simon responds by denouncing Jesus as a crucified Judean carpenter. On order from the prefect, Simon puts a young man to death, who is then restored to life by Peter, who meanwhile has brought back to life the son of a widow as well. When the wife of a senator requests that her son be revived from the dead, Simon can produce only the illusion of his restoration, but Peter demands that there be public, unambiguous evidence. The governor and the crowd turn against Simon as a fraud, while Peter brings the son to life, inviting the crowd to trust in Jesus, whereupon the people venerate Peter "as a god" (8). Again Peter performs a series of healings, while Simon puts on a public performance of flying over the city. Peter thereupon

pleads with God to discredit Simon publicly, as otherwise everyone will trust Simon rather than the God of Peter, who works
signs and wonders through him. At Peter's request, Simon falls
to the earth, breaking his leg in three places, and then dies at
the home of a fellow-sorcerer. The significance of the contest is
made explicit in the words of Peter to the crowd of curious onlookers: after healing and raising the dead "by the help of the
Lord," he declares: "Men of Rome, this is how the dead are restored to life, this is how they speak, this is how they walk when
they are raised up, and live for so long as God wills. Now, therefore, you people who have gathered to see the show, if you turn
from these wicked ways of yours and from all your man-made
gods and from every kind of uncleanness and lust, you shall
receive the fellowship with Christ through faith, so that you may
come to everlasting life" (8.28). Unlike those of Simon and the
sorcerers, the gifts that are offered to Peter by the beneficiaries
of his miracles are given to the poor, rather than kept by a greedy
fraud of a magician.

The conflict between Peter and Simon is set in a metaphysical
framework by the Clementine Homilies, which probably appeared in their original form in the third century.[107] After laying out a series of pairs of syzygies—God/Adam, Cain/Abel, Isaac/
Ishmael, Jacob/Esau—Peter portrays Simon as his opposite and
forerunner: "I, who came after him, followed him as the light
follows darkness, knowledge, ignorance, and healing, sickness. . . . A false gospel must first come from an impostor and
only then, after the destruction of the holy place, can a true
gospel be sent forth for the correction of the sects that are to
come."[108] Simon uses piety as mere pretence in order to steal
from men the fruits of truth (22.7). The Homily describes the
magical technique by which a boy's soul was separated from his
body, and how later the Magus fashioned him out of air by a
divine transformation (26.1–2). Simon, who is described as a Sa-

---

107. The possible stages in the development of the Pseudo-Clementine literature, including the Homilies, are sketched by J. Irmscher, in *New Testament Apocrypha*, 2:532–35.

108. Clementine Homily 5, The True Prophet, 15.1–17.5. Noted in chap. 6.

maritan and a follower of John the Baptist, had learned magic in Egypt (Homily 2). The charge against Simon, therefore, is not that he is a fraud, but that his powers are those of a sorcerer and not of divine origin. For the Pseudo-Clementines, Simon is the antithesis of Peter, the agent of God-granted miraculous powers. In Rome, Clement had heard reports of the exploits "a man" performed in connection with his proclamation of the Kingdom of God: "As proof that his speech is worthy of credit and is from the divine Spirit, he performs, so it is said, by his mere word many signs and singularly miraculous deeds, so that, as it were in the power of God, he makes the deaf to hear and the blind to see, makes the infirm and lame to stand erect, expels every weakness and all demons from men, yea, even raises dead persons who are brought before him, and besides brings healing to lepers whom he sees from a distance, and there is nothing at all that is impossible for him." On arrival in Palestine, Clement observes Peter, "a very highly approved disciple of the Man who had appeared in Judea and wrought with divine power many signs and wonders among the people" (Recognition 1.12.2). It is as the preeminent follower of this "Man" that Peter himself performs his healings and exorcisms, since he "has penetrated most deeply into the divine wisdom" (Recognition 1.12.6).

An important and recurrent feature of the miracle stories in these apocryphal writings is that of punishment. Although there are a few punitive miracles in the canonical Acts of the Apostles, the number and vehemence of them is greatly increased in this later material. We have already noted Jesus' striking down his playmates when they annoy or challenge him, according to the Infancy Gospel of Thomas (3–5, 9, 14, 16). In the Acts of John, the unrepentant are bitten fatally by snakes (70–80). In the Acts of Peter various impenitent or wicked persons are smitten with blindness or other ailments; and Rufina, who came from the bed of adultery to the table of the Eucharist is stricken with paralysis "from her head to her toe-nails" (1.2). Pagan shrines are destroyed, as is the case with the Temple of Artemis in the Acts of John (37–42) and the Temple of Apollo in Sidon (Acts of Paul 5). A greedy son is blinded (Acts of Paul 4), and a cup-bearer who struck Thomas is dismembered by a lion and a dog snatches his right hand (Acts of Thomas, First Act, 6–9). A young man killed his beloved, who would not join him in a vow of chastity after his conversion; later, when he took the Eucharist, his hands withered up (Acts of Thomas, Sixth Act, 51–52). After he confessed, his hands were restored. Conversely, the faithful are vindicated, the penitent are converted and restored. Caesar's cupbearer falls from the window to his death but is brought back to life by the Apostle.[109]

The intention of these punitive miracles and miraculous deliverances is twofold: they serve as warnings concerning the power of divine judgment, swift and effective, that will be unleashed against those who oppose God and his agents. And the narratives provide reassurance of divine support to those tempted to recant the faith or to separate themselves from the Christian community when it is under attack.

THE LIFE-WORLD IMPLICIT IN THE ROMANCES

The view of reality, both divine and human, that is assumed by those—both pagan and Christian—writing romances in the third and subsequent centuries may be readily inferred from these lively documents. Paramount is the conviction that the gods are in control of the course of human history—indeed, of the whole movement of the universe. Unlike the viewpoint of the earlier Roman historians, however, the divine control of history is evident not merely in the events surrounding the access to power or removal from power of the world leaders, but also in the course of the lives of simple, even despised, persons. The shaping of human destiny is apparent in the lives of Jesus and the Apostles but also in the experience of lowly believers. In their journeys, in their separations and reunions, in their losses and recoveries, in injustices and vindications, the divine hand is to be seen at work.

Those who are the special beneficiaries of the gods' control of destiny are characterized by lives of the highest moral quality; total control not only of sexual practices but even of sexual urges.

109. Acts of Paul 11; Acts of the Apostles 20:7–9.

Sex is regarded as the prime source of sin. The God of the Christians is pictured as bisexual, and the human race must eradicate the pattern of sexual relationships that has obtained since the fall of Adam and Eve. Paradoxically, the romances are filled with strongly erotic features, so that the preoccupation with sex reaches out to the modern reader, as it must surely have done, at least unconsciously, to ancient ones. But the tales of sexual aberrancy are told as warnings and serve to contrast with the abstemious life-style of the faithful.

Closely linked with the strong interest in erotic/ascetic narratives is the motif of divine rewards and punishments. There is no question of waiting until an eschatological judgment for divine commendation or retribution to take place. Rather, the gods act directly and immediately to sustain the pious and to punish the wicked. Accordingly, divine determination of human destiny is as evident in the experience of the unjust as it is in the lives of the just. The public nature of these manifestations of divine intervention in history is intended to serve as a warning to the opponents of the religious movement that God or the gods stand behind the proponents of this cult.

Miracles performed by Jesus and the Apostles are represented as public confirmation of the divine authority by which they work. The full import of these miraculous attestations is not always evident to the unbelieving observers, but they cannot mistake that something extraordinary is taking place, something which points to supernatural approbation of what is occurring in their midst. Unlike the miracles of Jesus in the gospel tradition, therefore, a fundamental aim of these miracle accounts is evidential: to prove that God is behind Jesus and his messengers. The divine authority is thus transmitted from Jesus to his Apostles and, presumably, to those who now carry forward the movement in their name. The continuity of authority is dramatically displayed in the stories of the continuing power of the Apostles which endures beyond their death, as in the case of the miraculous efficacy of the dust of the Apostles that remains in their tombs.

The specifics of the miracles and the motif of public contest between the Apostles and their opponents include features which tend to blur the line between miracle and magic. The protracted contest between Peter and Simon Magus has shown us some of the forms that the rivalry between Christian miracle-workers and other performers of marvels—labeled "magicians," of course— assumed. It is not surprising that these phenomena appeared in both Christian and non-Christian contexts in the Roman world of the third and fourth centuries, as this is precisely the period during which the Magical Papyri developed into the forms in which they have been preserved in papyrus manuscripts down to the present day. These synchronous developments should warn us, however, against the folly of beginning with observations about the ancient world based on—for example—the third century of our era and then proceeding to offer what pass for historical explanations of events or phenomena which date from centuries earlier. Thus, Philostratus's account of Apollonius of Tyana is wholly in keeping with its epoch, both in literary style and in the framework or life-world within which his travels and astonishing acts are interpreted.

But to offer Philostratus or the Greek Magical Papyri as historical evidence for events reported by writers of the first century, who were operating within a very different life-world, such as the writers of the Gospels and Acts, is historiographically irresponsible. What happened in the third century is that the church was moving toward centralization, which by the time of Constantine would take concrete form in the conversion of the emperor and the establishment of Christianity as the religion of the empire. Yet at the same time, there was a yearning for personal association with the gods, and especially for direct intervention of the gods in one's behalf. That aspiration in itself is age-old, but the detailed form it took, as represented by the propagandistic style of the romance, with its melding of magic and miracle, of the erotic and the ascetic, is distinctive to the third century of our era.

Also operative in these instruments of religious propaganda deriving from the late second and third centuries is a range of metaphysical assumptions significantly different from those apparent in the New Testament writings as a whole. Instead of the Pauline insistence on the difference between a physical body and a spiritual body, the Acts of Paul expects the resurrection of the flesh. This may be a reaction to movements competing with the mainstream of Christianity, such as the Gnostics, with their rejection of the material world as inherently evil. In place of the ethical dualism of the earlier period, with its conflict between the demonic forces and the power of God, there is a dichotomy between the material and the spiritual realms in Gnostic thought. In reaction to that negative Gnostic view of the created world, the Christians emphasized the tangibility, the corporeality, the materiality of the resurrection life that the faithful would enjoy. Although the term *resurrection* was used in both the first and the third centuries, the content of the concept altered radically in the course of that time. Sensitivity to the transformation of these central ideas must be present if faithful historical interpretation is to occur.

Some Observations about Method in the History of Religion

The Golden Bough has indeed broken. The history-of-religions cradle has come down, including the comparative method ensconced within it. There are signs of growing recognition of this collapse, even though many scholars at work in this field of study continue as though nothing had happened.

Mircea Eliade, as we have observed (pp. 24–26), is radically antihistorical, in that he rejects methods that interpret evidence in historical context, favoring instead the effort to uncover "the structure of transconsciousness."[1] Such an undertaking is intellectually worthy, especially when it is classified in the realm of psychology or aesthetics, but it cannot properly be designated as history. As G. Dudley has shown in his critique of Eliade, the latter is following the lead of Michael Foucault, who regards the method of verification by reference to empirical data as false and misleading.[2] Instead of providing some causal nexus for understanding the movement of religious thought in the continuum of history, Eliade offers only a paradigmatic relationship between archetypes and symbols. The history of religions becomes thereby an ahistorical analysis of religious language—primarily, the language that is textualized in myth and repeated indefinitely through ritual enactment of those myths. What Eliade

1. Eliade's work is thus characterized by Guilford Dudley III, in "Mircea Eliade as the 'Anti-Historian' of Religions," *Journal of the American Academy of Religion* 44 (1976): 348.

2. Dudley traces Eliade's kinship with Michel Foucault, who wants to reject all human sciences that inquire after causality—anthropology, sociology, and psychology—and all efforts to explain human nature, behavior, or history (348). Foucault seeks, rather, to find in language alone a means of conferring unity on what human beings experience as "the disparateness and unconnectedness of thought."

seeks is not historical development or change, but universal symbols, structures, and paradigms—none of them limited by time or culture.[3]

This enterprise closely resembles in its results the structuralist methods of Claude Lévi-Strauss, who has also been powerfully affected by the views of Foucault. The structuralist goal of discovering recurrent patterns in the human mind leaves out of account, and has no interest in, the unrepeatable uniqueness that is ingredient in every historical event. The legitimacy of this sort of enterprise—whether among literary critics, philosophers, aestheticians, or psychologists—I shall leave to others, but it should not be allowed to masquerade as historical investigation. To shift the image from broken bough to another nursery rhyme, no efforts by all the king's horses and all the king's men can put that history-of-religions construction—as historical study—back together again.

Within the field of historical-critical study, especially as it relates to the origins of Christianity, the method which arose in Germany in the nineteenth century and continues to be influential down to the latter part of the twentieth century, considers itself to be historical but makes its interpretive judgments on the basis of broad generalizations, or a "Gesamtkonzeption."[4] Thus, in interpreting the phenomenon of miracle in the early Christian literature, the followers of this school of thought relegate all the material treating of miracle in the Gospels to later tradition. According to this hypothesis, the real, historical Jesus was a teacher of pious wisdom, and it was the later converts to Christianity from Hellenistic culture who transformed the image of Jesus into that of a wonder-worker, thereby conforming him to the putatively universal image of a "divine man."[5] Mark in his

3. Eliade's method and aim are summarized by Dudley, "Mircea Eliade," p. 357.

4. Cf. Hans-Dieter Betz's notion of the comprehensive concept of the divine man in my Excursus below. Neither the image of the miracle-worker, which Betz identifies as the "divine man," nor the miracle itself can be described meaningfully in purely generalized terms.

5. Rudolf Bultmann's classic study of Jesus, entitled appropriately in the English translation, *Jesus and the Word*, trans. E. H. Lantero and Lucetta Mowry

gospel is understood by this school of interpretation to be com-
batting the rising notion of Jesus as a miracle-worker (= divine
man) by attributing this misconception to the disciples, whom
Jesus struggles to set straight on the subject: he is a messenger,
not a divine man. The argument is purely deductive, however.
The initial assumption is that the real Jesus could not have done
such an intellectually embarrassing thing as performing miracles. Their presence in the tradition is thus explained away.
The Q source is appealed to in support of this theory, as miracle
plays only a secondary role in that strand of Jesus tradition.[6]

Fortunately, there is a viable alternative to these methods, which
either take refuge from history in symbols or ignore historical
development while holding aloft the banners of sweeping generalization. The emerging method takes its cue from the approach to human understanding developed under the rubric of
sociology-of-knowledge. It enables the researcher to look with
fresh insight at familiar evidence, to avoid unwarranted, simplistic identification of parallels, to prevent mistaking neat
schemes of classification of phenomena for historical analysis,
and to see with new clarity how structures of religious experience and aspiration are transformed in changing contexts.

(New York: Scribner, 1934), sees no significant place for the narratives about
Jesus except for the story of his trial and death. Instead, what it finds essential is
Jesus' call to his followers to decide to obey God, which decision thereby actual-
izes the Kingdom of God in their midst. It is ironic that whereas the gospel
tradition itself announces the presence of the Kingdom of God in the midst of
Jesus' contemporaries in the form of the exorcism of demons, Bultmann assigns
all such embarrassing details to the later Hellenistic church and its recasting of
the Jesus tradition. Not surprisingly, scholars of the second and third generation
of Bultmannians are drawn to the Gnostic gospels, including the Gospel of
Thomas, which consist entirely of sayings, with no references to the activities of
Jesus or narratives about him. The Bultmann school now seeks to persuade others that the non-narrative—and hence, nonmiraculous—gospels are indeed the
oldest and offer us our best access to the historical Jesus. The controlling factor
in this proposition is not the persuasiveness of the new evidence, which many
find points to a much later stage in the development of the Jesus tradition, but
the attractiveness of a Jesus who is not involved in those embarrassing miracles.

6. Theodore Weeden, *Mark—Traditions in Conflict* (Philadelphia: Fortress,
1971). Thus thinks James M. Robinson, "Logoi tōn Sophōn," in *Trajectories through
Early Christianity*, with Helmut Koester (Philadelphia: Fortress, 1971).

In the course of our inquiry concerning the historical method that is appropriate and hermeneutically fruitful in the history of religion, our test-case has been the phenomenon of miracle. We have sought to carry out our analysis of this feature of both pagan and early Christian experience with awareness of and sensitivity to the range of settings in which the phenomenon appears, since the function of miracle differs from context to context. Perhaps as close as one can come to a general agreement on the significance of miracle in our period, from Alexander to Severus both within and without the Christian church, is to say that through miracle the gods or God disclose(s) the divine purpose for the world or for the chosen people within it through extraordinary events. The events are public; their import is often grasped only by those with insight to discern it. The events range from cosmic portents of change to direct divine intervention, which may take the form of healing, reward, punishment, judgment, or vindication. The specifics of the event are directly correlated with the life-world of the writer describing the occurrence, and that of the reading audience to whom the report is addressed. The details of the account must be searched to discover what life-world is presupposed in the narrative or inscription. There are no automatic or timeless links between a certain divinity and a certain meaning, or between one kind of act and one kind of import. The investigator must at every point raise contextual and presuppositional questions if the distinctive function of a miracle—or any other phenomenon—is to be discerned. For example, the range of meaning-frameworks and functions of miracle within our period may be summarized as follows:

1. If the primary value evident in the texts is the health or welfare of the seeking individual, as in the cults of Asklepios and Isis in Late Hellenistic times, then that is the form which miracle takes: ministration to personal need. Participation in or contribution to the cult is assumed, but it is not the primary factor. Gratitude to the beneficent divinity is expressed on an ad hoc, one-to-one basis.

2. If what is chiefly sought is union with the god, or disclosure of one's possibility for participation in divine cosmic purpose,

then that is itself the essence of the miraculous, as in the case of Aelius Aristides' revelations of life-purpose and heavenly transport through Asklepios, or Apuleius' being blessed by an epiphany of Isis. The benefits are personal, even individual, but the beneficiary senses himself or herself to be caught up in a larger cosmic scheme, rather than merely being on the receiving end of help for a specific need.

3. If the main concern is for the defeat of the evil powers and the vindication of the oppressed faithful minority, as in Jewish or early Christian apocalyptic communities, then miracle will not be a personal benefit at all, but rather a sign of the divine victory about to be achieved, of the triumph over the forces of evil, of the exaltation to positions of power and peace of those presently threatened and persecuted.

4. If the central focus is on the sovereign divine purpose being slowly worked out through the course of world history, then miracle will appear as portent, by which the divine discloses to the discerning person how the sovereign cosmic power is shaping the course of events, including especially the preparation for the line of succession of leadership among the world powers. Here the similarities between the Roman historians (Tacitus, Suetonius, Dio Cassius) and Josephus on the one hand, and Matthew on the other, are basic to recognizing the function of miracle in Matthew and Luke.

5. If the dominant interest of the writer is in religious propaganda, then we should expect an appealing narrative, in which both the prosperity and the problems of the faithful representatives of the cult are pointed up through accounts of miraculous occurrences, whether of difficulties or of deliverance, as in the Hellenistic romances and in the Acts of the Apostles.

6. If revelation is thought to occur through symbolic perception rather than through overt marvels, then the miracle stories will be told primarily as vehicles of hidden, mystical meaning, rather than as straightforward accounts of miraculous acts. In this instance, Plutarch's understanding of the miracles of Isis and John's presentation of the "signs" of Jesus in the Gospel of John perceive miracle in this mode of indirect communication.

7. If the major problems of the social or religious community

are stability, the maintenance of order, and the allegiance of the adherents, then we may expect miracle to take the form of divine attestation of the leader figure, as well as of punitive divine intervention to strike down the opposition. Miracle functions to glorify Apollonius of Tyana in Philostratus's portrait of him and his pilgrimages, while in a period of mounting official hostility toward the church on the part of the empire, and the attendant problems of apostasy, miracle serves in the apocryphal gospels and Acts to exalt the apostolic leadership. At the same time, the vacillating are promised miraculous support, or faced with the prospect of divine punitive action if they are unworthy or disobedient to the ordained leaders.

Methodologically central to the analysis of historical phenomena is the ideal type, as defined by Max Weber. Recognition of general similarities between a phenomenon and the ideal type is merely the preliminary stage of the historian's task: what must follow is the painstaking identification of the differentia which distinguish the object or events from its general type, and which therefore and thereby enable the interpreter to specify the uniqueness of a particular phenomenon.

The second crucial feature of sound historical method is the effort to locate the phenomenon in the larger framework of meaning in which it appears historically. That involves investigation of the assumptions about reality, human and divine, which are the presuppositions behind the documentation that has come down to us, and thus to recognize how phenomena which resemble those to be found at other times and in other cultures are to be understood in the specific context under investigation. Two major kinds of change take place: (1) *Forms*—whether literary, conceptual, cultic, or behavioral—undergo significant transformation as the cultural life-world changes. (2) Phenomena, which are superficially similar, will *function* in importantly different ways as the life-world changes, as the culture changes broadly, or as distinct groups with their own life-worlds emerge on the fringes of the larger culture. Chronology alone cannot serve as the basis of historical analysis, though it must be taken seriously into account, lest anachronistic historical links be contrived in the name of history. What is essential is the reconstruction, as fully as the evidence allows, of the specific context or life-world in which the phenomena arose.

In order to trace the outlines of the life-world of an earlier time and place the historian—including the historian of religion—must ask of the text or other ancient evidence under scrutiny the following questions:

Who is in charge? That is, what is the power or what are the powers that are understood as being in control of human destiny and of the fate of the universe?

What is the opposition? How are the forces of evil to be identified, and how are they at work to frustrate the divine purpose and wreck human aspirations?

What is the identity of those who understand? How are those persons to be recognized who have been granted the insight into the truth?

How and to what end does the divine manifest itself in human experience? Is the purpose of the gods to be observed in the course of public events, in the private experience of the individual, or by what other medium?

What are the privileges and responsibilities of the members of the community to whom these insights have been granted? What are the moral, political, cultic, and pious attitudes and actions that are to be assumed in light of the divine disclosure that has been made?

For these basic questions there will be a spectrum of answers. The issues, or variants of them, are pervasive. The historian's task is to identify the specifics of the answers that are given in a particular context. The more evidence available the better, but the identification of "parallels" cannot pass for responsible historical work. What is required is careful analysis of texts in context, including as thorough and sensitive as possible analytical reconstruction of the context. When historical work is undertaken along the lines here suggested, the romantic haze of the Golden Bough will have been dispersed. It is to be hoped, however, that the fog of intuition will give way to the brighter light of historical clarity and precision.

Excursus on the "Divine Man"

Hans-Dieter Betz, in *Lukian von Samosata und das Neue Testament*, Religionsgeschichtliche und Paränetische Parallelen (Berlin: Akademie Verlag, 1961), pp. 100–01, refers to a *Gesamtkonzeption* of the divine man as a tradition handed down from ancient Greek literature, which Lucian has merely accepted. Betz does not explore it fully but merely assumes that this conception of divine man provides the paradigm in terms of which Alexander was striving to represent himself through his miracle-working. Similarly, according to Betz, Lucian portrays Peregrinus as presenting himself to the gullible as a divine man by means of his apotheosis and his appearance in visions. According to Betz, this concept arises in times of fundamental uncertainty, "when through the *theios anēr* one seeks to recover the lost certainty through a *homo religiosus*, who is seen as a factor from outside the world." This phenomenon, Betz asserts, does not differentiate between religion and philosophy, but clothes the *theios anēr* in the role of a philosopher.

Betz notes that Lucian does not define the divine man sharply (102), and declares that it would be unrewarding to try to trace the links back from Lucian to the older Greek conception of the *theios anēr*. The fact is, however, that there is in Greek and Roman cultural history no uniform conception of a divine man to which Lucian or anyone else could appeal. Carl Holladay (in *Theios Aner in Hellenistic Judaism: A Critique of the Use of This Category in New Testament Christology*, SBLDS 40. Missoula, Mont.: Scholars Press, 1977) has shown that Josephus portrayed Moses, Joseph, Solomon, and Abraham on the model of the "hellenistic ideal of the virtuous (wise) man" (78). He never divinizes these patriarchal figures, nor does he do so for kings or figures in pagan history. Rather, *aretē* is defined in terms of Jewish law, and Moses' piety qualifies him to be called a *theios anēr*. Similarly, Philo of Alexandria recasts Israel's heroes in the model of the Stoic wise man, although Moses is never said to have received the divine nature. Philo goes out of his way to avoid taking Exodus 7:1—where the LXX calls Moses *theos*—literally. Nor is Moses called a divine man with respect to the miracles he performs. Artapanus rejects the analogy between Israel's heroes and the divinization of Dionysus (232).

David L. Tiede, in *The Charismatic Figure as Miracle-Worker* (SBLDS 1, 1972) has shown that it is not until the third and fourth centuries of our era that the earlier figure of a man as divine by virtue of his wisdom is combined with the shaman tradition to make Pythagoras—in historical retrospect—the model of *theios anēr*. The dominant paradigm of the divine man, as set forth by Plato (*Republic* 6.500.C-D), assumes that "the lover of wisdom by keeping company with the divine and orderly becomes himself divine and orderly in so far as it is possible for a human being." By the time of Plutarch (A.D. 46–120), there is disagreement as to whether it was his supernatural powers or well-trained reason that qualify Socrates for divinity (38), although Plutarch himself asserted that his divinity lay in his disciplined act and thought, his philosophical perseverance in the face of opposition and even of death, so that it was as a truly wise man that Socrates was divine. Only in the time of Philostratus (170–244) and Porphyry (232–305) in his life of Pythagoras do we have writers who clumsily juxtapose miracle-working and philosophical traditions (61). Tiede shares with Halladay the conclusion that in the Hellenistic Jewish writers, Moses is portrayed primarily as a wise man and as an agent of divine power and purpose (140–50), just as he is so represented by Ben Sira in his recital of God's mighty acts through famous men (Sir 45:2–3). Moses' *theiotēs* is seen by Josephus, both in his *Antiquities* and in the *Contra Apionem*, as evident through his receiving the divine law and through his being a model of virtue (221).

Ludwig Bieler, in his basic study of the divine man, ΘΕΙΟΣ 'ΑΝΗΡ. *Das Bild des göttlichen Menschen in Spätantike und Frühchristentum*, 2 vols. (Vienna, 1935–36; repr. Darmstadt, 1967), is unable to come up with an archetype and can only draw attention to the breadth of the variation in form and function of what he represents as the typical "divine man" (145–46). He acknowledges that later "ideal patterns" are projected back into the earlier times (147), so that the alleged paradigm becomes an ever-changing process in which there are no fixed points.

Lily Ross Taylor's classic study, *The Divinity of the Roman Emperor* (Middletown, Conn.: American Philological Association, 1931), provides a useful sketch of the Egyptian and Persian background of the divinization of Alexander and other Hellenistic rulers, and of the efforts to establish links between the Julio–Claudian rulers and the traditional gods. Especially significant are the portents which accompany the birth and death of the ruler. Vergil's *Fourth Eclogue* combines elements of Egyptian and Iranian religion to announce the birth of one destined to be a world-ruler (Octavian). But the theme of the divinity of the ruler is associated from the time of Alexander on with the principle laid down by Aristotle that "the man of preeminent political insight be followed 'as a god among men' for whom there is no law" (Taylor, p. 13). The only emperor with whom the ancient historians (including Tacitus, Suetonius, and Dio Cassius) link miracle-working is Vespasian (see above, p. 176). As we have noted, his wonders were performed in the shrine of Sarapis, the Hellenistic deity famed for healings and working miracles in behalf of his devotees. In the historical narratives, however, the miracles function to authenticate Vespasian as the choice of the gods for emperor, as the profound uncertainty of the year of the four emperors passed, and as the Flavians replaced the Julio-Claudian line. What is certain is that miracle-working was not a regular role of Roman emperors.

Recently Betz collaborated in a comprehensive study of the divine man: Gottmensch, in *Reallexicon für Antike und Christentum* (Stuttgart, 1982, Lieferung, 90). Betz's own substantial contribution to this study (Col. 234–311), shows that the title, divine man, was given in hellenistic and Roman times to healers, philosophers, seers and others whose knowledge and insights evidenced a special relationship with the divine. The generalizations which he draws, however, make no allowance for fundamental shifts in the cultural climate during these periods, with the result that distinctions are blurred. While Betz acknowledges that the "divine man" functions differently in the various gospels and in parts of the New Testament, he sees in all the New Testament the representation of Jesus as a divine being in human form—a least common denominator which is by no means the assured result of his earlier evidence, and which simply passes by much of the distinctive evidence in the New Testament writings. In spite of the detailed research and the impressive learning that his article demonstrates, his conclusions build more on the presuppositions deriving from the intellectual tradition in which he was trained than in the evidence itself. From that evidence at least one reader can only conclude that there is no such thing as a general conception of divine man in the Graeco-Roman period.

INDEX OF BIBLICAL REFERENCES

INDEX OF ANCIENT SOURCES

INDEX OF MODERN AUTHORS